Red Flags, Green Flags

Red Flags, Green Flags

Modern Psychology for Everyday Drama

DR ALI FENWICK

MICHAEL JOSEPH

PENGUIN MICHAEL JOSEPH

UK | USA | Canada | Ireland | Australia
India | New Zealand | South Africa

Penguin Michael Joseph is part of the Penguin Random House group of companies
whose addresses can be found at global.penguinrandomhouse.com

First published by Penguin Michael Joseph, 2024
004
Copyright © Dr Ali Fenwick, 2024

The moral right of the author has been asserted

Set in 13.5/16pt Garamond MT Std
Typeset by Jouve (UK), Milton Keynes
Printed and bound in Great Britain by Clays Ltd, Elcograf S.p.A.

The authorized representative in the EEA is Penguin Random House Ireland,
Morrison Chambers, 32 Nassau Street, Dublin D02 YH68

A CIP catalogue record for this book is available from the British Library

HARDBACK ISBN: 978–0–241–65368–5
TRADE PAPERBACK ISBN: 978–0–241–65369–2

www.greenpenguin.co.uk

For my beloved parents, who made me the man
I am today and who taught me to always give back.

To all my close friends, with whom I have
experienced the most beautiful moments in life.

And to my inner voice, who has always
guided me in the right direction.

Contents

Dating
Red flags in dating

CONTENTS

Preface

Writing this book has been such a joyous experience. Over the past years, I have been investigating how modern relationships have evolved and how technology, social trends and other global forces impact the way we think, behave and connect with others. It is truly fascinating to observe how fast our world is changing and how quickly we humans adapt. Every day new trends emerge across the globe and behaviours and social norms we once believed to be normal are no longer relevant or are even seen as strange. It's not a surprise that so many people feel confused and question if they should still behave or approach people in the same way, leading to reluctance to act and even overthinking. At the same time, we are expected to think on our toes. The world is moving so fast and being able to make quick decisions is seen as a strength.

However, quick decision-making can also trip us up, leading to faulty and biased outcomes. It truly is a masterful skill to be able to provide solid answers and make good decisions on the spur of the moment, while knowing when to slow down and think more critically about things. When it comes to making quick decisions, it is easy to label something we don't like in someone as a red flag. 'Bye bitch, next!' is the mindset many of us have nowadays, preferring to walk away when the going gets tough, which limits our ability to be more reflective in the moment. Because of this mindset, many people also find it hard to deal with difficult situations and prefer to run to the next best option rather than tackling the issue head-on. Learning to distinguish true red flags from green flags is an important skill set to develop, especially when you have to make a quick decision about something in your relationship; being able to recognize what is healthy and unhealthy behaviour can help you prevent a lot of drama down the road. Probably more important is being able to recognize when *you* are the red flag. Definitely not an easy task, and one that requires more introspection, which not everyone is comfortable doing.

Red flags and green flags have become very popular terms in today's culture, popularized through TV drama shows, youth culture and social media. The flags serve a purpose in society today, especially when it has become so hard to assess behaviours in a world where one thing one day can mean something else the next. Red flags and green flags help us to make better decisions, to think more reflectively about our experiences with others, and also to be more introspective.

However, red flags and green flags are also very subjective. For some, red flags are actually green flags, and for others, green flags are actually red flags. In certain situations, you may only see green flags in others, while they are as red as a lobster! Or seeing red flags in others may even be an indicator that you are the red flag. It's the way your upbringing, values, culture, life experiences and the media have influenced your beliefs and perceptions that make you judge what is red and what is green. Unfortunately, the brain's operating system is not without errors (cognition is prone to mistakes) and making quick judgements can lead our decision-making astray. *Red Flags, Green Flags* helps you to improve your decision-making using science, anecdotes, personal stories, tools and by helping you understand the latest behavioural trends impacting human relationships.

A quick decision or a process to improve how you think?

One of the reasons why I wrote this book is to help you reflect more deeply on what you are thinking and observing, providing you with a psychological lens to better evaluate human behaviour and everyday situations. That's why I don't want you just to see RED as RED and GREEN as GREEN. I want to empower you to make better decisions when it comes to red and green flags. And more than just helping you make quick decisions, I will also help you to slow down your thinking and make better decisions in the moment. Red for me is an acronym that stands for **R**eflect, **E**ngage, **D**ecide! On some occasions, going through the stages of RED can be fast. Some behaviours are truly danger warning signs that mean 'Run as fast as you can!' However, most of the time RED means, 'Stop, wait a minute!' like stop signs on the road. Stop, look left, look right and, when the road is clear, you drive. Even when we get the urge to run, it is always better to step away from automatic (or impulse-driven) thinking and reflect a bit on the situation before making a decision. Red flags come in various shades of red, so take time to interpret them well. Here are some examples of how to deal with a red flag more thoughtfully:

- **Reflect**
  - 'Wait a minute! That doesn't seem right to me. Let me focus on this a bit more and ask myself why I was triggered so much by this behaviour at work.'
  - 'Is this truly a deal-breaker in my friendship or could I be overreacting?'
  - 'I keep pushing potential partners away. I need to reflect on why I am doing this!'

- **Engage**
  - ○ 'OK, let me try to find out more.'
  - ○ 'OK, I am seeing now that my boss is using persuasion tactics to demand loyalty and have me overwork without additional compensation.'
  - ○ 'This is a complete deal-breaker for me. Let me check with my peeps if they agree or not with what I believe.'
  - ○ 'I am starting to realize that me pushing people away is linked to my own insecurities and trust issues. Let me talk to someone to get more perspective on myself.'
- **Decide**
  - ○ 'I have thought about this deeply and I don't think I want to continue anymore. Our values are completely misaligned.' (See more about this red flag on page 77.)
  - ○ 'This behaviour is not acceptable, but I do want to see how we can do better.' (See more about this red flag on page 50.)
  - ○ 'I have decided it is better not to date and to stay single for while. I need to work on myself first before I can attract love back into my life.' (See more about this red flag on pages 16 and 159.)

The more you learn how to deal with red flags, the better you will be at recognizing behaviours that need to be addressed and the more you will improve your abilities to deal with difficult situations effectively, even if you are not the best communicator or don't feel confident enough to speak up. The more you practise, the better you will become, and before you know it, it becomes second nature. If we all dealt with red flags effectively, we would not only improve our relationships in all areas of our lives but also make this world a better place.

Equally, GREEN flags also serve a purpose beyond the colour green. We associate green with 'go-ahead' or 'approval'. If it's GREEN, why should you devote any mental energy to something that already feels good or safe? Your brain naturally focuses less on things that feel safe. There is good reason to devote focus and attention to the behaviours you like in another person or that signal support, empathy or longevity. Positively reinforcing or reminding how you appreciate GREEN behaviours increases the likelihood that they will continue. That's why when you see GREEN, think **G**enuine, **R**espect, **E**mpathize, **E**levate, **N**urture. These words should in one way or another embody the GREEN behaviours you see in another person.

- **Genuine**
  GREEN behaviours are genuine. They come from the inside because that is the way the other person has been programmed through life. It's the way their spirit's energy functions. Examples of genuine behaviours are kindness, thoughtfulness and authenticity. Realness is what drives the behaviour.

- **Respect**
  GREEN behaviours are also respectful. Respecting your time, privacy and space when needed, respecting your perspective on life, and showing respect in their behaviours towards you and others. You should also make sure to respect green behaviours.

- **Empathize**
  GREEN behaviours are those that show empathy. Being empathetic towards others spans a multitude of behaviours within human relationships. Being a good listener and able to read between the lines, understanding

how someone feels in specific situations, and being able to adjust one's approach to meet people where they are at are core skills to keep any relationship alive and healthy. Make sure to empathize with the green behaviours you observe. Understand where they are coming from and why people engage in them.

- **Elevate**
  GREEN behaviours are also very elevating. When someone treats you right, supports you when it's needed most or responds effectively to difficult situations, it is very empowering and motivating to reciprocate the positive behaviours. Any relationship follows a simple equation: $1 + 1 > 2$, which means one plus one equals more than two. Green behaviours create synergies and positive emotions, which make you a better person and keep you going during difficult times. Always make sure to elevate green behaviours.

- **Nurture**
  GREEN behaviours are behaviours you should nurture. For any relationship to be sustainable, you need to nurture it. A plant needs water, sun and nutrients to grow and survive. Human relationships are the same. Nurture GREEN behaviours by acknowledging them, positively reinforcing them and respecting them. However, it's not easy to be sustainable continuously. That's why GREEN behaviours require nurturing from all sides and from everyone involved.

The framework to help maintain and strengthen green behaviours in others is also the framework we should apply to help others struggling with red flags. Being on the receiving end of compassion, empathy and respect from people close to you can help you become more self-aware and self-assured, and more willing to change unhealthy behaviours. Honing the green skills in yourself and in others encourages everyone to develop the important tools that help deal with many red flag behaviours. It's a win-win.

The default mindset versus the reflective mindset

Most of our decision-making processes and behaviours run on autopilot. This means that we are often unaware of why we make certain decisions and how the past informs our behaviours in the present. This automatic thinking (or 'default mindset' as it is often referred to) helps us to make quick decisions based on past experiences, values and beliefs. Who says that these automatic responses are the best decisions? They might be completely off. That's why it is important to watch out when we call a red flag in someone. Thinking of RED as a stop sign on the road helps us to metaphorically put a foot on the breaks, move away from default thinking and make better decisions in the heat of the moment. Let's compare the default mindset with the reflective mindset using the following examples.

Default mindset says: 'RED FLAG! I am being told I am delusional. I should just accept it!'
Stop, reflect and ask yourself:
'But why is my reality being challenged? I saw the text messages on my partner's phone. Am I being gaslighted?'

Default mindset says: 'RED FLAG! My relationship is getting boring! End it!'
Stop, reflect and ask yourself:

'Is my relationship really that boring or are the peace and stability in my relationship making me more aware of my inner chaos?'

Now, after carefully evaluating if the red flag is a 'you' problem or a 'me' problem, engage with the problem at hand.

Reflective mindset: 'It got physical after I asked to see those messages. My safety is in danger. What to do?'
Engage with the problem:
'I shouldn't allow my reality to be denied and I definitely don't tolerate abuse. My mother taught me that if someone hits you once, most likely they will do it again.'

Reflective mindset: 'Wait! I was brought up in a chaotic environment. I miss the drama!'
Engage with the problem:
'Now that I realize the boredom is a "me" problem, I should not end the relationship. If I end it, this will remain a recurring pattern in my life. Maybe I should decide not to fall back into old patterns of behaviour and tackle this for once.'

Note: Engaging with the problem can happen quickly, but sometimes it may take some time. You might need more time to think about things or you might want to engage your partner in further discussion to figure things out for yourself.

Now that you have engaged reflectively with the problem, it's time to make a more thoughtful decision about what to do next.

Reflective mindset: 'I will never tolerate physical abuse!'
(See more about this red flag on page 304.)
Decide:
'I am out! Run!'

Reflective mindset: 'This is clearly a "me" problem and I
want to do something about it.' (See more about this red
flag on page 265.)
Decide:
'Bae, I have been thinking about why I am feeling so bored
recently in our relationship and I realize that the tranquillity,
safety and predictability you give me are making me more
aware of my addiction to drama and chaos. I am telling you
this because I want to grow out of it and feel satisfied with
what I have with you. Please support me.'

How to use this book

I have written the book so that you don't need to read everything in sequence, just jump to the chapters you find most
interesting to read first. At the end of each chapter you will
find a brief summary under the heading 'What's the drama?'
where you will also find the red and green flags related to the
topic of the chapter. If you just want the drama, go straight
to the summary and the flags! But if you want more sub-
stance and to learn more about the psychology underlying
the drama and how to improve your own thinking and communication, then definitely read the whole chapter. At the
end of the book, I offer some exercises for you to start applying what you've learnt about red flags and green flags to help
you become more introspective and to tackle the problem

areas in your thinking and behaviour, and those of others. I highly recommend engaging in these exercises as they will help you put your new learnings into practise. Not only is practising a great way to experiment with new behaviour and ways of thinking, but it also helps to improve your ability to think reflectively, supporting you to foster healthier and stronger relationships. I am sure that the 24 red flag chapters will provide you with a deep insight into human behaviour, explained in a contemporary way, helping you to make better decisions in your life – be it with friends or family, in love or at work – eventually leading to more happiness and less drama (unless you enjoy a bit of drama occasionally).

Happy reading!

Dr Ali Fenwick

P.S. I have a surprise for you at the end of the book! A fun red flags, green flags game you can play with someone you are dating or with your significant other to foster a stronger connection and maybe even fall (deeper) in love.

Family and Friendships

Red flags in family and friendships

Family and friends are the cornerstones of your life. Your family, big or small, plays a significant role in who you have become today. Instilling into you values and beliefs about the world and teaching you strategies on how to survive. It is commonly known that our upbringing can have a huge impact on our well-being, ways of thinking and behaviours as we grow up. Not being brought up in a warm and healthy nest can negatively affect how you view/value yourself and how you form relationships later in life. Friendships are equally important and also heavily affect how we see and feel about ourselves. Once we leave the family nest, it is our friendships that mainly help form our identities and provide a sense of security. But what is truly considered a close friend? For many people today, online contacts, individuals they have never met in real life, are sometimes even considered 'friends'. This blurs the lines between true friends and mere acquaintances, which can influence how people value friendship in the modern world and how people treat each other.

Family and friends are a source of connection and sup-port and we need these close ties to understand who we are and where we belong. But sometimes family and friends can be a source of negativity and discomfort, which can severely impact our physical and mental well-being because of the psychological and emotional proximity they have with us. Strong family ties and friendships can change with time, becoming toxic and destructive. Feelings of jealousy, envy, anger, unhappiness and uncertainty can infect the positive connections we once had with the people we love the most. That's why it is important to be able to identify red and green flags in friendships and family relationships. Learning how friendships can change for the worse with time is crucial as it provides you with an opportunity to find ways to save your friendships, and, if needed, to let them go. Equally, learning how family ties impact your development and how you form relationships later in life can help you to pinpoint the problem sources of your behaviours in the present. The coming six chapters about red and green flags in family and friendships will help you uncover the intricacies of maintaining healthy and sustainable connections. All human relationships are challenging and the longer the relationship, the more we need to learn how to deal with everyday drama.

Red Flag 1 'Stop meddling in my life'

When parents keep interfering in your life

'No man should bring children into the world
who is unwilling to persevere to the end
in their nature and education.'
Plato

When parents keep interfering in your life

It's a blessing to have loving and caring parents. Caregivers who devote their lives to your upbringing and education, and who make sure you have everything you need in life to succeed: life skills, mental resilience, autonomy and self-determination. The quality of care you received from your parents is reflected to a large extent in who you have become today. The bond between you and your parents goes deeper than any friendship. It is often said that 'blood is thicker than water', and this is true even for those who don't have the best of relationships with their parents. The parent – child bond is sacred, and your parents' sacrifices naturally become your indebtedness. However, sometimes parents have a difficult time letting go of their little girl or little boy. They too have gone through their own trauma and once were their parents' little boy or little girl.

When children grow up and become adults, there comes a time when cubs have to fend for themselves and live their own lives. For some parents, the thought of letting their children go is a hard pill to swallow. In one way it means, 'I am losing my identity or authority as a parent,' and in another way it means, 'I am scared something will happen to them or I am losing control.' It's normal for a parent to experience fear, grief or sadness when the realization kicks in that the kids are growing up and want a life of their own. However, a parent's inability to let go can harm a young adult's development in life, and in some cases become so meddling that young adults don't want to see their parents anymore. People who have parents who interfere too much in their lives can also feel so indebted to their caregivers that they can't let go. It is especially difficult when parents play with your feelings as a way to stay in control and when you naturally find it hard to set boundaries.

Learning to understand when your mum and dad's engagement in your life is healthy and when it is unhealthy is important for your own personal development, mental wellbeing and for how you form relationships with other people. Understanding how to set boundaries for yourself is equally important but can culturally sometimes be very difficult. Being able to identify the red and green flags in your relationship with your parents or caregivers can help build a healthier relationship with them and provide you space to become the individual you desire to be. Continue and expand the healthy behaviours passed down from one generation to the next and aim to be the one who brings generational trauma to a halt.

The psychology of nosiness

There are various reasons why people can be overly nosy or interfering in your private life. Some parents genuinely are interested in everything you do, enthusiastic about your achievements, who you spend time with and want to know that you are safe and doing well. It is not unusual for many mothers or fathers to want to contact their children on a regular basis; vice versa, many people love to speak to their parents daily, even just briefly. A short call or a simple text message: 'How are you doing? Have a great day. Love you, Mum!' However, there are times when daily phone calls or continuously wanting to know what you are doing or who you are with feels awkward or even intrusive. Some parents have a hard time letting go. They continue to try and stay involved in your life out of fear of losing you or out of a need to control you, disregarding your own needs and well-being.

Culture and family enmeshment can also play a big role in how involved your parents are in your life, especially when social pressures require you to conform to cultural norms of how to behave, who to marry or how to continue your relationship with your parents when you grow up (or how to be a good parent). Cutting the invisible umbilical cord is not an easy thing but not letting go can have severe consequences for both parent and child. Research shows that people whose parents are overly controlling of their lives as children are more likely to develop self-esteem issues as they grow up, lack boundaries, have a higher risk of anxiety and depression, have a more difficult time adjusting to life and often develop relationship difficulties.

The narcissistic caregiver

Having a narcissistic parent can be very challenging for a child, even when they have fully matured. The narcissistic parent, being self-obsessed, often sees their child as an extension of themselves. Perhaps they try to live vicariously through their kids. Everything the child does is a reflection of them and setting high standards and being overly critical of their children is not uncommon. Besides demanding high achievements at school, the overly controlling parent can also dictate how the child behaves or even dresses. In some cases, money is used as leverage to keep children attached later in life.

Children of narcissistic parents often find themselves being overly self-critical, perfectionistic and never feeling like they are enough. Even when a child has left home, the narcissistic mum or dad can continue to exert control over their life, the child always feeling the invisible hand above their head controlling their behaviour or holding them back from being who they want to be.[1] This is especially true if your self-esteem has been negatively impacted because of being subdued by manipulation tactics to keep the attention on your parents, being constantly put down or believing that your parents' love for you was conditional. The more parents can make their adult sons and daughters feel like unworthy children, the more likely they will be able to control them. I have found that many of my personal development clients who have been brought up by overly critical or narcissistic parents occasionally (and unconsciously) project the same behaviours onto their romantic partners or even their own children.

DID YOU KNOW?
When your parents emotionally blackmail you

It is not easy to set boundaries in personal relationships, especially not with your parents. Some people are better at it than others. One's character, upbringing and mental state can make it hard to say no to others. When you value the needs of others over your own, people-pleasing tendencies can occur, which make you susceptible to wanting to meet your parents' needs beyond what would generally be expected. Over time, continuously putting your own needs aside for other people will take its toll on you. If not mentally, it will physically. If you don't say no and set boundaries, your body eventually will, potentially causing you irreversible harm. Learning to unpack why it is hard to say no to your parents is an important first step in realizing what holds you back from setting boundaries and taking back some control over other areas of your life.

One of the major reasons why it is hard to resist parents' unwavering demands is due to emotional control. Some parents can try to wind you up or emotionally blackmail you by saying, 'You owe me the air you breathe' or 'I sacrificed my life for you, you should do what I tell you' or 'You are nobody without me'. These words can hit hard. But if it is done (repeatedly) to manipulate you, you should realize that this is a red flag, and it is better not to react to such statements. Rather, focus on why these words keep you trapped in a loop.[2] Try to identify alternative beliefs and responses to such statements. This will give you back some control over time and make you less susceptible to such emotional manipulation.

Learning how to take care of your own needs

Learning how to take care of your own needs is very important in any relationship. However, it's not always easy to do. When parents are overly demanding or involved in your life, it is important to gradually create space between you and them. Parental attachment is often stronger than the attachment you have in your romantic relationship, and having your parents be too involved in your life can hurt your love affairs. A romantic partner can feel that he or she is competing for attention and eventually decide to leave if it becomes too much. At times, parents (or in-laws) can do this intentionally, out of fear of losing you or by a dislike of your partner. Even if you are in your late forties and married with kids, parents can still be overly meddling and dictate your life. There is no age limit to this obsessiveness.

Making some distance is also a way to deal with meddling parents, especially when your partner choices don't align with the expectations of your family or culture. Many gay/bisexual men and women, trans people and people who identify as non-binary are brought up in an environment where expressing one's identity or sexuality is not accepted, or is even deemed illegal, and they often choose to move away from their parents' home to explore their identities and develop a sense of self in a place where they feel safe and like they belong. Parental nosiness and prying can suffocate the self-development and attachment style of those who don't feel safe to express themselves fully at home.

If you feel your parents are too involved in your life and you want to start establishing some boundaries in your relationship with them, then here are some things you can say that can help create some distance:

- 'I understand that you want to know what's happening in my life, but I would appreciate it if you gave me some space to allow me to grow independently.'
- 'I know you love me so much. I understand your concerns about my partner, but please leave it up to me to make my own choices in life and also my own mistakes.'
- 'You can come to me to tell me what you don't like about my partner choices, but don't overstep your boundaries and directly contact my partner to voice your unhappiness.'
- 'Mum, I know you feel like you are getting less attention from me now that I have a girlfriend, but I can't have you interfering with my relationship because of your own insecurities.'
- 'I am happy to update you on my life but stop asking about my love life or when I am going to get married. Please respect that.'

When you start to create some distance from your parents, it's natural that you will face resistance. They might even get very upset with you and say terrible things to make you feel bad and reconsider your stance. But it's so important to protect your needs and learn to set boundaries as, over time, this will help you to develop more strongly as an individual and build healthier relationships with others.[3] With time, and to a varying degree, your parents will learn to appreciate your individuality and also learn to let go.

In India, it is generally the tradition that after a couple ties the knot, the wife moves into the house of the husband's parents. Shaadi.com (India's online marriage portal) reported that this tradition is steadily changing as more and more women prefer to start their own home after getting married away from the family.[4] Mother-in-law interference in the newlyweds' life is mentioned as one of the main reasons for the wives to opt out of living with the in-laws. With the presence of a new female in the house, it is not uncommon for some mothers-in-law to feel threatened by her presence and consequently want to dictate behaviour and set stricter rules.

When parents keep interfering in your life – what's the drama?

It is a blessing to have loving and supportive parents. It is not a given for everyone. However, it is a problem when parents or any other caregivers interfere too much in your life, especially when you are an adult and not living at home anymore. It can be hard to set personal boundaries with your parents as feelings of obligation and guilt can emerge. For parents, it can be hard to let go of their little girl or boy as they might experience a loss of control or meaningfulness in their lives. Some caregivers can be overly meddling, demanding or controlling due to various factors, ranging from environmental factors to mental health issues. Growing up with meddling parents can also impact your development and mindset, making it hard to set boundaries. Learning how to take care of your own needs and be less controlled by your parents as an adult is not only important for building a healthy adult relationship with caregivers but also important in terms of your own development and how you bond with others later in life.

It's a **red flag** if:
- Your father or mother (or other caregiver) keeps asking when you are going to get married.
- Your father or mother (or other caregiver) is dictating your life even after you have left home (e.g. forces you to study something they want you to study, dictates how you dress or who you engage with).
- Your parents or caregivers emotionally blackmail you to keep you within their control.
- Your parents or caregivers try to control you through money.
- You are not clear about your own needs, boundaries and/or demands and find it hard to express them clearly to your parents or caregivers. This allows others to meddle in your life.

It's a **green flag** if:
- Your father or mother (or other caregiver) respects your boundaries.
- Your father or mother (or other caregiver) doesn't pry in your life when you ask them to stop.
- Your family members respect the decisions you make for yourself when it comes to autonomy, romance and other life choices (even if they don't always agree with your choices).

- You are able to effectively balance keeping close ties with your family and ensuring you can live your life.

Things to consider when deciding if you want in or out

Keeping a healthy relationship with your caregivers is important for so many reasons. However, I realize this is not always possible. When you have very loving parents who just want the best for you, it can be hard to say, 'Please don't interfere in my life.' As the child, growing up independently can be very hard and, in some circumstances, close to impossible. Some caregivers can be very demanding and even manipulative, emotionally blackmailing you into doing what they want. Narcissistic mothers or fathers often put high demands on their children as they see their children as an extension of themselves. You need to decide how best to balance your own needs while maintaining a healthy and balanced relationship with your family.

Willingness to stay

- You can see that your parents' prying into your life is not meant with bad intentions. It is just a matter of time for them to get used to your adult life.
- When you ask them to stop meddling in your life, they eventually do.
- When they accept you as you are (even though they might not always agree with the choices you make).
- You improve the way you communicate with your parents. Through your effective communication, you find ways to build a much healthier relationship with

your parents while achieving more autonomy over your life.

Time to make some distance

- Your parents (or caregivers) interfere too much in your life.
- When your parents' interference is making you physically, emotionally or psychologically unwell.
- When your parents try to control you through manipulation or money.
- You cannot authentically be who you are at home.

Red Flag 2 'Why were you never there for me?'

The unavailable and unreliable parent

'It is a wise father that knows his own child.'
The Merchant of Venice, Act II, ·
Scene II, William Shakespeare

The unavailable parent

The quality of your thinking and the way you form relationships with others later in life are heavily affected by your upbringing, especially during your early childhood years. Growing up in a safe and warm environment, your emotional and physical needs will often have been met and you will have learnt how to develop a secure attachment with your caregivers. However, lack of care, attention or a secure environment when growing up can impact how you think about yourself, your ability to set boundaries, your willingness to engage in self-care and the choice of partners you make later in life. Especially when parents are physically or emotionally unavailable to meet your needs as a child, it can be easy to blame oneself for your parents' shortcomings.

As a kid, you can't imagine your caregivers not being able to provide what you need, so you start to believe, 'It must be me. I am not good enough to be loved and cared for', not realizing that humans lack skills in so many areas of life, including being a good parent (at times). Learning how to cope as a kid with an unreliable parent can lead to developing insecure attachment styles, a fear of abandonment and even self-esteem issues. These in turn can lead to behaviours that don't serve you well in forging secure relationships with others. Reflecting on how your upbringing has impacted your life today can be a fruitful starting point to find ways to be a better person in many areas of life, including being a better person for yourself. We can go through life on auto-pilot and often we are not aware of how past experiences can affect how we think and behave in the present moment. Becoming more aware of our unconscious processes is key to one's personal development and the ability to identify situations that can trigger the red flag behaviours inside of us. Increasing our self-awareness and learning how to escape from the shadow of unreliable parents can help us to detach from negative parenting influences and even generational trauma to an extent. As adults, we can't change our parents or their behaviours, but we can learn how to heal our inner child and find ways to reparent it as the mature self. Remember, 'We are all a product of our past, but we don't need to be a prisoner of it' – a saying that resonates so well with this dilemma. Your past impacts who you are today, and to a certain extent how you think and behave, but it doesn't define who you want to be. We always have a *choice* if we really want to change. The power is in your hands if you choose to become more self-aware of your default behaviours and thinking patterns and are intentional about wanting to change them for the better.

The psychology of unavailable parents

It's an unfortunate fact but not all parents are great caregivers. Even when some parents have good intentions, they can fail at being a good provider. Let's face it, parents can't always be on their best behaviour and mistakes will happen along the way, but if being emotionally neglected is the norm, then there is something wrong. There are numerous reasons why some parents are not able to provide the love and attention a child needs. Not being able to care fully for one's child can come down to personal issues,[1] lack of financial resources, lack of parental skills, lack of emotional intelligence, the environment you are brought up in,[2] their parents having mental health issues, ill intent or drug and alcohol abuse, to name a few. A powerful insight I like to share about emotional neglect is that it is not something that happens to you as a child, rather it is something that fails to happen to you as a child: the lack of acknowledgement, recognition, awareness, commitment, love or validation.

Understanding where your parents' unreliability and/or unavailability comes from helps to put the behaviour into context, but it definitely doesn't justify their behaviour or the impact it has had on you. Though not always easy to decipher, learning to understand *why* your parents couldn't provide the necessary care for you as a child can provide the objectivity that is needed to find ways to detach from the past if that is something you are aiming for.

On some occasions, you can have very loving parents, but still feel neglected. This is very common when parents are unreliable in their behaviours. They habitually make promises they don't keep; they are not there for you during your important moments in life; or, at times, they are very warm, while at others they are distant and cold. Having an unreliable parent can make you feel less loved, less trusting,[3] socially withdrawn[4] and even susceptible to being attracted to unreliable partners later in life.[5] The unpredictability in interpersonal relationships can also become an addiction, with you waiting for the moment they finally do show up or show love and affection again. The psychological impact of emotional neglect on one's well-being can be huge and is considered a form of trauma.[6]

The neglected child

Chronic neglect is a hard thing to process, and everyone deals with it in a different way. Experiencing traumatic events in your life doesn't always have to lead to a negative mindset or behaviours later in life though. Everyone is different and will respond to hardships in different ways.[7,8] However, a common consequence in adult life of chronic emotional neglect during childhood years is the processing of emotions.[9] People can become fearful of deep emotions, either positive emotions like those experienced in romantic partnerships or negative emotions, such as the fear of abandonment. In both scenarios, pushing a partner away when they get too close, or the moment you see the first red flag, could be a response to not knowing how to deal with deep intimate emotions. Pushing emotions away feels familiar and safer. Dealing with your emotions (even positive ones) might make you feel exposed; you might equate it to coming across as weak to others, or that you are losing control of yourself. Fundamentally, both these responses have to do with a lack of trust and a fear of getting hurt.[10]

On the other side, emotional neglect and unreliable parental care can also lead to people-pleasing tendencies. Going out of your way to be nice to others or trying to meet people's demands at the cost of meeting your own needs can come from the belief that, 'I need to make you happy, and when you are happy, then I am happy.' This often reflects a lack of a strong sense of self and being conditioned to believe that love is conditional and that by 'giving you what you need, I will get attention, respect and ultimately love in return'. People-pleasing tendencies are often related to low esteem[11] and fear of rejection. The neglected child wants to do what they can to make the other person happy in order to feel accepted.

The neglected child inside can heavily dictate the behaviour of the adult in the present (even when there is no need to be scared). Learning to become more aware of one's inner child is an important step to take in trying to address one's trauma responses in life and relationships. Once you become more aware of how your inner child dictates your behaviours in the present, you can embark on a journey of self-healing by acknowledging the inner child and finding ways to soothe and reparent it as the adult version of you. Inner child work is a great way to start changing the default script in your mind and validating one's own needs and emotions.

DID YOU KNOW?
Writing a letter to your inner child
Many people ask me how to work with their inner child and there are various ways you can go about connecting. In my TikToks and Reels, I talk a lot about the impact of the inner child on our behaviours in the present moment.

People's reactions online often are 'Damn inner child is ruining my life. How can I kill the inner child?' to which I respond, 'You don't!' First and foremost, it is important to acknowledge that everyone has an inner child. Getting in contact with your inner child is a way to strengthen your well-being and feel more connected to your inner self. It is a way to understand why certain situations trigger you and why you respond in the way you do, making the unconscious conscious again. The inner child is your younger self, which carries the pains and neglect from the past into the present. It helps us understand why, as adults, we can be so mature at times but during other times respond like the hurt child inside of us. It is important to learn how to manage the inner child as our pains can also be a source of our drive and success in life.

When do we allow the inner child out and when do we tame it? And, as adults, can we find the compassion and courage to reparent the inner child to give it what it didn't receive before, but wants so badly? Can you hug your inner child and tell it, 'Everything is going to be fine. You're safe now. I acknowledge your pain. I forgive you for being upset. And, as the older you, I will give you what you need'? Writing a handwritten letter (or a letter on your computer or phone) to your inner child is a great way to tell it all of the above in full detail, and can be very healing. It can help you to build a more productive and happier relationship with your inner self. Though you can do this from the comfort of your home, it is advisable to work with someone who can guide you through the process.

Adele has spoken openly about how the absence of her father impacted how she navigated relationships later in life. To avoid getting hurt, she reportedly would be the first one to hurt her partner as a way to protect herself.[12] Feeling abandoned or neglected by a parent can negatively impact how we form romantic relationships in life. Inadvertently, we can repeat the dysfunction we saw in our parents in our own relationships.

The unavailable and unreliable parent – what's the drama?

Our formative years are the most important in terms of creating a healthy basis for our adult life. Being brought up in a warm nest with much love, care and attention positively affects one's physical and mental development, and even contributes to one's success in life. Growing up with parents who are not emotionally available or are unreliable can negatively impact one's mental development, emotional regulation, sense of self and ability to form healthy and lasting friendships and romantic relationships later in life. As a child growing up, it is not uncommon to start believing that you might be to blame for the emotional and physical neglect from your caregivers, questioning yourself, 'Why doesn't mummy or daddy love me?' or 'What am I doing wrong that they won't tend to my needs?' In your default mind as a child, your caregivers are good people supposed to protect you. It is important to realize that not everyone is capable of being a loving parent or knowing how to express that love in a healthy way conducive to good child development. It is also important to become aware of how your childhood years impact your mindset and attachment later in life, especially if it impacts your ability to foster healthy and long-lasting relationships. However you decide to mentally deal with the past or the influence of your inner child on your behaviours today, remember that you have the power to change and be different. The past does not have to define who you will be tomorrow.

It's a **red flag** if:
- Your father or mother (or other caregiver) doesn't show up in the most important moments of your life.
- Your father or mother (or other caregiver) didn't provide you with a safe environment growing up, which makes you comfortable living in chaotic relationships later in life.
- You believe it is your fault that your parents didn't give you the attention you needed as a child. Remember, it wasn't your fault. Not all parents are capable of giving the attention and love that is needed.
- You fail to be introspective to identify self-limiting beliefs and emotional triggers that have stemmed from your earlier years.

It's a **green flag** if:
- Your father or mother (or other caregiver) is open to talking about the past with you whenever you feel it is the moment to address things that have hurt you.

- You acknowledge that parents make mistakes, and you also understand that you are not a prisoner of your past. You have the ability to forgive and to change.
- You acknowledge that neglect is not something that happens to you, rather it is something that has failed to happen to you as a child.
- You embrace the inner child (not kill it) to find ways to nurture and reparent it as a way to reconcile the inner conflict between the past and the present. You find ways to address the mental programming from the past and find ways to improve one's thinking and behaviour in the moment.

Things to consider when deciding if you want in or out

Deciding if you are in or out in this chapter means if you want to let your past decide your future or not. Not coming from a warm, caring or loving nest doesn't automatically mean that you will be affected by it later in life. Luckily, we are all different. However, the likelihood of you being impacted by parental neglect and unreliability is high. If you see that the decisions you make in life don't serve you well due to your upbringing or that you find it hard to build long-lasting healthy relationships with others, then maybe it's a good idea to start working on your default mindset. Learning to become more introspective is a first step in uncovering how the unconscious is influencing your decisions today. Which situations trigger you and why? Why are you the first to walk away when you see the first red flag? Why do you cause chaos when there is peace in your relationship? Asking yourself these questions can bring to light how the past might be influencing the present. Remember, we are all a product of our past, but we don't need to be a prisoner of it. We always have a choice to break away from the shadow of the past.

Want to learn more about how
your past impacts your present

- You want to learn more about how your past shaped your behaviours today.
- You realize that the way your parents raised you holds you back in various ways.
- You realize that the neglect you experienced in the past negatively affects your ability to build healthy relationships in the present.
- You want to learn how to create a more sustainable relationship with your inner child.

Not ready yet to explore how
the past impacts the present

- You are able to form healthy relationships with friends, colleagues and/or romantic partners. You're happy as things are for now.
- Regardless of your upbringing, you are capable of making healthy life choices.
- You have found a way to turn past pains and childhood traumas into a source of positive motivation, which has become a core driver of your success in life.
- You currently don't feel secure enough to address the past. You will consider it once you are ready for it.[13]

Red Flag 3 'Middle Child Syndrome'
The impact of birth order on sibling rivalry

'Brothers and sisters are as close as hands and feet.'
Vietnamese Proverb

The impact of birth order

Sibling relationships are one of the most enduring relationships, but having siblings can be a blessing and a curse at the same time. This very much depends on how your relationship evolves with your older or younger siblings. Having a positive relationship with a brother and/or sister (or multiple siblings) has multiple benefits to one's development as a child. It teaches you critical skills in how to navigate relationships, such as social skills, empathy, the ability to negotiate and a willingness to share and support each other. Some studies even show that having positive sibling relationships can contribute to better health in later life.[1,2]

Older brothers and sisters can also serve as role models and protectors, especially when they take on more serious responsibilities within the family. However, having siblings doesn't automatically mean they will be a positive ray of light in your life. Many people have a bad relationship with their siblings, which can have adverse effects on one's development and mental health. There are many factors that impact your relationship with your siblings, from family dynamics and the environment you were brought up in to personality. A less understood factor of influence on sibling behaviour is that of birth order. Can the order in which you were born impact how you are treated, your outlook on life and who you become? Are men who have an older sister by default a green flag? And if you have a younger *and* an older sibling, could you be the victim of middle child syndrome?

Understanding how birth order can shape the way parents treat you and the development of your personality over time is a perspective of human relationships worthy of consideration. It provides a lens to evaluate your existing relationships with siblings and an opportunity to explore how brother and sister relationships have impacted who you are today. Sibling relationships are one of the strongest bonds that exist and, unlike with a friend, you can't easily walk away from a toxic brother or sister relationship and be rid of the drama. Identifying the red and green flags in sibling relationships can help you break away from negative dynamics and patterns of behaviour and build stronger bonds with those you share the same bloodline with.

Birth order effects: pop psychology or the real deal?

Have you ever wondered if the order you were born in could impact you in any way? Well, this is a question many people believe to be true. Austrian psychiatrist Alfred Adler was one of the first to theorize that birth order can impact the personality development of siblings. However, when it comes to later research, there are many who would disagree.[3] Various studies

investigating birth order effects have produced some interesting findings, but nothing that is conclusive enough to state as
a generalizable fact (partially due to the difficulty of studying
such complex relationship dynamics). But dismissing the
impact of birth order effects on personality and behaviour,
and the compounding role of gender, culture, wealth and
family size, would leave out a degree of understanding of how
family ties impact life outcomes.

Nature versus nurture – a behavioural perspective

We already know from the psycho-dynamic perspective of
psychology that getting more or less attention as a child can
have an impact on your quality of thinking, personality and
attachment style later in life.[4] So, it's natural to think that being
the first, middle or last born in the family will one way or
another impact how much attention you get and the role you
play as a brother or sister in the family. Culture also plays a
strong role in birth order effects. Some cultures prioritize
first-born children, giving them more authority, receiving
more respect from younger siblings or having more rights
over property later in life. In Aboriginal culture, there are
even names indicating birth order for each gender. In other
cultures, first borns might experience more pressure to take
on family responsibilities, leading to higher levels of anxiety
and depression compared to their younger siblings.[5] Personality has a genetic component to it, but it is mainly shaped by
one's upbringing and environment. This development is often
referred to as nature versus nurture. From a behavioural perspective, being a sibling with a certain birth order means that
you will have to learn certain behavioural strategies over time

to be able to compete for attention, resources, uniqueness and position in the family. Your birth order can therefore influence who gets more or less of these resources, making you more prone to develop certain birth order traits.

Birth order traits

Whether anecdotal or research-based, certain behavioural and personality characteristics have been associated with one's birth order. The following describes the characteristics often associated with the different birth orders and how these are potentially shaped by the family dynamics.

First borns

First borns are the eldest of the siblings, hence timewise receive the most parental attention. Because first borns are the parents' first child, they are often given a lot of (detailed) attention and care from parents. It is often said that first borns develop the strongest bond with their parents and therefore later in life want to make sure to meet their parents' expectations. This can make first borns more responsible, goal-orientated, conscientious and outgoing, but also neurotic, conservative and bossy. There have been some ideas that first borns are slightly more intelligent (higher IQ) than younger brothers and sisters due to the *tutor effect* of having to educate younger siblings.[6] However, hard evidence that this is the case is missing.

Middle children

Middle children often find themselves between the best of both worlds. The first born with its privileges and the last born with its privileges. This can lead to many middle children feeling left out, ignored or excluded, making it feel hard to fit in. This can lead to the middle child feeling the least favourite of all siblings and the need to compete or be the peacemaker. This unique position is often referred to as *middle child syndrome* (note, this term is not used or seen as a mental disorder, it's merely a popular term). Middle child syndrome highlights that the middle child will often be less happy, more angry and more attention-deprived due to their birth order, causing all kinds of issues later in life. Lacking a clear understanding of their role in the family, the middle child may, as a consequence, also lack one in the world. Middle children are therefore believed to be the least connected to the family and often the first to leave home. However, other proponents of the middle child birth order argue that being the middle child actually has more positive qualities than the other birth orders do, such as being more diplomatic, independent, tentative, flexible, empathetic, easygoing and better at negotiating.

Last borns

Last borns often receive the most attention and care from all the siblings, making them feel more protected and cared for. They are often seen as the baby of the family, sometimes spoilt and seen as someone who can't do anything wrong. This can make last borns more agreeable, open, charming, popular, creative and have high self-esteem compared to older siblings, but they are also more risk-taking, rebellious and likely to become more dependent on others later in life.

DID YOU KNOW?
The impact of culture and gender on sibling position

To think of birth order as the only factor that can influence behaviour and personality in sibling relationships is too narrow. Human behaviour is complex and there are other factors that can influence human behaviour and family dynamics. Besides birth order, there is also something called sibling position.[7] If you are the only girl born into a family of five boys, you could receive more (special) attention, parents seeing you as the princess of the family. If a child is born with a disability, then more care is given by the parents and also by the other siblings to the disabled child, even if one's birth order would dictate otherwise. Or if a child is born after the death of a child, more care might be given to the newborn (or they may be overprotected). The impact of sibling relationships on self and others should always be visited through a multi-dimensional lens.

Is all of this fact or fiction? Like with horoscopes, it is easy to associate with the broad spectrum of the characteristics of birth order traits as they are very relatable. Whatever the case, there is truth in how birth orders can impact behaviour in the short- and long-term, albeit in a complex way. However, it is important to note that every family, family dynamic and situation is different, so it's hard to claim hard facts about someone's personality or quality of life based on one's birth order alone. What I believe is more important in determining how your relationship with your siblings impacts you is to evaluate if the behaviours you observe on a daily basis are healthy or unhealthy, and to figure out if/how sibling and family dynamics play a role in this behaviour. Even though parents like to believe that they treat all their children equally, they in fact don't – they have a different relationship with each of their kids. Parents often change as they get older and have more children, so each child gets a different version of their parent. If you feel impacted by your relationship with your siblings in the past, it might also be an idea to sit down and write out exactly what you feel has impacted you and how, and then to choose a moment to speak to your brother or sister about it. That one conversation later in life could be the catalyst to help you release old pains and maybe even rebuild a lost connection.

Red flags in sibling behaviour

Regardless of birth order, it is important to understand the origin of sibling behaviour and the impact it has on you. Identifying how family dynamics can motivate certain behaviours puts you in a better position to address unhealthy behaviours within parent–child and sibling–sibling relationships. Here are some examples of how to address family dynamic problematic behaviour:

Rivalry

Your brother or sister feels the need to compete with you. You feel that they always want to be better than you but not in a nice way. Ask yourself, are they naturally that way with other people as well or are they only more competitive in that way with you? Could the behavioural impact of your birth order have made your sibling want to compete with you more? If you believe so, then addressing the family dynamic and the feelings attached to perceived experiences with your sibling will have a more positive effect on changing the behaviour and the accompanying emotions, rather than just talking about the competitiveness alone.[8] As siblings, it is important to inquire about how the other person experienced growing up with you. Though you might think you know what is driving the other person's behaviour as a brother or a sister, you might be surprised by what you hear.

Controlling siblings

Some siblings can be very controlling in their relationship with their brother(s) and sister(s). This is especially true for older siblings, who naturally feel more in charge because of their age and position in the family and can be particularly bossy. Besides the eldest sibling, middle children can become bossier as new siblings join the rank. Controlling siblings can use manipulation techniques, such as lying, gaslighting, threats and guilt-tripping, to make you do what they want. To counter such behaviour can be hard because it is often an older brother or sister you're dealing with. Learning how to set boundaries is important within sibling relationships. If you feel pressured by a sibling, take your distance from them or minimize contact as much as possible. You can also set an ultimatum or explain what the consequences will be if they continue to control or manipulate you. It is important to follow through on the consequences you lay out to them if bad behaviours continue. Not doing so can worsen how they treat you moving forward. Finally, find ways to improve your communication skills. Unravel the sibling dynamics causing friction and find ways to diplomatically address the issues through communication, especially when you experience power imbalances in your sibling relationships (e.g. dealing with a physically stronger sibling).

A great example of someone who hasn't been affected by her middle-child status is reality TV superstar and successful businesswoman Kim Kardashian. Kim has clearly carved out an identity for herself. And if she did suffer from any lack of attention as a child, she definitely doesn't today.

The impact of birth order on sibling rivalry – what's the drama?

Having siblings can be a blessing and a curse at the same time. Sometimes you're lucky and have a fantastic relationship with your brothers and/or sisters, and sometimes you're unlucky in your relationship with your siblings. A personality mismatch between you and your siblings is often a cause of conflict between brothers and sisters or maybe a specific event triggered ill feelings towards each other, which jeopardizes the relationship. But could you ever imagine your birth order being a possible source of drama in sibling relationships? Some people believe it to be true and there is even some research that supports it. Being born first, last or somewhere in the middle can impact how your parents treat you and how you feel about yourself. Though not all research supports the birth order impact on mindset and behaviour, from a behavioural perspective, being a sibling with a certain birth order means that you will have to learn specific behavioural strategies over time to be able to compete for attention, resources, uniqueness and position in the family. First borns are believed to be the most conscientious and responsible out of all siblings. Last borns are often stereotyped as being carefree and the most creative, while middle children are thought to be the least happy and attention-deprived, hence the popular term middle child syndrome. All of this, fact or fiction? Popular language can create stereotypes or biased realities, which can be used for self-validation purposes. However, there is truth in how birth orders can impact behaviour in the short- and long-term, albeit in a complex way. Use common birth order beliefs as a guidepost, but always remember, every family environment is different. You should always look at your family situation from a unique perspective and try to uncover how family dynamics and sibling relationships have evolved over time and how they have shaped personalities and influenced behaviour.

It's a **red flag** if:
- As a parent you deprive your middle child of attention.
- As a parent you don't acknowledge the impact family dynamics can have on adult behaviours once kids grow up.
- You still hold grudges as an adult for how your parents treated you and your siblings differently. Learn to let go and forgive where possible.
- Your first-born status makes you more controlling in your romantic relationships, which can negatively affect your love life.

It's a **green flag** if:
- You understand that your birth order can impact your personality, beliefs and behaviour. However, you also realize it is not a given. Each family is different.
- You positively embrace the good characteristics of your birth order. The first born being results-driven and responsible, the middle child being empathetic and a great negotiator and the last born being positive and creative.
- You try to reconnect with siblings to talk about the past and find ways to soothe lingering pains and concerns as a way to free yourself and others from self-limiting beliefs.
- As a parent, you prevent middle child syndrome from happening. Make sure to give the middle child the attention they deserve.

Things to consider when deciding if you want in or out

Keeping good relationships with each other is an important goal for any family member, especially for siblings. However, it is not always possible to keep good relationships with brothers and sisters. You might not agree about how the other person is living their life or you might hold a grudge against one of your siblings for how they treated you in the past. It could very well be that your birth order, gender or other personal characteristic (or life event) made you more responsible or less seen or taken care of in the family. So many things can happen that can jeopardize family ties and one's willingness to stay connected. Your relationship with your siblings is important to your own development and finding ways to reconcile the past when needed is a learning journey every family member should engage in to maintain healthy relationships moving into the future. However, that is not always easy and sometimes impossible.

You don't feel negatively impacted as an adult by your birth order

- You value the importance of family and believe that blood is thicker than water. Every family member needs to find a way to deal with individual differences.
- You realize that your birth order has impacted your personality and your relationship with your siblings, but it doesn't define how you continue to engage with them as an adult.
- You find ways to talk about the past with your siblings as a means to address past pains and heal. Your siblings are also open to having the conversation with you.
- As the eldest child, it is highly probable that you may feel the most responsible for the family and the most willing to keep the sibling relationship strong.

You do feel negatively impacted as an adult by your birth order

- When the way your parents or siblings treat you negatively impacts your mental and physical health.
- When your parents and/or siblings don't accept who you are as a person.
- When your siblings have intentionally created an ill relationship between you and your parents.

ЧAS

- As the first born, you feel more responsible and as a consequence may feel more lonely or isolated. As the middle child, you have learnt to be the mediator in the family, potentially leaving you feeling less important as a sibling within the family unit. As the last born, you might feel less able to express yourself, or become more introverted due to overprotection or experiencing limitations to one's personal freedom.

Red Flag 4 'OMG, did you hear what happened to Wendy?'

When friends and family gossip

'Words have no wings but they can
fly a thousand miles.'
Korean proverb

When friends and family love to gossip

Communication, in spoken words or in writing, is an important tool for everyday life. It helps to create closeness, solve problems in relationships and inspire others to go above and beyond. Our language helps others understand who we are, how we think and what we find important. Words are powerful, not only because they convey a message, but also because they affect how people think and feel about themselves and how they think and feel about others. Unfortunately, not all types of communication are positive. Certain styles and forms of communication can be very destructive. Think of lying, gaslighting, swearing and manipulating. There are also other forms of communication that, depending on their usage, can be either positive or negative. Gossiping is an example of such an ambivalent communication style and is a form of dialogue that friends and family often engage in. Across cultures, gossip serves a social and psychological purpose in human relationships (it brings people together and allows for friends or family members to share pains or unhappiness with each other).

According to one specific study,[1] the average person gossips for approximately 52 minutes a day. However, gossiping can be extremely harmful and a form of aggression aimed at destroying close friendships or ruining someone's reputation. That's why it is important to understand why people gossip, specifically in which situations, and what can be done about it. Diving into the psychology of gossiping can help explain why friends and family members gossip and how positive banter can turn into negative bad-mouthing. Some friends or family members might use gossip as a weapon to destabilize existing relationships, and it is important to recognize the signs of positive and negative gossiping behaviour to prevent it from negatively impacting your life. Being able to identify the red and green flags in gossiping not only aids in building stronger relationships, but also equips you with the knowledge and tools to become a better communicator. Time to turn gossip into a tool to build stronger connections among the people you love the most.

The psychology of gossiping

The psychology of gossiping is extremely interesting. Gossiping is the act of speaking about someone in a good or bad way when they are not present. Gossiping generally has a negative connotation to it. When we think of gossiping, we often think of spreading rumours or talking bad about others to damage their reputation or relationships. However, there are also positive aspects to it and it can even be considered constructive to human relationships. People engage in gossip to bond with others, share information and maintain social order. Gossiping can also help deal with negative emotions and overcome psychological discomfort. From an evolutionary perspective, besides bonding, gossip is a communication strategy to influence social systems through reputation and establish rules within the group to keep people in check. Gossiping can be seen as a survival strategy. And according to some research, up to 67 per cent of daily conversations are related to other people and/or social topics, with women engaging more in gossip than men.[2] It seems shocking to hear that we 'gossip' so much, but in social settings we generally like to talk about others and share social information. Everyone gossips. Recent research also shows that gossiping releases oxytocin, which makes people feel happier and closer together.[3] The way gossip is used to regulate oneself and facilitate relationships determines if it is used for good or for bad. That's why it is important to become more reflective of when and why you or others gossip, and which function it plays in one's social life. This also makes it easier to determine when gossip is a red flag or when it's a green flag.

The dark side of gossiping

Gossiping and spreading rumours with the intent to hurt others is a malicious act and a sign of aggression. The psychological reasons behind this behaviour are often related to fear, jealousy, insecurities, retaliation, wanting to feel important and loneliness. People often engage in bad-mouthing when they don't feel strong or confident enough to address people or situations head-on. Taking an indirect approach to hurting others is less confrontational and can be done without the other person directly noticing what's going on. There are also psychopathological reasons why people gossip. People with narcissistic personality disorder, for example, often try to ruin the reputation of others they fear or dislike, scared of being called out on their own bad behaviours or as a way to self-promote. People who score high in dark triad personality traits, which besides narcissism also include Machiavellian and psychopathic tendencies, actively engage in reputation smearing and spreading rumours without feelings of remorse. They even see negative gossip as entertaining.

What's so fascinating about gossip is that if you are in good standing within your social group, gossip fosters collaboration. People hear about you in the corridors and through other group members. Your reputation surely precedes you and others reach out to work with you or to socialize with you. 'Success breeds success', as they say and people like to be around people who do well. But this positive reputation also attracts the bad actors in the group who are fearful of your success and positive vibe. Steadily you will experience microaggressions at work or among friends and family, which put you on your guard. When you try to protect yourself by not engaging with bad actors, your disengagement and pushback are used against you. And slowly a positive reputation can turn into a bad one if not managed strategically. It's no surprise that high-performers in organizations or successful friends and family members are the target of negative gossip by peers or people who are close to them due to jealousy and insecurities. They become the target of bad-mouthing and rumours. It can also be the organizational or family culture that facilitates this negative behaviour to keep people in check, especially in big families or in professions where individuals stand out and competition is high, like in the media, academia and sports. If you have become a victim of bad-mouthing or negative gossip without solid grounds, always remember when people talk about you, you're probably important, because if they speak of themselves, no one would listen. Keep your head high and move on. Let karma do its work.

Who gossips more: men or women?

Both men and women engage in the act of gossiping. However, according to various behavioural, gender and clinical studies, women tend to gossip more than men[4] and there are differences in the topics both genders gossip about. There are various reasons for this. One specific reason why women engage more in gossiping among other women is to compete with peers for potential mates (romantic rivalry threat).[5] Gossip can also be used as a weapon or as an act of aggression. While men generally tend to express aggression physically, women engage more in reputation smearing and gossiping as a form of aggression. Specifically, highly competitive women engage more in aggressive forms of spreading rumours than less competitive women. Another reason why women engage more in gossip is that gossip fulfils intimacy needs and, compared to men, women seek more closeness with others as a way to feel informed, feel safe and stay connected.

When is gossiping healthy and when is it unhealthy?

Gossiping takes on various forms and, as was explained above, there can be different reasons why people gossip. Not all gossip is bad and some can actually be very positive. But what is the difference between healthy and unhealthy gossiping? The following breaks down how positive and negative gossip is used and provides examples of what is said in each scenario:

Healthy gossip

Sharing positive news about friends and family members :

- Talking about someone starting a new job, getting promoted, being in a new relationship or buying a new house
- Talking about future plans of loved ones as a way to support or to feel inspired

Unhealthy gossip

Sharing negative news about friends and family members:

- Spreading rumours
- Talking about someone's behaviour
- Damaging someone's reputation
- Trying to create animosity between friends

Learning the skill of positive gossip

- Consider if gossiping is going to serve a purpose in your conversation (for yourself or for the other person).
- Don't gossip to advance yourself or for personal gain.
- Don't be negative about others. If you want to warn, then warn, but only to serve the needs of the group (not yourself).
- Don't change the story or distort information.
- Try to focus on the positive points of another person. Also, when you hear gossip, choose to stay neutral and counter the information with requests for positive comments about the person in question.

DID YOU KNOW?
Gossiping is so central to human behaviour that different cultures around the world have peculiar names they give to people who love to gossip. Some of my favourite names given to gossip queens and kings in different parts of the world are:

Radio Mileva (Serbian) – which means something like 'gossip central'

Chismoso/a (Spanish) – someone (male or female) who spreads rumours even if they are not true

Roddeltante (Dutch) – literally translated as 'gossiping aunty'

八卦 (Bāguà) (Chinese) – someone who enjoys talking about other people's private affairs

Koutsombolis (Greek) – gossiper

Marites (Tagalog) – a way to call someone a gossiper in the Philippines

Yenta (Yinglish – a Yiddish loan word in English) – gossiper or blabbermouth

Fofoqueiro/a (Brazilian Portuguese) – someone (male or female) who loves to gossip

Mchongezi (Swahili) – someone who speaks badly about others

When friends and family gossip – what's the drama?

Conversing, in words or in DMs, is an important tool for everyday life. Our conversations with others help us to bond, solve problems and even influence the minds of others. Gossiping is a specific form of conversation that has the power to connect but also to destroy. Gossip serves various purposes in human relationships, from simply sharing information to dealing with negative emotions and overcoming psychological discomfort, and also as a way to influence social systems to keep people in check. Gossiping generally has a negative connotation to it, and rightly so, because not everyone is capable of positive gossip. Positive gossip is one's ability to share positive information about other people, which elevates their status and reputation within social groups. Negative gossip, on the other hand, hurts relationships and can ruin someone's reputation and even career prospects. Unfortunately, many people engage in negative gossip due to various reasons, such as personal insecurities, fear, jealousy, retaliation, wanting to feel important, ill intent and/or loneliness. You can't fully protect yourself from gossip, but you can learn how to not let it affect you. Equally important is to develop a habit of not engaging in spreading hurtful rumours and, where possible, to protect others whom people speak ill of. Speaking up can challenge the intent of people's reasons to engage in negative gossip and even make them more reflective if they should continue their crusade.

It's a **red flag** if:
- You, your friends or your family engage in bad-mouthing or gossiping.
- You, your friends or your family engage in reputation smearing out of jealousy, spite, self-esteem issues or mental health issues.
- You, your friends or your family engage in unhealthy gossip as a form of aggression.
- You allow yourself to be too much affected by what other people say about you.

It's a **green flag** if:
- You can distinguish the difference between healthy and unhealthy gossip and choose to stay away from unhealthy gossip.
- You understand the role of positive gossip in social relationships and use it to bond with others, only sharing positive aspects of the people you speak about.
- You protect people whom others gossip negatively about in your presence or challenge the bad-mouthers on their intentions for spreading such rumours.

- You know how to counter attacks of gossip. You know when it's time to be quiet, to push back or to leave.

Things to consider when deciding if you want in or out

Let's face it: people love to gossip! It's human nature and who doesn't enjoy getting in on the beef? Engaging in positive or negative gossip has various psychological benefits to it. It helps you to bond with others and at times it can even help alleviate psychological discomfort. However, it is important to think twice before gossiping about, or bad-mouthing, others. Ask yourself what your true intentions are of wanting to engage in spreading rumours. Are you upset? Do you feel important by putting others down? Or do you want to be a moral crusader? Whatever the reason, always start by acknowledging your intentions and consider what the potential consequences will be of your actions (either directly or indirectly). If you enjoy gossiping, why not engage in positive gossip? You never know how the universe will reward you for your kind words.

What promotes unhealthy gossip

- Not being in a good headspace.
- The organizational culture you work in showing that spreading bad rumours about others is acceptable and a way to survive and thrive.
- You engage in gossiping to show how much on top of new developments you are, which makes you feel important.

- You see gossiping as a way to influence the social circles you operate in to keep people in check.

What prevents unhealthy gossip

- You realize the impact spreading rumours can have on others (including yourself).
- You become more aware of the underlying reasons why you engage in gossip and want to change your behaviours.
- You want to protect people in your social circle. You challenge others when they gossip about people you know.
- You prefer to address people directly when there is something you don't like about them rather than to gossip about them behind their back.

Red Flag 5 'My lovely idiot'

When friends try to put you down

'Be careful who you call your friends. I'd rather have
four quarters than one hundred pennies.'
Al Capone

When friends become fiends

Having close friends is important. Friends have your back,
help you grow and tell things how they are. I always like to
say that friends 'buffer the pain and help you gain'. No matter
how difficult it is to hear the hard truth at times, when it
comes from the people closest to you, you know it often
comes from a good place. Your good friends have your best
interests at heart. But sometimes besties change and treating
you well is not a given anymore. At first, you might not notice
changes in a friend's behaviour, but over time you start to
pick up on the subtle remarks or condescending tone. 'You're
too old to be partying so late' or 'You don't look that pretty
like you used to', poking at your insecurities or purposefully
trying to bring you down. Sometimes friends are too judgemental about your lifestyle or who you are dating, criticizing
how you live your life and who you spend your time with,
which can make you feel like you are continuously being
judged and leaving you feeling drained and unsupported.
Negativity in friendship can also start when your friends stop

complimenting you about your achievements or not acknowledging the progression you are making in life. Whatever the reason for the change of heart and behaviour, it is always important to address it. Many people prefer to turn a blind eye to the problem, not wanting to hurt the friendship or hoping that things will pass over time. But this is how problems are fostered and friendships eventually end or turn nasty. Being able to identify the red flags in your social circle is important to allow you to address problems quickly and find out what the reasons are for the change in behaviour. Not all negative behaviour is callous; sometimes friends act out of character because of insecurities and fears. And not all unhealthy behaviours are severe in nature, nor can they always be solved. Understanding the psychological drivers of bad behaviour within the realm of friendships can provide you with the tools to better understand why a good old friend can turn into a bitter old fiend and how best to address the issue at hand. Sometimes, enough is enough, but sometimes we need to help others realize the hard reality of their behaviour. That's what good friends do!

What makes friends change character

It's hard building strong and deep connections in today's fluid world. It is easy to call someone a friend, but a true friend transcends mere acquaintance. Friendships are powerful bonds between two or more individuals, which strengthen through shared experiences and a deeper understanding of each other. Close friends provide you with a sense of reality and mental and physical support in times of need, which help buffer negative events. It's hard to build close friendships, so once you have them, you invest in them, and you are OK to give more slack to them when things don't go well. That's what friends are for, to support you in your good moments and in your bad moments. But why is it that some people act out of character and become negative, especially after you have known them for years? As you can imagine, there is no clear answer to this question, but there are some common reasons why friends might treat you differently over time.

Jealousy

One common reason why friends will you treat you differently is because of jealousy. You might have found a new boyfriend or girlfriend and decide to spend more time with them than with your friend. The new relationship brings a sudden change to your long-standing friendship, which can make the other person feel unhappy that the contact has become less frequent. They might be jealous of your new relationship and therefore start to treat you differently or talk ill of your new partner, fearing that if the romantic relationship continues your friendship will be lost.

Fear and insecurities

Another very common reason why friends change their behaviour towards you is due to insecurities. If you are someone who likes to grow and work on yourself, this might leave friends feeling left behind in their own development. As you further develop, some friends might see a distance emerging between you and them to which they react negatively. It's not you they are actually reacting to, it is the gap they believe is developing between you and them because of your personal development. This can create feelings of insecurity, competition or even animosity as a way to reconcile internal frustrations of not developing oneself or not being happy for someone else's growth.

Bitterness (unhappy with self)

Not everyone is very happy at the moment, especially with so much turmoil and uncertainty happening in the world. People can become bitter, often due to emotions such as anger and sadness, which develop gradually over time. One's bitterness is often expressed in disappointment or irritability, which can cloud how a friend normally engages with you. Their bitterness can make them more judgemental of you or more demanding of attention. They might not be as supportive anymore and even see your friendship as a source of frustration. When a friend becomes bitter, it is important to listen to why they are sad and disappointed, and to discuss how best to support them moving forward, even when they try to project their bitterness on to you and bring you down.

Self-centredness

Another source of behavioural change is when friends become self-centred. Caring about yourself is never a bad thing. In fact, it is very important at times to focus on yourself. But sometimes friends can get a bit carried away in their self-indulgence. Self-centredness is characterized by people only wanting to talk about themselves and their achievements. Even when you want to share about what is happening in your life, some friends make it all about them. You might hear them saying, 'I also had such a bad time this weekend' or 'That's not as bad as what happened to me.' Becoming more self-centred in life can be due to various reasons, such as upbringing, trauma related to neglect or abuse, personality disorders or social media or society overemphasizing the need for individualism and self-love. Recognizing when friends are more focused on themselves and care less about keeping friendships alive is a good starting point to have a solid conversation about how to bring more balance to your mutual bond.

DID YOU KNOW?
Why is it so hard to let go of a worthless friendship?
Solid friendships take years to develop. You invest so much time in building a strong bond with someone you care about that it's natural not to give up on people close to you when things don't go so well. Every kind of relationship has its ups and downs, but sometimes, some downs keep dragging on and eventually become toxic. So, why do so many people keep hanging on to friendships that they know are not good for them anymore? The answer is not that straightforward as there are various psychological reasons that hold people back from letting go. One key reason is the belief that you can fix someone or have the ability to change people. If a friend is misbehaving and continues to mistreat you even after all your efforts to try to change their behaviour, you might still tolerate their abuse by making excuses for their bad behaviour. You might say, 'They had such a bad childhood' or 'I know they are a good person on the inside.' Thinking you can fix people actually prevents them from changing their behaviour. It is better to create distance when friends disrespect you. It sends out a clear

message that 'enough is enough' and maybe it's time to change. Another reason why people find it hard to let go of bad friendships is due to a sense of loyalty. 'Friends to the end' is the mindset many people grow up with and in some communities being loyal to friends is even socially demanded. Don't get me wrong, loyalty is an important virtue to have in a friendship, but sometimes your loyalty is taken for granted or even misused. It is important to realize when certain friendships become hurtful or hold you back from growing, and that a loyal person can be pushed to a point that they don't care anymore. Finally, not wanting to end a friendship could be linked to one's own self-esteem. Not believing you are worthy of good friends, you hold on to those people who don't treat you right. If you find yourself hanging on to someone who is intentionally bringing you down or mistreating you, then you will do yourself a favour by letting go. Remember, respecting yourself makes others respect you more.

When friends speak behind your back

When you think of good friendship, the last thing you expect is that your friends will speak behind your back. Having your back and protecting you in front of other people is a hallmark of good friendship. So, why do 'friends' talk ill about you to others? A common reason why friends talk behind your back is because they are angry with you but don't want to tell you to your face. Instead, they out their frustration about you to others. Friends can also feel the urge to talk bad about you if they feel that you have let them down or made them feel inferior in some way. Because they don't feel strong enough to confront you about it or want to hurt you in a passive-aggressive way, they will gossip about you to others as a means of retaliation (see Red Flag 4 for more about gossiping). When you find out that friends have spoken badly about you to others, it can be a painful experience that can damage the trust you have as friends. When friends feel the need to talk behind your back, always remember that their behaviour says something about them more than it does about you. Good friends know how to have difficult conversations with you when it is needed and to tell you when something you have done has hurt them. Even when friends do talk behind your back, always confront them. Have that conversation. Eventually, it has to stop otherwise it makes no sense to remain friends.

When it comes to friendships gone nasty, there are many to talk about. Out of the many celebrity friendship bad-mouthing accounts, the Katy Perry and Taylor Swift feud definitely stands out. Katy and Taylor were friends at the start of their global stardom. However, over time, both singers got entangled in various fights due to supposed back-stabbing and bad-mouthing incidents. In 2019, reportedly both singers were finally able to put their differences aside and are now on good terms again.

When friends try to put you down – what's the drama?

It is important to have close friends. People you know who understand you and who have your back. A good friend tells you things exactly how they are. They don't sugarcoat what needs to be said. What they tell you can be a hard pill to swallow sometimes, but you know it comes from a good place. It takes time to invest in building trust and a solid friendship with someone. Unfortunately, good friendships can turn sour for reasons you didn't see coming. Someone you love and trust as a friend can eventually turn on you. It is hard to guess what the reason is for people's change of heart, but as friends you should always address the elephant in the room. Maybe you have changed and they don't like it or maybe they are going through a rough time and are projecting the bitterness onto you. Being treated badly by a friend can be a very painful experience and you might not be willing to address the problem so as not to hurt the other person or hoping that things will pass with time. Unfortunately, this doesn't always work and can lead to even more resentment or problems down the road. Being able to identify the red flags in your social circle is important to address problems soon and to decide how to address them.

It's a **red flag** if:
- You allow yourself to be put down by your friends and make excuses for their bad behaviours towards you.
- Your friends or family members (subtly) joke about you in a negative (or condescending) way.
- Your friends' bitterness is projected onto you by receiving negative comments or being snapped at.

- Your friends only talk about themselves and show little interest in listening to you.

It's a **green flag** if:
- Your friends and/or family members joke about you but not in a mean way.
- You understand that in a long-standing friendship support, time and distance are required to allow people to go through their difficult phases – especially when you can't always see eye to eye.
- You are able to start a conversation with a friend to discuss the change in behaviour or character and can tell when their answers are genuine or not.
- When the time is right, you're able to let go of people who don't treat you right.

Things to consider when deciding if you want in or out

It can be very painful and confusing to realize someone you consider a good friend has started to treat you in a bad way. They start to put you down in front of others, they make (subtle) negative remarks, speak badly about you or they remain silent about your success but enjoy it when you are not doing well. There is always a reason for a change in behaviour and it is important to figure out why it is happening. In many cases, by having open and candid conversations about the situation, you can eventually figure out the reason for the change in behaviour. However, sometimes people are not willing to talk about what is really bothering them. If you can't figure things out and things don't improve after various attempts to find a resolution, maybe it's better to say goodbye, which can be a hard thing to do depending on your sense of loyalty. But also remember that loyalty can be abused. People come on your bus in life and also get off. Some stay for a while, while others remain for a lifetime. As you grow mentally, physically and spiritually, you decide who you want to keep in your life bus and who not. Bringing new people on the bus who can help you grow requires emotional space and time in your busy schedule. Focusing more energy on the new and less on fixing what sometimes can't be fixed is a mental shift you will need to make.

Willingness to stay

- You understand the importance of a good friendship and aim to unearth the underlying reasons why your friend is treating you in the way they are today.
- You have a strong sense of loyalty to your friends and saying 'goodbye' is not an option for you.
- You realize that you have changed and your friends are (indirectly) reacting to that. Time for a deeper conversation.
- You figure out that your friend is bitter and projecting their bitterness onto you. Be a supporting and loving friend through these difficult times.

Time to leave

- After repeated attempts to solve the problems in your friendship, you find there is no change.
- You are being mentally and emotionally affected by how your friend is treating you.

- You realize that people naturally change and that you can't fix people. If people are not willing to improve themselves to keep the friendship alive, then so be it.
- Your friends are not happy for your recent growth or success and try to put you down as a way to keep you in place.

Red Flag 6 'Can you pay this time?'
Dealing with selfish friends

'No one has ever become poor by giving.'
The Diary of a Young Girl, Anne Frank

Dealing with selfish friends

It is important to have good friends in your life. By good friends, I mean people you feel strongly connected to and to whom you can open up to share the personal things happening in your life. The good and the bad. Good friends are people you meet up regularly with in real life. I start with this definition because friendship can mean different things to different people. In today's world, people have multiple contacts they call 'friends', who they have never even met in real life (just online) but nevertheless feel close to. In this chapter, I am referring to friends who you meet with regularly and have a strong and meaningful connection with (or have built up in the past and stayed connected to at a distance). It is often said that you can count the number of close friends you have on one hand, which means it's hard to find people you can really relate to and trust. And when you do find them, you make sure to invest in your close circle of friends as much as possible to keep the bond strong, even when due to work or other circumstances you are physically worlds apart from each other. Spending quality time with your friends is core to building connection, intimacy and trust. Investing means giving. However, giving is not everyone's strong part. Some friends are naturally not that giving, but still good friends. Others are nice people but see friends as a way to get further in life, taking more than they are giving. But it can also happen that good friends suddenly stop reciprocating like they did in the past (which they themselves are not always conscious of). It could very well be that something has happened in your friendship that has made the other person less willing to share or give. Or maybe it's your over-giving nature or people-pleasing tendencies that have made your friends less generous.

Whatever the reason, learning about the importance of giving in relationships is important. Also, being able to identify when the friendship has become unbalanced in a give-and-take way is important if you want to find ways to address the issue at hand and save your friendship. It's easy to say goodbye to a friend when we see something we don't like in them because we believe there are so many other people out there to meet still, but good friends are hard to come by and maintaining strong connections is central to mental and physical health. Identifying red and green flags in your friendship is important for deciding if continuing the bond is still worth it.

The law of reciprocity

Sociologist Alvin Gouldner declared in the 1960s that reciprocity was a fundamental law in human relationships and helped facilitate strong human connection. 'You scratch my back, I scratch yours' or 'Tit for tat' are the proverbial sayings that reflect the importance of reciprocal exchanges in all types of relationships. We evaluate the strength of a relationship on how positive these exchanges are and if our give and take between friends happens in a balanced and fair way. Not only humans but also primates engage in reciprocal behaviour as a way to bond and create social cohesion within groups.[1] We can learn a lot about human behaviour by observing animal behaviour and it is no surprise that nature has provided scientists with many interesting insights about what creates strong bonds among humans and the factors that drive cohesive behaviour. Primates grooming each other, for example, is a form of altruistic or mutualistic behaviour. You can do things because you inherently want to do things for others or you can do them because you know it will benefit you in some way (e.g. inclusion, protection, receiving other kinds of resources). Reciprocity is a social service that underlies both animal and human relationships. Though no one is expected to pick fleas from friends' heads as an act of friendly service or a sign of appreciation, we humans engage in various exchanges with friends to build service and connection. And it's natural to expect friends to do the same for you (albeit not always in the same way). Psychologically, inviting someone to your place for dinner creates an internal pressure for the other person to eventually do the same for you. Paying for a dinner will most likely lead to the other person paying for you next time. Exchanges don't have to be mechanical ('I do it so you need to do it next') but you know and can feel when it is time and necessary to give back.

The emotional bank account

Being good friends for years, you have built up an emotional bank account. An emotional bank account is a metaphor I like to use for how many brownie points someone has acquired in your mental scorecard. After building a solid and trustworthy connection, you're not always counting what your friends are doing for you. There will be moments when you or your friends will be in a difficult situation, not being able to mentally, emotionally or physically give back. Because they have built up goodwill in your bank account, you accept and even support them where possible, expecting things will get better in the future. However, if things don't change and people keep on taking, you might not pay too much attention to it at first, but your emotional bank account does get depleted. How big the emotional bank is and how much deficit it can take before filing for bankruptcy differs from relationship to relationship and person to person.

How to identify when friends act like leeches

The unfortunate truth is that some friends are absolute leeches. They just want to take as much as possible from you without giving anything in return. And when you have nothing else to give (or when you are in need of help), they move on to the next person to leech further. There are various reasons why some friends engage in this behaviour.

Selfishness

Selfishness is a big word that needs to be unpacked. Some people are selfish by nature, which is a trait that is hard to change. It doesn't mean that selfish people are always thinking about themselves, but that in some areas of their lives giving is less of a priority. Besides personality, selfishness can be linked to life experiences and circumstances. Losing wealth or health or going through a divorce can (temporarily) make someone more focused on themselves and thus less willing to give. Circumstantial reasons for being less generous can have short-term or long-term effects. Once things resolve, people normally go back to their giving selves again. However, that is not true for everyone. Some remain in a taking mindset or even become extremely selfish in various areas of their lives (doing so unconsciously). This can be linked to trauma or to enjoying the benefits previous circumstances provided. Whatever the reason, only taking and not giving will make it hard to sustain a healthy friendship in the long run.

People pleasing

If you are a people pleaser or someone who is naturally more generous, it can happen that your behavioural tendencies in friendships can unbalance the reciprocal nature of a bond. Though you mean well, giving too much is never a good thing. In essence, you are conditioning the other person to receive without the need to give back. Some friends who have less regard for giving back can take advantage of your good intentions. A good friend, on the other hand, will eventually reciprocate your actions or at least tell you that you don't always need to pay or do stuff for them. They might even ask you, 'Why do you always want to please? It's OK to get something in return' or 'I love you as a friend. Giving me stuff won't make me love you more. Just being you is more than enough for me.' Once you start to realize that your people-pleasing tendencies can actually hurt your relationships and you try to rebalance the reciprocal nature of your bond, don't be surprised if your friends start to get upset with you or call you less. Let them take their distance and reevaluate if maintaining a friendship with you in a more balanced way is still worth it for them. If not, let them go. Sure, you will feel anxious and guilty about it (which could trigger your people-pleasing tendencies again), but acknowledging that people should like you for who you are (and not only for what you do for them) is important. Creating stronger friendships starts with becoming aware of how our own behaviours can disharmonize existing bonds. Empathy without self-respect will lead to self-sabotage; you will always see the good in other people but you will use that as an excuse to allow them to hurt you.

DID YOU KNOW?
Today's economic climate makes it hard to meet in person
With rising food and energy prices, many people are thinking twice about spending money on restaurants, partying and travel. The lack of leisure spending is also impacting the number of social moments people are having with friends, as well as the busyness of today meaning people also don't spend much time meeting

---

friends at home. Which is a shame, as you can meet friends anywhere you want. Many people feel ashamed to speak about their financial situation to a friend, which can also be culturally related, but good friends will always be understanding of your situation. Instead of meeting outside, consider bringing people inside. Instead of going to a restaurant, for example, have a culinary tasting at home on a rotating basis, like in the British reality series *Come Dine with Me*. It's a great way to spend quality time with friends and to appreciate each other's cooking skills as well. Definitely worth a snap or a story on Instagram! Instead of going to the cinema, organize a Netflix binge night. Popcorn, bites and giggles, fun guaranteed! Or play a fun card game. Spending quality time with others doesn't have to cost much, but at the same time is priceless.

*What are the best ways to deal with
people who just want things from you?*

Once you realize that you have friends who are only taking and not giving, you might wonder what you can do about it. Here are some steps you can take to address the one-sided relationship:

Acknowledgement

It is important to start by acknowledging why you feel your friend is taking more than they are giving. Which behaviours do you observe? Do they only talk about themselves without asking what is happening in your life? Do they never pay for drinks or dinner when you go out? Do they only want to meet you when they want something? Identify the behaviours you find most annoying and try to figure out the reasons behind them. This will help you to address your observations and concerns to your friend.

Express your needs

When you decide to speak to your friend, it is important to explain how their behaviour is impacting you and your relationship. It is also very important to express your needs if you felt that your needs in the past were not being met. Remember, your friends are not mind readers, so it is important to express what is important to you. You might be worried about having the conversation with your friend, scared you might hurt them, but not addressing the problem at hand can have more severe consequences to your relationship than potentially hurting someone's feelings by telling them what bothers you or what you need.

Consider the consequences

It is important to think carefully about the outcome of the conversation (or of not having any conversation at all). What do you want to achieve in the end? Do you want to improve the relationship through a candid conversation? Or do you want to take some distance from your friend for a while? Perhaps you are willing to end it if the selfish behaviours continue? Planning through the different scenarios is a good way to prepare for different outcomes and will give you more confidence in managing difficult conversations. Remember, there is a natural evolution to friendships. When shared emotional bonds or personal interests diverge, it's OK to let things go. Maybe there will be a time later in life when it makes sense to reconnect again as friends.

In the story *A Christmas Carol*, Charles Dickens writes about Ebenezer Scrooge, a cold-hearted miser who is visited by three spirits on Christmas night that show him his past, present and possible future if he doesn't change his ways. The visit by the three spirits weighs heavily on his guilty conscience and Scrooge decides to become more giving. Though the story of Scrooge embodies the spirit of Christmas – giving – I think it's important that we always reflect on the power of giving in any relationship at any time.

Dealing with selfish friends – what's the drama?

Reciprocity is central to human relationships. Every good friendship is based on a balanced and fair exchange of give and takes. Even among primates, there is a 'you eat my fleas and I'll eat yours'. It helps them to bond and to feel a sense of safety. We humans are no different. Though we don't eat each other's fleas, we generally know when and how to give back when we receive a favour or an invite from a friend. However, not everyone is willing to reciprocate or sees the need to do so. And some people are just downright stingy and just take, take, take. It can happen in a good friendship that people go through difficult times and are financially or emotionally not able to give back like they normally do. But because you have built trust and an emotional bank account with your good friends, you are not expecting to get anything back immediately, as you just want to help. Many people in today's world call random people they meet online a friend, so it is not surprising that there is no emotional investment in people you meet online to reciprocate favours received. However, when true friends stop giving back or keep on leaving their wallet at home every time you go out for drinks and dinners, it's to re-evaluate the basis of your friendship. It could very well be that you have been too giving in recent times, which some friends (unintentionally) have become used to. It is also we who need to evaluate our own behaviour when we want to maintain a healthy and well-balanced bond with others.

It's a **red flag** if:
- Your friends ask for more than they give. They act like leeches.
- Your friends don't invest in your relationship with them.
- Your friends only text you when they need something.
- You believe that you need to give first before you deserve to get something in return.

It's a **green flag** if:
- You understand that reciprocity is a law that facilitates all social relationships. There is always a give and take, which should be mostly balanced.
- You invite people over for drinks or dinner (or dine out) when you are invited by others.
- You understand that if friends are not giving back in the same way all of a sudden there might be something

happening in their lives that is preventing them. You choose to inquire in a non-judgemental way.

- You understand that there is a limit to everything. If your emotional bank account is empty, maybe it's time to make more difficult decisions about the friendship.

Things to consider when deciding if you want in or out

When you start to realize that your friend has become less giving, it is very important to figure out what the reason is behind it. There could be various factors impacting someone's change in behaviour, not all of them bad. On the contrary, there are legitimate reasons why some people can't give back in the moment. The problem is that they might not be as open about the reasons, so it is always good to reach out to them to see what has changed in their life. Good friends should be able to have open and candid conversations with each other, but sometimes it requires a nudge from a buddy. But what should you do when close friends are only taking and not giving back? Is there a sense of entitlement or don't they see a future anymore with you as a friend? Or perhaps they are going through a difficult time and it's time to figure out what the reasons are for a change in character. Figuring out the cause can help you to decide how to help out or how to continue your friendship.

Willingness to stay

- You value your friendship and want to try to figure out what has caused the change in character.

71

- You understand that your close friend is going through a difficult time and you don't mind temporarily giving more than receiving.
- Your friend has always been a bit on the tight side, but you value your bond and know how to maintain a healthy relationship that feels fair.
- You understand that your people-pleasing tendencies or generosity has unbalanced the reciprocal nature of your friendship; you giving more and the other person taking more without feeling the need to reciprocate like before. Time to reconsider your approach to restore the balance.

Time to leave

- Your friend only takes and doesn't give anything in return, and you can't identify any logical reason for this change in behaviour. Maybe it's time to distance yourself from your friend.
- Your friend doesn't see a future with you anymore. Time for a chat or time to take some distance.
- You keep inviting your friend but don't see it being reciprocated. Remember, you can't squeeze blood from a stone, so stop inviting.
- The one-sided relationship is making you deeply unhappy. Time to focus on yourself.

Work Relationships

Red flags at work

We spend a solid one-third of our awake lives at work. Work plays a significant role in our lives and helps shape our identity and sense of self-worth. The psychological impact of work, and within it work relationships, on our mental and physical well-being is huge. It is important to make sure we work in an environment that is secure, supportive and positive. Building strong and healthy relationships in the workplace with peers, managers and other members of the organizational tribe not only motivates you to do your best at work but can also help you advance your career and feel a sense of safety and belonging in the organization. Especially in today's volatile and uncertain business environment, people want to feel safe, connected and inspired. Unfortunately, not all colleagues have good intentions and at times you might face precarious situations, such as micro-management, harassment and political attacks. If you haven't been subjected to such behaviours in the past, it can be very hard to identify, and by the time you realize something is wrong, your mental health could already be at stake or you might be out of a job. Learning to identify red and green flags at work is important to ensure you build healthy relationships with the people around you in the workplace. It is said that people often leave the organization because of a bad relationship with a manager, so knowing how to identify healthy and unhealthy behaviours in the person who supervises your work is an important skill set to develop. You

RED FLAGS, GREEN FLAGS

minimize the chance of being subjected to bad behaviours and you maximize your ability to progress in the organization, knowing that there will always be people who prefer to see you crumble than rise up. For both you and your manager, working well with others and rising to power come with responsibility. Identifying your own red flags in work settings and work relationships is equally important to help you foster strong bonds at work and advance your career in an ethical manner. Work relationships are about give and take, but sometimes people prefer to take more than they should or take at the expense of your livelihood and sanity. Learning about red and green flags at work helps you stay focused on what will get you further, allows you to push back professionally when people overstep their mark and helps you see the psychological reasons why people do what they do in the workplace. The coming six chapters about red and green flags in work relationships will help you create stronger relationships at work and advance your career success through others and improved decision-making.

Red Flag 7 'This company is your family'
Managers demanding unwavering loyalty

'Family is the most important thing in the world.'
Princess Diana

Being part of the corporate family

It's a wonderful feeling to know that you are part of a loving family. You are taken care of, you know that you belong and you've learnt that together everyone achieves more. Almost everyone knows that building and sustaining a family takes a considerable amount of time, and much is needed from your side to make it work. Love, protection, loyalty and sacrifice are central tenets of family life. Besides the family you get, there is also the family you create, and many people develop strong bonds with friends, who can feel like the brother or sister they never had, as willing to love and protect as any family member. Similarly, organizations (especially the leaders and managers running the show) try to create a family environment at work to help people feel safe, productive and like they belong. Some companies do an excellent job recreating a family environment in the workplace, enticing enough to inspire employees to be productive and weather difficult times together. Especially when the world outside feels so unpredictable and uncertain, knowing you have a company that feels like a family can help you feel safe. However, some managers play the 'we are your family' card to demand loyalty from their employees while having no intention of investing time, money or effort into developing and retaining workers, especially when the going gets tough. Building meaningful connections at work is essential to your career success and your well-being, so being able to differentiate between authentic and false family praise at work is essential to figure out if you are in the right environment. This chapter explores the fascinating psychology of attachment at work and uncovers when work culture and management practices to develop strong bonds are a green flag and when they are a red flag.

Why is having a strong connection at work important?

When you go to work, you are bringing your whole self to the workplace. Even though you might not show your true colours or keep parts of yourself hidden, your mind, body and heart are with you when you are doing your job. And because you are not a robot or zombie, you need to feel a connection with the work you do and a sense of belonging in the workplace to be able to do your job properly. No one can be engaged at work if they don't feel somehow emotionally connected to their job. The difference between feeling a connection at work and feeling no connection at all is like saying to yourself, 'I love my job!' versus 'Fuck, get me the hell out of here!' Behavioural studies show that having meaningful relationships at work and feeling emotionally connected to one's job can be beneficial in more ways than one, leading to all kinds of positive outcomes, such as higher productivity, less absenteeism, more willingness to go the extra mile, increased resilience when faced with difficulties and improved mental health.[1,2,3] Establishing positive attachments at work is beneficial to both the employee and the employer. Seeing that you spend on average a third of your life at work (and as we are getting older, we have to work longer), it is important to find something you like to do and also develop healthy work relationships. Otherwise, it could be detrimental to your health.

Managers and leaders play an important role in helping employees feel engaged and willing to remain in an organization. Low productivity and high turnover can severely hurt a company's performance and also negatively impact employee morale. As a manager, your task is to make sure employees feel happy and productive at work. You can achieve this by providing support where needed, acknowledging, praising and rewarding people's effort and contributions, being transparent and role modelling good/ethical behaviour. As an employee, feeling you have a manager who appreciates you, you can trust and who has your back when you need it most, is what creates a strong bond between the both of you. It is often said that employees get attracted to a company because of what it stands for but often leave because of a bad relationship with a manager. Unfortunately, not all managers are great, so learning how to deal with a difficult boss is an important skill set to have.

The psychology of workplace attachment

You've probably never consciously thought about how psychological attachment is established in the workplace. You might think that it is something that just happens when you like the company, and this is partially true. However, building a psychological attachment in the workplace can be done very intentionally. HR and people managers are experts in this and design policies and work practices that help develop strong bonds at work.[4] In a nutshell, well-orchestrated work procedures can make you feel psychologically attached. I will explain to you how this is done.

Employee/employer relationship

To improve how an employee feels at work, it is important to focus on the relationship between the employee and the organization, and not just on the employee. The quality of the relationship will dictate how emotionally connected someone becomes towards their work. Just like a friendship or love relationship, you need to work on the connection to make the other person like you and be willing to invest more of their mind and heart into you. (See Red Flag 6 for more on reciprocal relationships.)

If you promise, you need to follow through!

So, how to work on the connection? Strong emotional connections are initially formed by setting clear expectations about the relationship. Being clear about how and why you want to work together is an important first step in setting up a solid employee/organizational relationship. Just think about the interview procedure. You get invited for an interview, you learn more about the company and the position, the company evaluates if you are a good fit for the job, and then if it is a match, you agree to the terms of the agreement. These initial steps are super important in establishing a connection at the onset because they set clear conditions of what you can expect from engaging with the organization and which obligations you both have towards each other.

Psychological contract

Once you start working at an organization, you take your time to see how the working conditions are, you socialize with your colleagues and your manager and perform your tasks. Not only are you judging the experiences you have at work, but you are also evaluating if what you have agreed to is being met. This is often referred to as the 'psychological contract'. A physical contract is what you sign on paper, but the psychological contract is how you mentally keep track of whether the organization is following through on its promises and meeting its obligations. At the start of your job, you might be keeping scores to see if you receive training on the job, if the organization is truly inclusive and transparent and if you are allowed to work from home two days a week as was promised during the interview. If the organization follows through on its part of the deal and you meet yours, then over time meeting each other's expectations will lead to more positive attachments and eventually more trust. The stronger the emotional connection, the more trust, the safer you feel and the less you need to be concerned about continuously evaluating the relationship (though you never really stop evaluating the relationship, just less frequently). This helps you to think more freely, be more engaged in your job, and consequently perform better.

When expectations are not met

When expectations are not met anymore or the organization has experienced significant changes, the exchange relationship can become unbalanced. When this happens, you can become again more cognitively focused on the relationship, questioning whether your needs can still be met or not and making sure that you are being treated fairly during times of change. Having a bad experience with a manager can also make you more focused on the psychological contract, which can hurt the emotional bond you have with the company. Just imagine being a top performer for many years in the organization and all of a sudden your boss, for whatever reason, becomes a complete a-hole with you or a colleague tries to sabotage your work. In the beginning, you might shrug it off as just a phase, but if it persists, your level of enthusiasm and engagement will go down. If the deteriorating relationship is not remedied quickly, the relationship can be ruined for good, making it pointless to continue working for the organization. You can imagine that at this stage there is no connection anymore and you're thinking, 'Get me the hell out of here!' People often stay in a broken relationship if there are no other options available and you need the money. However, the longer you stay in a broken relationship, the worse it will be mentally and physically.

The power of identity at work

With so much change happening in the world, it is impossible to keep people only happy with positive exchanges. Any change or unexpected situation will definitely impact the psychological contract. Why is it then that some companies are better than others at motivating and retaining people, especially in times of difficulty and unexpected change? The answer is that the better-performing companies also build psychological attachment through a process called organizational identification. Identity has become a hot topic in companies nowadays. When you think of identity at work, you probably are thinking of gender, ethnicity, usage of pronouns and sexual orientation. Identity definitely plays a huge role in these topics. However, identity (and organizational identification) goes much further than that. Identity at work not only helps employees feel connected to the job and the organization, but also helps to answer the question: 'Who am I?'[5] Your identity is a dynamic construct, continuously evolving and adapting to the social groups you feel strongly connected to (e.g. family, work, sports teams, religious groups, political parties). The more you identify with specific social groups, the more likely you are to incorporate the ideals, norms and behaviours of those groups into your self-concept.[6] In other words, the more you identify with your work, the more you allow work to define you and the more likely you are to feel emotionally and psychologically connected to your job.

So, how is this process of identification facilitated? Companies that have a clear purpose, strong organizational values, a positive work culture, inspiring job titles and who champion diversity and inclusion are able to establish a deep psychological attachment to work through identification (which can happen faster than trying to meet each other's expectations the whole time). The reasons why people feel a need for identification at work are multiple. Identifying with the company's values or purpose helps you understand who you are and why you do the work you do. Feeling *one* with the organization also helps you feel a sense of belonging and safety. Consequently, feeling understood, safe and protected makes you more resilient, especially during difficult times. I can tell when people are highly identified at work. They often embody the company's DNA, they are very protective of their organization and often use words like '*we* architects . . .' and '*our* prospects . . .' instead of 'I' or 'mine'. The *me* turns into *we* for highly identified employees.

Why do managers create false connections at work?

Not all companies value their employees the same way. Some organizations really invest a lot in their people. These organizations spend a lot of time making sure you feel comfortable at work and create environments where people feel included and respected. Especially in today's world of work, there are not enough people to fill all the available jobs.[7] Companies need to start focusing on creating better workplaces (work environments and conditions that help employees to win at work). Even with companies outsourcing work to low-cost labour countries and automating work processes using AI and other technologies, there is still a shortage of qualified labour. Post-pandemic, people's attitudes towards work have drastically changed. Many people don't want to go back to a 9–5 job or work five days a week from the office. Companies are having a difficult time retaining their people. Truth be told, why the hell would you go back to a company that overworks you and doesn't appreciate your efforts? Most people need more than just money to keep them motivated on the job.

Seeing how difficult it is to keep employees engaged and

committed, it is not uncommon for company managers to make false promises or create false attachments to keep you as long as possible in the company. Breaking promises kills morale and loyalty (and even promotes counterproductive behaviours, such as lying, cheating and stealing, as a way to 'even the score'), but in challenging times some people don't really care as long as they reach their targets. Also, companies are very good at applying the same psychological techniques to make you accept less than favourable conditions. Which again, in the name of business, is seen as acceptable behaviour. Let me share some examples of how certain managers do this:

'We are your family!' This phrase is used in my opinion too loosely in organizations. Some companies truly live up to family norms and virtues by prioritizing employee well-being beyond normal standards, providing a good work–life balance and job security. However, many cannot continue to provide such amenities in today's world. Many managers haphazardly use this term to create a kumbaya-like feeling in the office without providing all the benefits that come with being a family. Sadly, some managers misuse the 'see us as your family' to create fake group associations to demand loyalty and excessive work from their people. As can be seen on social media, today's younger generation has developed an 'ick' towards this term!

'Your colleagues are your friends.' Hell no! Your colleagues are not your friends, they are your colleagues. Period! Sure, friendships can develop over time from being desk buddies, but by default they are work acquaintances. Most people don't bring their authentic self to work, so you don't know who's truly hiding behind the corporate mask. When friendships develop in the workplace, professional relationships and identities intertwine with your personal life. This can complicate things, making it hard to keep work strictly business or your personal life strictly personal. If colleagues have bad intentions due to personal dislikes, jealousy or rivalry, they can pretend to be nice to you to get closer and use personal information against you in the workplace (giving rise to the popular term 'frenemies' – a combination between friends and enemies). I have heard too many horror stories of workplace incidents, reputation bashing and dismissals because of people getting too personal with colleagues at work.

'This is what we can offer you. Please understand that everyone earns this amount here.' A very common HR tactic applied during salary negotiations to unconsciously pressure you to accept the salary they offer you. This tactic is based on a persuasion technique called *social conformity*[8] and it is very powerful because you might believe that by not accepting the offer you are antisocial or not a team player. People who are susceptible to peer pressure are especially vulnerable to such social influences. Always remember that even if salary negotiations are capped by labour unions/collective agreements, you can still negotiate upwards if you believe you are worth more (within all reasonableness, of course). Otherwise, find somewhere else to work that is willing to pay you your worth.

'You remind me of myself when I was younger. You're such a fighter and I am sure you will help us grow significantly. I can see a bright future here for you!' This is actually a very nice thing to hear if it is genuine and you truly are someone the organization values a lot. But it is also used as a way to keep someone attached. False promises without a clear path of progression or development remain vague. If this is said, make sure to get further guidance on how to have a bright future at the company and have your manager and HR develop a career plan or a growth strategy for you, with regular check-ins to evaluate your development and the goals you have achieved.

'I can't give you more money at this stage but let me promote you to customer happiness manager.' Sometimes companies just don't have more money to give. Instead, non-monetary benefits are offered (for example, working from home opportunities, health insurance coverage, company car). One effective way to motivate an employee without money is through job promotion. People are willing to take a better position in lieu of future salary increases. Employees see the elevated status and organizational power they receive with the promotion as a reward, especially if status is important to them. Some managers intentionally promote people or come up with creative job titles to keep employees motivated with increased task responsibilities without additional pay. It is up to you to decide if you are OK with this. You can take on the cool position of customer happiness manager, but just remember that customers will only be happy if you are truly happy.

Quiet quitting

In the past few years, *quiet quitting* has become quite the phenomenon in the workplace. Quiet quitting is not actually quitting your job, but slowly not showing up anymore or going the extra mile.[9] When employees don't feel connected to the workplace (anymore), they get work done, but nothing more. Examples of quiet quitting are not speaking up in meetings, not participating in voluntary work events, leaving at exactly 5 p.m. or regularly putting one's online status to 'busy' when one is just relaxing when working from home. Quiet quitting in terms of giving the bare minimum has been around for years, but the pandemic has definitely impacted people's beliefs and priorities about work. People today are especially feeling the crunch of having to work harder and for less money. I don't believe quiet quitting will remain as a trend, but it will transform into a general mindset about work. Many people don't want to work themselves to the bone to fill the pockets of corporations at the expense of their mental and physical health. And with mental health issues on the rise, companies that don't protect employee well-being and create a positive work environment will soon find themselves heavily understaffed, with high turnover and health-related absenteeism.

DID YOU KNOW?
What do organizations and terrorist groups have in common?

Terrorist groups and cults also use social identity to get people attached to their organization. The persuasion techniques terrorist groups and cults use to create attachment are the same as those applied in organizations, albeit more sinister.[10] Very often, terrorist groups or cults will target people who are emotionally vulnerable, lonely or have a weak self-identity as they are more influenceable by social pressures and coercion (e.g. intimidation, indoctrination).[11] Once a cult group gets you into their circle, socialization tactics are applied to create a strong sense of belonging through cult membership and psychological dependence, eventually severing ties with the outside world. This eventually leads on to 'drinking the Kool-Aid',[12] an expression often used to reflect the unwavering loyalty and obedience cult members have towards the cult and cult leader. The stronger the cult membership (identification), the more likely you will do what the group tells you to do.

When companies truly live up to their family status

Some companies really do a good job living up to their family status. I find family-run businesses to have a strong people-first mindset. Having worked as an adviser to various family-run businesses, I often hear stories of how members of the family will go out of their way to retain their talent or give special attention and support to an employee who is in need or seriously ill. I often say if you really want to know how people behave, then you should pay attention to how they act during times of crisis. During challenging times, organizational leaders and managers are more likely to show their true colours. The recent pandemic is a great example of that. During the global pandemic, not every organization or their leaders who had 'people first' as a core value were willing to provide employees job security. Some leaders even after the first fiscal quarter at the beginning of the pandemic let people go to cut losses and maximize profits. Not very people first, hey! However, many did decide to retain their staff and provide support during those unprecedented times. Living up to your core values and expressing those values through impactful behaviour is what truly gives a company a family-feel hallmark.

The family in Japanese companies

Japanese companies are known for preaching the family ana-logy at work. And rightly so. Most Japanese corporations provide lifetime employment (that is changing though) and when they hire new employees, they tend to look more for a value fit than a skill set fit (they often hire people straight out of university). Because a job is often offered for life, many benefits are provided to employees for their loyalty. Job security, handsome pension benefits and full coverage health insurance, to name a few. As with any family, you spend a lot of time together (also after work) and you don't disregard family members that easily when things don't go well. Rather, you put them in a corner as punishment or temporarily exclude them from other activities with the rest of the family.[13] These engagement and punitive behaviours are very common in Japanese companies with strong family values. Socializing outside of work is very common in Japan (often referred to as 'after five' in Japanese business culture), and going for drinks, dinners and karaoke with your colleagues and boss is seen as a must. Many important deals and corporate discussions are discussed and decided outside of regular work time. With limited personal time, employees can quickly feel overworked.

The term 'this company is your family' is a heavy burden to carry. Using the Japanese context as an alternative perspective on company as family, I don't recommend companies using this term without thinking about how they can ensure the positive aspects family life at work brings while minimizing the negative aspects.

There are many examples of how trying to create a family-like work environment can become toxic. Demanding unwavering loyalty can make some highly committed employees behave in unethical ways or fail to report wrongdoings in the workplace to protect the company.[14] In 2015, Volkswagen was found guilty of rigging car pollution-detection software to pass government emissions tests. The company Chairman said during a press conference that the emissions scandal was caused by a chain of different wrongdoings internally and a broken work culture tolerating rule-breaking.[15] Dysfunctional families exist in the real world and the dysfunctional family culture also exists in organizations. Even when appropriate checks and balances are in place, the culture, and within it the tolerated behaviours, can prevent people from doing the right thing.

Managers demanding unwavering loyalty — what's the drama?

Feeling connected at work is important. It benefits your well-being, helps you stay productive and provides a sense of belonging and protection, especially when the world outside is changing so much. Some companies can feel like an extended family, going out of their way to make you feel like you matter, listening to your concerns and actively looking for ways to make your life more enjoyable and productive in the workplace. However, not all companies do this, and specific work cultures can even make you feel like a number. Still, regardless of the work culture or environment you work in, many managers love to say to their employees, 'This company is your family.' This term is used too loosely, and sometimes even misused to demand unwavering loyalty or justify overtime at work. Not only that, but managers also apply other psychological attachment and social influencing techniques to influence employee behaviour to their benefit. Younger generations entering the workplace today particularly have an 'ick' for the 'see us as your family' analogy to foster attachment, which reflects a much broader attitude change towards work. Since the pandemic, people have learnt to prioritize other aspects of their lives, such as alone time, well-being and family time, and are not willing to compromise their physical or mental health to benefit an organization, let alone work five days a week from the office. Organizations are having a hard time keeping employees motivated and committed and will need to rethink how they hire, treat and retain their talent. There is a war for talent nowadays. Money is not enough to keep people happy and productive in a rapidly changing world. Employees are looking for meaningful work, work-life balance, personal growth, and positive relationships at work. Companies need to do more to create a resilient form of psychological attachment in the workplace, which benefits both the employee and the employer in the long run. Creating a true family feeling at work, where people feel respected, valued, protected and allowed to express themselves authentically without retribution, comes with responsibility. If an organization says 'this is your family', then they should be!

It's a **red flag** if:

- Your company says to you 'this company is your family'. Most organizations can't live up to the commitment and responsibility of being a true family.

- Your company uses psychological attachment and other persuasion strategies to demand loyalty, obedience, overwork or pay less for your time. Become more aware of how these strategies are applied in the workplace.

- You find yourself doing bad things at work to protect the company. Because of your strong affiliation with the company, you rationalize mistreating or bullying employees. Think twice before engaging in such behaviours and always remember karma exists!

- You get too friendly at work. Remember that over time it can become difficult to separate your business life from your personal life, which can cause problems at work, relationship- or reputation-wise.

- Your organization makes promises about future pay or promotions but doesn't follow through on them. If they do this once or twice, most likely they will do it again. Document everything!

It's a **green flag** if:

- Your company focuses on your well-being at work: you feel accepted, respected and protected. And when things go wrong, they quickly take action to try to remedy it.

- Your organization has good leadership. Leaders and managers that are excellent communicators and put

93

people first, and when difficult times arise live up to their people-first values!

- You feel like you belong in the workplace, regardless of age, race, sexual orientation, religious beliefs or disabilities. Work cultures that create a feeling of oneness for everyone are a major green flag!
- Regardless of the company's work-from-home policy (if your line of work allows you to work from home), you still feel like going to the office because of the camaraderie and the warm connection you have with your colleagues.
- Your personal values and purpose align with those of the company. The more aligned, the stronger the fit and the connection you will feel. People who embody the organization's values often get promoted (if they also meet other job-specific requirements).

Things to consider when deciding if you want in or out

You need to decide if an organization is truly a family to you, based on your evaluation of the actions and behaviours you see in the workplace. If both employee and employer meet their end of the bargain and deliver what they promise, great things can happen. Not only do you trust more, but you feel happier and are more productive. However, positive transactional and relational exchanges at work are not enough to keep people attached in today's world. When things are changing so rapidly outside, we need to find ways to connect more from the inside, and identity at work can help to achieve that. Having an elevating purpose at work can help you understand what gets you out of bed in the morning besides pay alone, while feeling a sense of belonging at work can help you feel valued and protected. However, when these things are missing and you feel excluded, bad things tend to happen, which can negatively affect your mental and physical health. Time to rethink if you should stay or leave.

Willingness to stay

- Your company respects and accepts you as a valued individual.
- You feel a strong and positive connection to the work you do and the colleagues you work with.
- Your company follows through on promises!
- You can set up clear work–life boundaries with your employer and they respect agreements made.
- Leaders and managers actively model the values they preach.

Time to leave

- You are not respected for your work or your personal identity. Go where you are celebrated, not where you are tolerated!
- Managers don't value your input and don't take action when they say they will do better.
- Your company promises you growth, but in the end doesn't provide training, job rotation or promotion opportunities.
- Your manager demands you work more but doesn't provide the supportive environment or adequate pay to go along with the increased pressures.
- You found a better opportunity somewhere else. Don't worry about leaving. There is an end to loyalty in today's business environment.

Red Flag 8 'Can you work this Sunday?'

Not respecting boundaries at work

'One finds limits by pushing them.'
Herbert A. Simon

Respecting boundaries at work

Boundary setting is an important skill to learn and master. Our lives are continuously being bombarded with changes, uncertainties about the future and personal requests from others. It is important to learn how to set boundaries for ourselves, not only to limit what other people request from us but also so as not to become too overwhelmed internally by the external world. Setting boundaries at work is no different than setting boundaries in any kind of family or romantic relationship. It's human nature for people to ask more than is needed or to take more than should be taken. 'You give a finger, they take a hand' is a common saying that reflects such behaviour. With so many competing goals and personal needs at work, it is common for people to ask you to do more work than you can manage or to work on days you are free or on holiday. At the same time, it is hard to say no to a boss that demands an immediate response when you are not in the office. Though it is your free time, you fear that not responding will make you a bad team player or potentially lower your chances of promotion. But at the same time, you realize that not communicating your needs allows other people to suck you dry, eventually impacting on your performance at work and your mental health. There are various reasons why we find it hard to set boundaries at work, which are often personal by nature. In this chapter, we will deep dive into the psychology of setting boundaries and explore why some managers and colleagues like to over-step the boundaries of others. We will also investigate why for some it is hard to set boundaries and what can be done about it with specific strategies that you can apply at work. Setting boundaries might seem scary at first, but soon you will realize how important it is to do and how it actually helps you to gain respect.

The importance of setting boundaries at work

One of the most important factors impacting how well you perform on the job is job clarity. Understanding what is required to do the job well should not be underestimated. You need to know which tasks to perform and at which level. You have to be able to assess if you are capable of doing your job properly and which skills you need to improve to achieve high performance at work. These skills are not just technical skills, but also interpersonal skills, such as being a good collaborator, capable of influencing others effectively to get the work done and managing oneself in terms of stress and time management. These latter skills are import-ant at work because you can easily lose yourself in your job at times, not taking enough breaks or not being able to switch off from work, like when you are on holiday or working on the weekend. Job clarity helps you to understand the boundaries of your work in terms of your role and the time needed to complete tasks. If you don't set clear boundaries for yourself, then you can eventually become overworked and burned out. Equally important, is knowing when to say no to other colleagues if they ask you to do additional tasks that don't fall within your responsibility. Of course, it is good to help others, but be mindful that other people are also good at passing their responsibilities on to others. It is particularly difficult to say no to a manager, especially when they ask you to take on more tasks than you can handle at once or when they ask you to work overtime, like during your weekends or time off. Occasional overwork is expected, and work life is always about give and takes, but there are limits. And it is important that you take responsibility for setting boundaries for yourself, because no one else will.

What holds you back from setting boundaries at work?

It can be hard at times to say no to someone asking you to take on extra tasks or to work during your off time. The work culture can also dictate the need to work more than is normally expected. People who go above and beyond are applauded for being 'on top of things' and 'going the extra mile to get shit done'. However, in an *always-on* culture, burnout and disgruntlement are not too far away. It is even more troublesome when you are being micro-managed, which puts even more pressure on you. So, why do so many people find it hard to push back when their boundaries are overstepped? Often, fearing to speak up to a manager can hold someone back from being assertive about their own needs. Fear of retribution or losing one's job can also underlie one's lack of assertiveness to speak up. Another common reason for people not to push back is *people pleasing*. A desire to satisfy the needs of others as a way to feel accepted and liked, or due to low self-esteem issues. Colleagues and managers pick up quickly if someone is a people pleaser and you become an easy target to dump more work on. Another reason why it can be hard to set boundaries at work can be related to prolonged remote work or working as a freelancer. The freedom of remote work can be very attractive to many but working remotely or for yourself also requires personal effectiveness skills to know when to switch off. Not having clear work and life boundaries can cause some people to overwork. During the pandemic, I was studying how working from home (WFH) impacted employee attitudes and behaviour. I found that many people were working harder than normal, not because they were increasingly productive, but more because they were anxious due to lack of visibility and connection. I called this behaviour 'panic working'.[1]

The importance of self-awareness in boundary setting

Learning to identify the reasons why you find it hard to set boundaries is the first step in learning how to set boundaries for yourself. Boundaries are not just physical boundaries (e.g. asking people to respect your time and space), but can also be mental (e.g. routines and structure) and emotional boundaries (e.g. not allowing other people's emotions to affect you) as well. Self-awareness is key, together with building confidence in speaking up and expressing your needs. Here are some underlying reasons why it is hard for many to set boundaries at work (and to stick to them):

People pleasing

A common issue for people pleasers is that once they try to set boundaries at work for themselves, feelings of anxiety and guilt emerge because setting boundaries is something so foreign to them. Besides the fear of the unknown, people pleasers also have a hard time setting boundaries out of fear of hurting other people's feelings or being rejected. These negative emotions can quickly trigger people-pleasing tendencies again, falling back into the old patterns of behaviour that make it so hard for people pleasers to stick to boundary setting.

Perfectionism

Perfectionism can also be a core reason why people find it hard to set boundaries at work. As a perfectionist, you aim to be your best at work and ensure everything is done correctly. This can push you to work more hours than you should and go beyond normal standards to deliver the work quality you feel comfortable with. If we look deep under the hood, one's perfectionism can be driven by various factors. One of the main reasons people are perfectionists is due to the fear of disapproval or judgement by others. Working on every single element of your project can give you a false sense of control over your environment, which minimizes the risks of being wrong or not doing your job right. Setting boundaries for yourself lowers your ability to exert your control over the environment, which can trigger fears of failure again and consequently failure to stick to the boundaries you set for yourself.

DID YOU KNOW?
If you can't set physical boundaries, learn how to set mental boundaries
When working from home, you need to balance your work life with your private/family life. Being able to decide when and how to work is necessary to have a sense of control over your life. This is particularly difficult if you live in a small house or flat where you don't have extra space to work in to separate your work life from your private life. One effective strategy is to create mental boundaries. Examples of mental boundaries are following strict routines, like waking up in the morning and getting dressed for work as you normally would, taking breaks and finishing work on time. The mind likes to compartmentalize life as it makes it easier to shift between personal and work identities. Mental boundaries can help you separate your work and private lives even when you are working in the same space you are living in.

How to professionally say no to your boss or colleagues

In a business environment where more needs to be done with less, there is a big chance that bosses and colleagues will try to put more work on your plate. Not only because companies are trying to be more cost-effective or have a hard time finding talent, but also because people are inherently lazy. If they can pass work onto you and you are willing to take on the extra load, then often they will. So, learn how to push

RED FLAGS, GREEN FLAGS

back and say no professionally so that you don't become overloaded and colleagues don't get used to dumping work on you that you don't have to do.

Your boss says, 'I want you to work on this now'

It may be very normal for your supervisor or boss to make last-minute decisions concerning work planning and prioritization. However, if your boss keeps moving and reprioritizing your work, it becomes very frustrating not having a completion date in sight or control over your work process. If this continues for too long it can lead to burnout, so finding a way to respectfully push back or reprioritize your own work is needed. Here is an effective strategy to use when dealing with a boss who requests immediate action. You reply, 'I understand that this work requires immediate attention and I am happy to work on it now. To make sure I can finish my other tasks on time, can you help me decide which task can be taken off my list or deprioritized?' If your manager pushes back on this request, remind them how long each task takes as they might be unaware. Providing your manager with an overview of your work and expected timeframe for each task can help address this concern.

In the American version of the famous TV series *The Office* (a sitcom that depicts everyday office life), directed and produced by Greg Daniels, Regional Manager Michael Scott says to temp worker Ryan, 'I need you to come in early and get me a sausage, egg and cheese biscuit on the way in.' When Ryan arrives at the office early and gives Michael his breakfast, he realizes that that was the only reason why he had to come into the office early.[2] A somewhat funny scene from the TV show, which unfortunately reflects how some managers treat employees. Respecting boundaries at work is important, but due to certain relationship dynamics in the workplace or just ill-behaviour, some people can demand or interfere more than they should.

Not respecting boundaries at work – what's the drama?

Today's business environment is tougher than ever. We need to do more with less. Also, because of working from home, the boundaries between work and home have become blurred. We work in an always-on culture, glued to our devices and expected to respond quickly to get things done. If we don't, we might lose an opportunity or just forget to take action. In this environment, it is easy for managers to demand more than is expected from you or to not respect traditional work–home boundaries. It's no surprise that more people nowadays are feeling disgruntled and burnt out at work. It is important to learn to set boundaries for yourself at work, especially if you are sensitive to external pressures and find it hard to say no. There are many reasons why you might find it hard to say no to your boss, such as the fear of losing your job, people-pleasing tendencies or being a perfectionist. Setting boundaries helps you to manage your energy and maintain good physical and mental health when working under pressure. If you have a natural tendency to overwork, then learning how to set boundaries is equally important. Being effective at boundary setting at work requires a good dose of self-awareness[3] to identify why you are not setting boundaries in the first place and also how to overcome the resistance. Another important factor in setting boundaries at work is how to tactfully and respectfully say no to your boss.

It's a **red flag** if:
- Your manager tells you that you can't take longer off than a week for your holiday.
- Your manager tells you that you need to work (again) on Sunday.
- Your company tells you that you will be promoted if you put in the extra hours and take on additional tasks for a while.
- You are sick and your company tells you off for not answering emails.
- You lack boundaries at work, which makes you say yes more often to requests that you actually prefer not to do.

It's a **green flag** if:
- As a manager, you respect your employees' boundaries at work and at home.
- As a manager, you provide your employees with clear job descriptions, so that they know what falls within their responsibility at work and what does not.
- You know how to effectively communicate your needs and how to professionally say no.
- You know how to switch off from work.

Things to consider when deciding if you want in or out

It's normal for people to feel pressured at work and to be asked to work overtime. Especially in today's rapidly changing world, you are considered a good worker if you are 'switched on' and give your all to the company to get shit done. Such a work environment can easily make managers overstep personal boundaries way too often. Finding a fine balance between meeting expectations and protecting your sanity and your health has become an even more important balancing act in today's day and age. If your colleagues and managers overstep your boundaries, it is important to verbalize your limits and your needs. If your needs are not respected and you find it hard to maintain a balance between your work life and your home life because of work pressures, then maybe it's time to rethink the importance of your existing job in your life.

Willingness to stay

- You feel that your boundaries are overstepped too often, but you know when enough is enough. You're happy to stay where you are for now.
- Though your boss can be overly demanding, the work culture in general is positive and supportive.
- You can express your needs and boundaries clearly to your boss. As a response, they minimize sending requests to work overtime or during your time off.
- You learn how to better manage your energy and time at work.

Time to leave

- As a manager, you respect work–home balance, but the work environment forces you to demand more from your employees, even when you can see that they are overworked.
- Your manager keeps on overstepping your boundaries after you have clearly expressed what they are.
- Being asked to deliver on the spot the whole time and to work during your free time is impacting your mental and physical health.
- When your manager continually or deliberately undermines your authority.

Red Flag 9 'Don't complain! That's how we do things around here!'

When there is no consideration for employee well-being and mental health

'If you can't handle me at my worst,
then you sure as hell don't deserve me at my best.'
Marilyn Monroe

Prioritizing employee well-being

Work plays a significant role in everyone's lives. Not only does your job help you earn money, but it also provides you with various emotional and psychological benefits, such as a sense of belonging, purpose, status and personal growth and it can even boost your self-esteem. Because so much of your life is spent at work, it is important to work in an environment that is positive and protective. The experiences you have in the workplace and the connections you forge there heavily affect how you feel both in and outside the workplace, and how you perform on the job. Positive work environments make you feel energized and happy and can even improve your mental and physical health. Toxic work environments, however, can have the opposite effects, leading to all kinds of health issues, such as burnout, depression and even death. As our personal lives are becoming increasingly intertwined with work due to the rise of remote-work setups and an always-on work culture, it is important that organizations find ways to help employees set clearer boundaries for themselves. Let's face it, today we need to do more with less and it doesn't look like this trend will end soon. However, many work cultures are not very employee-centric or consider employee well-being a key priority. And in some organizations, HR means more *human remains* than *human resources*, focusing more on squeezing the last drop of sanity and health out of your body in the name of efficiency and profit maximization. Prioritizing employee well-being is hard to achieve if the work culture dictates a 'Suck it up! Don't complain!' attitude. Being able to identify work values and practices that support employee well-being and mental health is important to deciding if you want to work for a company or if you want to remain in your job longer. 'That's how we do things around here' can blind you to what has changed in today's world of work and the need to prioritize your health and overall well-being at work.

The importance of focusing on employee well-being and mental health at work

With the rise of diversity and inclusion in the workplace and more companies prioritizing mental health through all kinds of workplace policies and initiatives, well-being is becoming a hot topic in the workplace. The 2020 global pandemic scare, which caused massive layoffs but also many employees to voluntarily resign from their jobs (often referred to as the *Great Resignation*), was a pivotal moment for many to re-evaluate life priorities and their relationship with work. Enforced lockdowns during the global pandemic, alongside fear of infection and domestic violence, contributed to increasing cases of loneliness, anxiety and depression. These unfortunate developments made companies more conscious of the importance of prioritizing employees' well-being as a way to retain (and attract) talent. Diversity and inclusion initiatives also prove that putting people first not only benefits employees, but also positively affects the performance of the organization.

How do you define mental health at work?

In recent years, mental health has become an important topic to focus on. Besides dealing with mental health issues caused by overwork and mistreatment in the workplace, many companies acknowledge the impact modern life has on how people feel and think. Not to mention the impact digital devices and platforms have on the changing nature of relationships and well-being. However, mental health initiatives in organizations are still in their infancy and many challenges need to be overcome before people trust and see the benefits of mental initiatives at work. Still, there is a lot of stigma around mental health at work and people don't want to be labelled as having a mental health disorder as the question arises, 'What then?' There are fears that being labelled in this way will make them less of an employee and they may not know what services there are for ongoing support.

The topic of neurodiversity (acknowledging the different ways people process information and make decisions beyond neurotypical thinking) often finds itself caught between diversity and inclusion and mental health, unclear if neurodiversity should be seen as a strength or a disability that requires support. People with ADHD or on the autism spectrum are more willing today to speak about their neuro-diversity at work, and as many studies show, are often highly intelligent, creative and successful people. However, not everyone sees it as a strength, as behavioural traits that accompany these types of cognitive styles are often atypical (e.g. hyperactivity, hyperfocused, less social than normal, no filters in communication). An important aspect about mental health I believe is how you frame what mental health is. Do you see mental health as a state of illness and therefore a deficiency that needs accommodation? Or do you define mental health as a state of productivity, coping strategies and resilience (in other words, a state of well-being)? The latter definition completely changes what mental health means and how you foster it, and how employees engage with it. Personally, most of my work has looked at the individual from a state of well-being and resilience and not from a state of illness. The clinical model is just one paradigm by which to evaluate human cognition and behaviour. A great example of this in practice is how the United Arab Emirates refers to people with mental or physical disabilities as *people of determination*. The way we label things in our lives can hold us back from seeing new possibilities but also energize us to be more. Choosing how to define mental health at work is probably one of the most important steps companies should take when aiming to make employees flourish.[1]

Organizations that prioritize productivity over health

It's unfortunate, but even in today's world with so much focus on improving mental and physical well-being at work, there are still many companies that don't give much attention to, or even care about, the well-being of their employees. Cost reduction and efficiency improvements are prioritized over employee well-being. Take, for example, the implementation of AI in the workplace. Many people are fearful of losing their jobs to AI and receive little emotional or psychological support in workplace transitions. In addition, work environments that promote a 'that's how we do things around here, so suck it up!' culture often leave people feeling left out and unsupported. Work culture is something that is built up over years and the modern workplace is changing so rapidly that the culture often can't catch up in time to support the needed change. This can often be seen in how managers naturally respond to topics related to mental health and well-being. And this can even be the case when employee well-being initiatives and policies are in place. The unwritten rules of not taking long holidays, working overtime regularly without pay or being asked to be on call when you are on holiday are clear red flags that your company doesn't prioritize your well-being and that organizational culture makes it hard to adopt healthier work behaviours, even when new policies are in place.

DID YOU KNOW?
Psychological safety
Psychological safety reflects how safe you feel at work to speak up, engage in critical debate and tell someone when they have made a mistake, take risks and experiment with new ideas without the fear of retribution. Psychological safety has been found to increase team performance and innovation outcomes and to enhance physical and mental well-being. Building psychological safety in an organization takes time, especially if you work in an environment

where everyone is too scared to speak up or challenge the status quo. Often companies will start focusing on psychological safety because employees have experienced harassment or bullying in the workplace. New legislation can also trigger companies to focus more on building psychologically safe work environments. During these initial stages, most employees don't believe in the initiatives and are cynical about them. Over time, as companies walk the talk building and rewarding psychological safety and employees engage more in speaking up at work, that's when a cultural shift can happen. Developing a psychologically safe environment at work should be done intentionally and diligently, understanding that behavioural change and trust-building take time.

How to distinguish between a people-first and a people-last mindset

You would think it would be easy to identify when an organization prioritizes well-being at work. And you are right, in many cases it is easy to evaluate if a job or organization is good for your mental and physical well-being. However, in some situations this is not that obvious. The fact that your organization engages in well-being practices and has mental health policies in place doesn't automatically mean that they are good for you. Also, working in a high-powered environment can go very well for a long time, but what happens when, due to changes in the workplace or the business environment, you don't feel you can handle it anymore? How well you feel supported in dealing with job stressors and demands is an important criterion for evaluating how well your organization truly supports you. Here are some interesting work situations that at first sight may seem positive, but require more consideration to conclude if they are truly people-first practices:

'We don't have mental health policies in place, but we do have Pizza Fridays!'

'Sure, you can work from home, but to make it fair to the other employees in the office, can you also do some work over the weekends?'

'If you want to be promoted in this company, you need to go above and beyond.'

'Tell us about your mental health issues and let us know how we can support you.'

In May 2023, I gave a keynote presentation for the World Bank Group during one of their virtual town hall meetings. During this keynote, I spoke about the importance of psychological safety to enhance well-being at work, and the strategies organizations as big as the World Bank Group can incorporate to build a psychologically safe environment. One key take-away from this talk was that psychological safety can mean different things to different people around the world and should be approached using a cross-cultural lens. Another important lesson to keep people motivated towards building safer and more trusting workplaces is to make people aware that enhancing psychological safety at work is an ongoing journey.

When there is no consideration for employee well-being and mental health — what's the drama?

The topic of employee well-being and mental health is high on the agenda for most companies nowadays. Today's business environment is demanding a lot of people, from dealing with unforeseen scenarios, like the pandemic and the wars in Ukraine and the Middle East, to multiple organizational transformations happening at the same time to make the workplace more inclusive, digital and sustainable. Work pressures are increasing, and people are finding it hard to deal with it. If on top of that you have a manager who tells you 'Don't complain! That's how we do things around here!' then you can conclude that your well-being is not high on their personal agenda. If you feel that your mental and physical well-being is suffering at work due to job demands or the organizational culture, then it is important that you speak up and express your needs. However, not everyone feels safe to speak up in the workplace, which shows that there is a lack of psychological safety. Psychological safety is the belief that you can take interpersonal risks to be your authentic self and voice concerns in the workplace without fear of retaliation or losing your job. Not feeling safe at work impacts your productivity, well-being and your mental health. You need to think carefully if you want to remain in an environment that focuses more on numbers than on people.

It's a **red flag** if:
- Your manager tells you to not complain and 'Suck it up! That's how we do things around here!'
- Your company asks you to disclose your mental health issue to them when they don't have clear policies in place on how to manage mental health effectively at work.
- Your manager doesn't believe in mental health and says to you that you are often negative and that you just need to cheer up!
- You throw yourself into work as an escape from your personal issues.

It's a **green flag** if:
- As a manager, you regularly review the workload of your employees and actively delegate tasks towards or away from them so as not to overload them.
- Your company promotes an environment where it is safe to speak up, which creates psychological safety.
- Your manager shows empathy and vulnerability at work, modelling caring work behaviours in the workplace that foster a sense of belonging.
- You know how to maintain a healthy work–life balance, making use of free time, delegating work where possible, working from home and spending quality time with friends and loved ones.

Things to consider when deciding if you want in or out

Companies are actively trying to find and keep their talent in a world where loyalty towards each other is rapidly disappearing. Not prioritizing employee well-being and mental health in today's chaotic and volatile business environment will definitely boot you off the 'employer of choice' or 'best place to work' global rankings. And even when companies do make such listings, it's not a safeguard that your well-being and mental health will be protected. Luckily, many companies are learning how to do better and trying to find ways to improve management practices and the organizational culture. If you find yourself dealing with a workplace that doesn't care about your well-being and mental health, then maybe it's time to rethink where you belong.

Willingness to stay

- You are a resilient person and enjoy your job. The lack of interest at work in your well-being doesn't bother you. When it becomes too much, you will leave.
- You are able to speak up to your manager to request a change in how your work is conducted or a decrease in workload to make it more manageable for yourself.
- Your organization is in transition, prioritizing more good people-management practices. You are hopeful that things will improve.
- You are unhappy in your current job due to excess demands, but you currently don't have an alternative to move to.

Time to leave

- You don't feel psychologically safe at work, which prevents you from speaking up and being your authentic self.
- You are not feeling physically or mentally well due to ongoing work pressures and your manager tells you to 'Suck it up!'
- Your organization promotes a toxic work environment where being highly political and cut-throat are seen as strengths and a way to survive organizational life.
- When you feel undervalued and tolerated. Time to look for a place where you will be celebrated.

Red Flag 10
'Why don't you do it this way?'
The micro-managing boss

'It's my way or the highway.'
Unknown

The micro-managing boss

Having a good manager at work is important. Good managers set you up for success in the workplace, provide you with resources to help do your job and give feedback and guidance to help you deal with work-related matters and interpersonal issues. Your relationship with your boss is crucial for your success and survival at work. In a lifetime, you will have various bosses and eventually you might become someone's boss or more. Managing people is very different from managing tasks. Tasks you have control over, people you don't. Good managers know how to get the best out of their people and know how to delegate effectively. Unfortunately, there are many managers who don't have good people-management skills. Sometimes it's due to a lack of competencies and sometimes a lack of trust (or other interpersonal abilities). Lack of skills can be related to being new to management, e.g. being promoted to manager because there is nobody else qualified to take on the role. Whatever the issue underlying bad management, it is important to know when your boss is not performing well on the people-management side and understand what to do about it so that someone else's bad skills don't become your professional demise. Identifying the red flags and green flags in management behaviours (and the underlying psychology) can not only help you deal better with your boss, but also identify the skills you need to have to be an effective people manager.

What is micro-managing?

Micro-managing is the act of wanting to know everything your employees are doing and dictating every step and move they make in their work. It can be an effective management style for new employees on the job, but not for a long period of time. Micro-managing can be very frustrating to employees, as it undermines an employee's autonomy and shows a lack of trust in someone's ability to get the job done properly. Micro-managing can lead to employees feeling very frustrated, and thus less productive. Not only that, but micro-managing can hold employees back from growing, and also be a cause of mental health issues in the workplace. The loss of autonomy and feelings of distrust can make someone feel very uncomfortable and stressed at work, leading to all kinds of health issues, such as burnout, anxiety and depression. Micro-managing occurs frequently in organizations and it can be a problem to deal with if you are subjected to it.

The psychology of micro-managing

There are various reasons why bosses micro-manage their employees. Most of these reasons relate to deficiencies in people-management skills and the ability to trust others. From a competency perspective, being able to delegate work to others is very important. Newly minted managers especially may still have to transition their mindset from being a manager of tasks to being a manager of people. This basic but fundamental shift in mindset is a cause of a lot of mismanagement at work. A manager might think, 'I need to make sure the job gets done properly! My employees are not doing the work the way I want it to be done', believing that it's their way or the highway. New managers suffer from this functional fixedness at work because they often link their way of working to the behaviours that got them promoted to manager.

Another reason why managers micro-manage is due to trust issues. Trust issues can stem from past non-work-related experiences. Being less trustful of others by nature, some managers by default see colleagues as less trustworthy, with no apparent reason to distrust a colleague other than their own insecurities or mental programming. Mistrust can also be a consequence of an organization's work culture. Some work cultures are characterized by cynicism and mistrust and are full of paranoia. The work environment can make managers less trusting of other managers in the organization and even their own direct reports. In this case, mistrust is more of a systemic problem within the company. Mistrust breeds mistrust, and when working in a toxic environment, it is hard to tell if your micro-managing boss is on your back because they are scared you can't work properly or if they are purposefully trying to undermine you to make you look bad . . . or make themselves look good. During the pandemic, some over-controlling bosses took micro-managing to a whole new level, using online tools to monitor employee presence and activity. Another reason for managers not to trust employees and therefore choose to micro-manage is when employees repeatedly make mistakes or misbehave in the workplace. A manager might want to intervene in a controlling way to rectify the matter temporarily or go into full-on micro-managing mode to ensure no more mistakes are made. The severity of micro-managing in this case can depend on the personality of the manager or if the mistakes made by others impact his or her performance reviews. Whatever the issues underlying lack of trust at work, not being able to trust as a manager will hurt their own performance (and potentially lead to burnout), their objective perceptions of others and the performance and well-being of the people they manage.

Finally, micro-managing can also be triggered by bosses who want complete oversight. Even the highest-ranking executives can be serial micro-managers. This level of micro-management is very unhealthy as it shows wanting to have complete control over every situation out of fear of something hurting the company, their reputation or opportunity for promotion.

DID YOU KNOW?
The Peter Principle
In organizational psychology, there is something called the Peter Principle, which reflects the relationship between competence and career advancement. The Peter Principle states that people in hierarchical structures are promoted to their level of incompetence, which means that people continue to get promoted until they can't perform well any more.

Interestingly, the Peter Principle also states that people who realize that they are incompetent are generally unhappy with their situation, while those who do not realize it are generally happy and unaffected. However, in many (work) cultures the Peter Principle does not always apply, as people can also be promoted to positions above their skill level due to favouritism, close ties, nepotism and political connections. In the Middle East, the concept of *wasta* (or having strong connections) is essential to develop to help you get or stay in your job or to help you get out of trouble. Having wasta in the Middle East can get you into positions way beyond merit and performance alone. Being promoted based on having strong ties happens everywhere, but in some countries it is just more prominent than in others. It is often said that 'your network is your net worth' and having strong social ties is pivotal to your career success.

How to minimize micro-management at work

So, what to do when a boss is micro-managing you at work? There are various strategies you can apply to gain more autonomy and decision-making power without compromising your relationship with your superiors. The approach to apply heavily depends on the reasons why your boss is micro-managing you. It is also important to ensure that addressing micro-managing behaviour is done on a regular basis (not just a one-off), which requires frequent check-ins. The following strategies will discuss how to counter micro-managing depending on whether your boss's controlling behaviours are personality-driven or workplace driven:

Personality-based micro-management

Your boss tries to micro-manage you by saying, 'I don't like it to be done that way, I want you to fill it out this way.' Having a boss watching over your shoulder the whole time and dictating how to do your job undermines your ability to think and work independently. It is important to push-back at times so that you have the ability to navigate your work with more personal freedom (otherwise hire a robot to do the job). This is what you can say to respectfully push back: 'Thank you for your input. I will consider this approach. Is there a specific reason why I can't do it the way I have done it so far? Your input can help me see how best to work on these kinds of projects more independently moving forward.'

Workplace-driven micro-management

It is hard to build trust in a work environment where mistrust has become part of the organization's culture. Work cultures that breed mistrust are often highly competitive, filled with politics and a place where employees often experience unfair treatment (for more on organizational politics, see Red Flag 11). Bosses who thrive in an environment of cynicism and mistrust have embodied the organizational culture to some extent in their way of working. This sometimes leads to workplace-driven micro-management, which is not always linked to someone's preferred management style. The lack of trust in the organization or due to the nature of the work can make managers less trusting of employees. In these scenarios, it can be beneficial to establish a close relationship with your boss. Trust and accountability go hand in hand, and finding ways to establish personal trust with a micro-managing boss is your best strategy when it is hard to find in the organization. You can start building a strong relationship with your boss by trying to understand what his or her main concerns are in terms of reliability and accountability. Once you understand the main concerns, you can try to address them by providing opportunities to show that you are reliable and accountable for meeting work objectives in the most transparent way. Something you can say to start establishing a stronger connection could be, 'I understand that it is hard to trust in our current work environment. However, I want to assure you that you can rely on me to get the work done effectively and with full transparency. Please let me know how we can build a strong, trusting and open relationship together.'

An example of a demanding and micro-managing boss to the extreme must be Meryl Streep's character Miranda Priestly in the movie *The Devil Wears Prada*. She is known for her need for perfection, cut-throat behaviour, being condescending and ruthless and enjoying belittling her assistant in front of others. A textbook example of a micro-managing boss who will make your life hell.

The micro-managing boss – what's the drama?

Having a good manager is pivotal to your performance and development opportunities at work. It is often said that people get attracted to a company for its reputation, but often leave due to a bad relationship with a manager. The quality of your relationship with a manager can make or break you at work, so it's important to develop a trusting connection with your boss. Despite your good efforts, you can find yourself working with a tyrant who doesn't trust you or allow you to work independently. Welcome to the micro-managing boss! For many, an employee's worst nightmare. Micro-managing bosses want to dictate exactly how you do your job and often don't trust that you can do the work well. Working under a micro-managing boss can be a dreadful and draining experience, which can negatively impact your performance and even your mental health. Learning how to communicate effectively with your micro-managing boss is an important skill to develop if you want to find ways to build trust and maintain your autonomy at work. As micro-managing often impacts the whole team, it is also important to address the problem as a group (e.g. during a team meeting). Learning why your boss is micro-managing you is an important first step to take when aiming to address the conflict at work. Often micro-management comes from a place of fear and insecurity, need for control, lack of trust and/or a lack of management skills.

It's a **red flag** if:
- Your manager gets upset because you don't do the work in the same way they do it.
- Your manager shows you (directly/indirectly) that he or she doesn't trust you.
- Your manager uses online surveillance tools to monitor your presence and work activity when working from home.
- You allow yourself to be micro-managed due to fear of making mistakes or losing your job.

It's a **green flag** if:
- As a manager, you give your employees the flexibility and autonomy to do their job.
- As a manager, you trust your employees when they work from home. You focus more on productivity (quality of employee output) than on how many hours your team clocks in every day.
- The company culture is more of a learning organization, where making mistakes is not seen as a crime but as an opportunity to learn and grow.
- Your manager gives you feedback on how you are performing and how to improve without dictating.
- You use effective language to speak up against micro-managing and help your micro-managing

manager to build trust in how you do things, while also respecting their positional authority.

Things to consider when deciding if you want in or out

It's hard to decide if you want to continue working for a boss who doesn't trust you and wants to dictate your every move. Even if you really love your job, not being able to work effectively with your manager can be draining and demotivating. Making your own decisions and finding ways to do your work in the most effective way possible is not only important to boost your productivity on the job, but also improves your self-esteem and confidence. It can be hard to build trust with people at work, especially if you work in a toxic environment, but you will always encounter difficult bosses, no matter where you work. Learning how to deal with a micro-managing boss can be tricky, but not undoable. Deciding if you want to stay or go will very much depend on how well trust can be established between both of you and how well you can convince your boss to allow you to work more independently.

Willingness to stay

- Your manager is a good person but lacks proper management training to manage the team well. You find ways to help your manager gain more trust in your capabilities and work methods.
- You are fine with receiving direct instruction and regular oversight, especially during the early stages of your employment.

- You address the micro-management issues directly with your boss and find ways to work together, which can show them that they can trust your judgement and way of working.
- You know your micro-managing boss won't stay for long, so you will sit it out.

Time to leave

- Despite your efforts to address the micro-managing at work, your boss remains controlling and distrustful.
- You feel that your growth opportunities are being jeopardized because of being micro-managed.
- Being micro-managed negatively affects your well-being.
- Your micro-managing boss has isolated you from everyone else in the organization, making it hard for you to get support for your issues.

Red Flag 11 'You can trust me!'
Office politics

'In politics, stupidity is not a handicap.'
Napoleon Bonaparte

Office politics

When you go to work, engaging in office politics is probably the last thing on your mind. You want to go to focus on the tasks at hand and have a bit of chitchat with colleagues during coffee breaks or lunch. Not everyone loves their job, but at least you want to make sure that you can do your job peacefully and without too much stress. Engaging in office politics is too time-consuming for most people and those people who do engage in it are probably backstabbing creatures you don't want to be engaged with. That's the mindset most people have when they think about office politics – something negative and too time- and energy-consuming. Also, you don't believe in elbow rubbing in the organization. Your results are all that matter. Unfortunately, career success is not based on merit alone. It also heavily depends on your support network, allies, reputation, goodwill and your ability to influence up, down and sideways. Office politics is more than just toxic behaviours in the workplace, it is a multi-disciplinary skill set that you will need to learn if you want to advance your career success and eventually grow in positional and situational

power. However, most business schools and executive education programmes won't teach you about the art and science
of office politics. You are often left to fend for yourself and
to figure things out alone. Unnecessary! In this chapter, we
will deep dive into what office politics really is, why it is
important, go under the hood and explore the (dark) psychology driving political engagement at work, and learn how to
identify political behaviours in the workplace and how to
counter them. Recognizing red flags and green flags in office
politics will help you identify and neutralize negative actions
quickly and with confidence, while leveraging the positive
behaviours that can help you improve your reputation at
work, build strong alliances and rise in position and power (or
at least protect your position).

What is office politics?[1]

When we think of office politics, we often think of something negative. Certain colleagues engaging in bad behaviour
at work to hurt others and/or to advance their own careers by
throwing others under the bus. We also often associate the
term office politics with toxic behaviours such as 'gossiping',
'backstabbing', 'sabotage' and more negative workplace consequences, such as 'layoffs' and 'mistrust', and something that
is 'taboo' and should not be spoken about. These negative
beliefs hold strong in our minds, keeping most people away
from partaking in political embroideries. Being involved in the
wrong political battle could cost you your job and that is something most people don't want to sacrifice. Also, many people
see office politics as elbow rubbing and don't believe sucking
up to a boss is the best way to get the next promotion. 'Only

my work matters and this should be the only thing that gets me promoted' is the mindset many people have when they go to work. However, regardless of office politics, we all know merit alone won't get you far in life. It is also important who you know and how you mobilize people to help achieve your goals or that of the organization.

Office politics is more than just the ill treatment of others or engaging in back-handed activities. Once you start seeing office politics as an important skill set to learn, which can be a force for positive change in the organization, you can improve how you foster relationships at work. Office politics reflects the behaviours, dynamics and strategies people use at work (individually or in groups) to increase their influence and power and achieve goals. To be able to succeed in navigating the political arena at work, you have to be smart about building connections throughout the organization (and not just with your boss and direct colleagues). Very often people are so preoccupied with their job that they invest less in purposefully getting to know people across the organization and figuring out people's needs and concerns. The proverbial saying, 'It's not WHAT you know, but WHO you know', is key to successfully engaging in politics at work. It is no surprise that less capable people, who are great at networking and understand the importance of building strong connections and allies at work, stay longer in organizations and sometimes advance faster than those who have more knowledge or experience.

Why you should care about office politics

What bewilders me is that hardly any business school or corporate education programme teaches people about office politics, despite it being so vital to your career success. Like with anything political, there will always be rotten apples behaving badly, but this doesn't come close to what office politics truly entails. Dealing with toxic behaviours at work is just the tip of the iceberg in terms of competencies that are needed to effectively navigate politics in the workplace. Office politics is about forging strong relationships in and outside the organization, identifying allies and opponents and knowing how to work with them effectively, building a strong personal brand and reputation at work, and being able to manage oneself when gaining power in the organization. Developing these skills will catapult your career success and productivity and help minimize stress levels. Not to mention, help you protect yourself and your team's interests when organizational challenges occur.

The psychology of office politics

Psychology lies deep at the core of office politics in general. It helps to explain the invisible factors driving people's attitudes and behaviours. To be able to master political skills at work, it is important to understand the psychological drivers of behaviour and the deeper reasons why people behave as they do. If your boss tries to take credit for your work, then this behaviour can be driven through fear, lack of confidence or entitlement, and reflect an underdeveloped skill at being able to manage effectively. Similarly, a colleague who always wants to take on leadership roles or be the spokesperson for the team can be driven through power and status, which in itself is not a bad thing.[2] However, the pursuit of power and status can motivate some people to behave unethically. There is a dark side to the psychology of office politics and this helps explain why people behave badly or mistreat others in the workplace. Understanding what motivates such behaviours is extremely important for finding ways to identify and neutralize toxic behaviours at work.

Power

Power is a central tenet of organizational politics. People engage in office politics to elevate their power or the power of the group they represent. There are different ways to achieve power in an organization. The first way to get more power is by climbing the organizational ladder. People higher in the organizational chain have more power over social and organizational resources. However, positional power is not the only way to gain more power in the organization. Situational or personal power is held by those who are good at forging strong relationships throughout the organization, often bypassing existing chains of command and formal structures. Being connected with the right people in the organization, especially more senior people, can give you more access to job opportunities and protection during times of change. Expert power is another form of power achievement in organizational settings. Being an expert in a specific field, such as AI or having knowledge of a specific market, can give someone expert power, which increases their status and value within the organization.[3]

Machiavellianism

Machiavellianism is a personality trait that uses manipulative and deceptive behaviour to gain power and money. People who are Machiavellian deceive and use force to control or coerce the behaviour of others to grow in power. The word Machiavellian is derived from Niccolò Machiavelli (1469–1527) who wrote *The Prince*, celebrating cunningness, deceitfulness and aggressive behaviours as political astuteness. It is believed that one of the reasons why people today view politics as something negative is due to Machiavellianism. Many people also still try to exercise aggression and manipulative tactics to attain resources and power in the workplace, driven by a belief that politics is cut-throat and you need to be forceful to climb the ranks.

Personal motives

Human behaviour is driven through various motivations. Power is just one of many factors that motivate individual and group behaviour. Often related to power is the need to control. The need for control can be born out of a need for predictability and order, but also from anxiety and insecurity or from a need to be better than others. I often say A players choose A players and B players choose C players, because B players lack the confidence to work with bright-minded people out of fear of not looking competent or the fear of losing their job. Another personal driver of political behaviour in the workplace is recognition. Some people are so driven through recognition and wanting to be seen that they will go above and beyond to achieve that goal. Also, when no recognition is given to people who deserve it, this can lead to political situations in the workplace as well. A deep need to be recognized stems from various areas of life, some being childhood trauma, and it can drive workplace behaviours in positive and negative ways. Finally, autonomy can also be a major driver of workplace behaviour. A division or project team might engage in office politics in an attempt to gain more autonomy in decision-making or resource allocation.

Organizational culture

Organizational culture plays a strong role in how willing people are to partake in office politics. In some organizations, it is vital to be political; otherwise you won't have a long career path. Rubbing elbows with the right people or forming alliances with colleagues to get people fired can be part of a toxic work environment. I would not advise working in such a workplace, but some people truly thrive in such environments. However, office politics can also be a positive thing. Especially in big organizations, such as corporations or institutions, where there are many groups of people with opposing interests, having an organizational culture in place that provides resources for mentorship and interest groups is important for learning how to forge close relationships across different divisions and leverage differing motives to achieve a common goal.

DID YOU KNOW?
Five per cent of executives are psychopaths!
The occurrence of psychopaths in the general population is normally around 1 per cent, but in organizations this number seems to be much higher. Psychopaths are not always in jail, sometimes you find them in the boardroom as well. The number of executive and senior leaders exhibiting psychopathic traits is anywhere between 5 per cent and a staggering 20 per cent according to some sources. [4] It's hard to assess if someone is a psychopath without proper clinical assessment, but behavioural traits are easier to pick up on. Psychopaths are power-motivated and seek out positions that give them power and control over others (specifically social

---

and material resources).[5] Many successful psychopaths display traits such as charisma, decisiveness, confidence and immunity to stress, which are often associated with effective leadership.[6] Especially in today's rapidly changing and unstable times, corporate psychopaths can flourish.[7] Psychopaths don't feel empathy or can't resonate emotionally or understand feelings intellectually, which makes it easier for them to make tough and cold decisions, which can negatively impact the environment they operate in. Companies with weak checks and balances in place and who pride heroism and charisma over collaboration are particularly vulnerable to psychopath behaviour. In their book *Snakes in Suits*, psychologists Dr Robert Hare and Dr Paul Babiak provide a detailed description of psychopaths in business and how to deal with them.

Advancing your career by playing the game right!

Office politics is not something you should shy away from. On the contrary, it is something you should master. Being political is often believed to be a dark trait. You are either political or not. I want to change this false belief because being political is not a trait, it is a skill set you can learn. I have developed a framework that I call the 5Ps framework of organizational politics (go to my website www.drfenwick.com to find an illustration of the framework), which explains the four inventories of skills and competencies you need to develop to become better at navigating and utilizing political

situations at work. At the core of the model is the psychological inventory, which helps to explain the psychological
aspects of the four inventories and the importance of power.

The left side of the framework reflects your personal influence, both internally and externally. Internal influence (or the
personal management inventory) is your ability to manage
yourself when confronted with political situations at work. Do
you address the situation or do you walk away from it? Personal
management also deals with your personal beliefs and fears
about office politics and how well you can deal with power as
you climb the organizational ladder. The external influence (the
politics inventory) reflects how well you are able to influence
others politically in the organization. This can be how well you
engage in conflict management or how well you are able to
protect your interests. But the politics inventory also represents
the political games and toxic behaviours that happen in
the organization.

The right side of the framework reflects your ability to
influence others internally and externally. The internal ability to influence others is how well you can build a personal
brand or enhance your reputation (the personal reputation
inventory). Personal reputation reflects your ability to
advance your career by building a positive reputation inside
and outside the organization. Being perceived as a collaborator, positive and credible can help you in various ways at
work, from promotions to being chosen as a spokesperson
or representative. The more visibility you have in the organization, the better the chances of being promoted and
rising in power. Externally influencing others is done
through forming strong alliances and strategic partnerships
inside and outside the organization (the partnership inventory). When trying to make change work in the organization,

you need to be sure that the biggest stakeholders are on your side. Understanding the needs of different constituents in the organization and beyond can help you form alliances as a way to achieve your personal and group goals. Learning how to master the skill sets and competencies related to the different inventories of organizational politics will help you navigate the political landscape at work with confidence, as well as leverage work relationships to achieve your personal and team goals.

When the ambitious military commander Julius Caesar rose to political power, he didn't achieve this by himself. He was supported by many allies in his quest. One of his close allies was Crassus, a wealthy Roman general. Crassus was Caesar's financial patron and provided Caesar with the necessary connections. Forging strong alliances with key stakeholders is necessary if you want to progress up the ladder. And learning how to leverage the needs of your stakeholders and weave them into your grander scheme is necessary to remain and grow in power.

Office politics – what's the drama?

Political behaviour in the workplace is an inescapable part of organizational life. Whenever groups of people work together, power struggles and resource competition occur. People with opposing interests will try to engage in zero-sum games to gain more power, either by taking individual action or forming alliances to achieve common goals. One or multiple times in your career you will have been subjected to political attacks or yourself engaged in office politics to stand your ground and protect your interests and your job, or to gain power and bring others down in the process. However, office politics is not only about sabotage, back-stabbing or gossiping at work. Office politics entails a variety of key skills and competencies every employee should master, such as being able to forge alliances and partnerships, establishing your personal brand and reputation at work, and learning how to use multiple intelligences to grow effectively as a leader and not allow oneself to be corrupted by power. Building your political skills and intelligence in the workplace will help advance your career success and support you in your leadership transition, both in and outside the company. Psychology is foundational to office politics to help explain the motives, both good and bad, behind political behaviour. At the same time, the psychological lens also provides a roadmap on how to effectively neutralize political attacks at work by deciphering the reasons why people behave politically.

It's a **red flag** if:
- Your boss tries to take credit for your work.
- Your boss tries to isolate you from important information and people in the organization.
- Your colleague spreads rumours about you.
- Your organization has weak checks and balances in place to identify and deal with bad behaviours in the organization and a culture that promotes individual results and charisma instead of group collaboration. Also, it is an issue when the reward system at work propagates negative political behaviour.

It's a **green flag** if:

- You learn how to build strategic partnerships and allies in the organization to help achieve individual, group and organizational goals.
- You work on your personal branding and reputation at work. You build relationships throughout the organization based on trust and excellence and are seen by others as someone who can serve and protect the interests of others.
- You learn how to deal with power effectively. Not only how to gain power, but also how to protect yourself from being corrupted by power.
- You deal with political attacks at work effectively. You prevent them from happening through strategic manoeuvres and tackle them head-on when they occur.

Things to consider when deciding if you want in or out

Deciding to stay in an organization that is highly political is a hard choice to make. However, it doesn't matter where you go, you will always be exposed to political games and unfortunate political manoeuvres one way or another. It is therefore important to not only develop your political skills but also to know in which environment you want to thrive.

Willingness to stay

- You enjoy the work you do and understand that it is important to learn how to play the game. Wherever you go, office politics will always be present.

- You have found a way to build expert power in the organization to protect your position for as long as possible. You are not interested in participating in political discussions, other than keeping good relations with your boss and colleagues.
- You like to be the social butterfly in the organization. You like connecting with people across the organization and see the value in doing so to help you achieve your goals.
- You understand the importance of building strong alliances in the organization. You like to stand for something and you are willing to fight for what you believe in. Engaging in office politics you see as a must to protect your people and advance their needs.

Time to leave

- You have been the target of a political attack – a mean one – and now you believe it is time to move on.
- You work in a toxic environment that doesn't fit with your personal values. You know staying in this job or organization will eventually corrupt you and make you like them, which you don't want. Time to leave!
- You don't get along with the people who are currently in power. You expect to be treated badly or become the victim of bad behaviours at work.
- Engaging in office politics is becoming detrimental to your physical and mental health. It is causing you stress every day and it is affecting your work and relationships both in and outside the office.

Red Flag 12 'Next time, you will achieve your targets!'

Bosses who keep moving the goal posts

'When it is obvious that the goals cannot
be reached, don't adjust the goals,
adjust the action steps.'
Confucius

Moving the goal posts

Having clear targets at work is important to help you stay focused on what needs to be done. Not only do they help you to stay motivated on the job, but they also help to evaluate how well you are performing to achieve them. Goals and targets psychologically work like mental goal posts, guiding your daily decisions at work and what to prioritize. People have both short-term and long-term goals, which are either imposed by others or self-created, the latter having the strongest impact on motivation. Goals are very energizing and help guide work-related behaviours, especially when goal achievement leads to monetary and non-monetary rewards. Managers use targets and goals to keep employees focused on the objectives of the organization and to elevate performance. However, it happens a lot that managers change targets and objectives on the go, making sales targets and project completion ratios hard to achieve or completely unattainable. In other situations, work-related objectives are vague and unclear, and how to achieve them is left open for interpretation. At times, this is done on purpose as a way to minimize costs or to deceive employees, not realizing how detrimental these practices are to employee motivation and job satisfaction. In this chapter, we will dive into the psychology of goal setting and learn how goals guide and motivate behaviour in the workplace. We will also learn how to recognize red flags and green flags in how managers motivate performance at work and how you can minimize the chance of being subjected to fake goals. And probably more important, what you can do yourself to stay motivated on the job without the need for external reinforcement or monetary rewards – a key skill to develop that will serve your career and personal life well.

The need for goals in life

Having goals in life is an important way to stay focused on what you want to achieve. You can have both short-term and long-term goals that you aim for, and which guide your behaviours at different stages of your life. Your life goals can be imposed on you by your upbringing and surroundings, such as the need to get married, to buy a house or to work in a profession that your parents want you to do. Goals can also be self-imposed, giving you direction and meaning in life. Just think of your purpose and guiding passions and how they inform the decisions you make in everyday life. They become a (moral) compass to help your decision-making in times of uncertainty and change or as a way to feel guided by something higher than yourself. Goals activate and energize behaviour and are a powerful source of motivation.

How goals impact motivation and behaviour

Goals are an important source of motivation. They help you to stay focused, put effort into your work and decide how to engage with others to achieve your goals. The emotional and cognitive significance people give to goals and the accompanying rewards are core to workplace motivation. Often people believe that money is the only factor that will motivate behaviours at work and, let's be honest, you can't really motivate people if the topic of money is left unaddressed. Get the topic of money off the table though and you will quickly find that employees are motivated by so many other things as well, like wanting to be recognized, a sense of belonging, social status and power, being creative and innovative and personal mastery. For me, besides money, *autonomy* and *seeing other people grow* really motivate me to do my best and to find ways to continuously improve my skills. I will also work five times harder if someone allows me to work the way I want. It is important to identify the factors that not only motivate you extrinsically (e.g. rewards, status, punishment) but also intrinsically (e.g. sense of achievement, ambition, creativity). Intrinsic motivation is the most powerful and sustainable source of motivation, which helps you to stay focused on your goals even when the going gets tough.

Why managers keep on changing the goal posts

Setting goals and clear targets is an important way to motivate people in the workplace. It helps achieve an organization's overall goals and sets clear expectations for what kind of performance and behaviours will be appreciated and rewarded. However, not all managers create clear targets or at times even change the goal posts to make targets harder to achieve (if achievable at all). This is often done intentionally if sales targets are easier to achieve than expected or as a way not to pay employees for their efforts. It can happen that managers create vague, non-quantifiable business objectives that make it hard for anyone to truly understand what needs to be achieved and how to be correctly evaluated. Even when objectives are clear, evaluating someone's performance as 'under-performing', 'good performance' or 'excellent performance' is also extremely subjective. This is best described as 'management discretion', which can be coloured by all kinds of personal or political motives at work. The negative impact of changing the goal posts, setting unrealistic targets or keeping business objectives vague is that it can significantly demotivate employees. It also destroys trust at work and can even lead to counter-productive behaviours, such as theft, fraud, bullying, sabotage and high turnover and absenteeism.[1]

DID YOU KNOW?
Vroom's Expectancy Theory
Vroom's Expectancy Theory is a well-known motivation model to help explain why people do and don't put effort into achieving their goals. Vroom's model states that employees will only put effort into achieving their goals if:

1. They believe targets are attainable (expectancy)
2. When they achieve their targets they will be rewarded (instrumentality)
3. The rewards are what they want to achieve (valence)

If, as an employee, you don't believe that your targets are attainable, then you will not put effort into achieving them. This can be caused by having goals that are too hard to attain or not having the proper skills to do your job properly, or be due to political issues. Once you achieve your goals, do you then believe you will be rewarded appropriately? This depends on if your manager actually pays you for achieving your targets or purposefully changes the goal posts to make it impossible for you to fully achieve. Performance reviews can feel like war, with your employer battling to get out of having to pay you full remuneration for your work instead of evaluating your performance fairly. Finally, do you find the rewards appealing to work towards? These rewards don't only have to be monetary rewards like bonuses but can also be promotions or employee of the year awards, reflecting more intrinsic needs, such as recognition and achievement.

Signs your company doesn't keep its promises

As you read in Red Flag 7 'This company is your family', making sure you keep your promises is important to building strong and positive relationships at work. When promises are not kept, the psychological contract you have with your company becomes violated, leading to less engagement and less trust. Promises are easily made but also easily forgotten. Often managers will verbally make promises about the future but also forget that they made these promises later. You can't always blame a manager for this, because he or she has many things to take care of. However, making false promises on purpose to achieve personal goals is downright bad management and will hurt the work relationship. If you have been subjected to false promises, it is important for you to decide how you want to continue the relationship with your manager. It is said you get attracted to a company for what it stands for, but you often leave because of the relationship with your manager. Instead of just waiting for promises to be broken (which will never turn out well), it is better to be prepared for different scenarios. Here are some red flags to watch out for when your manager makes agreements with you and how to prevent or counter them:

Creates vague goals – 'By next year, I want you to increase the brand awareness of our new product.'
Any goal that is qualitative by nature (non-numerical) is open for interpretation and will be subjectively evaluated. In some organizations, managers set such goals on purpose to give themselves that discretion. However, the problem with such performance evaluations is that the human brain can't

remember or evaluate all events and experiences equally. Nor does a manager have full insight into someone's behaviour and performance at work. More often than not, specific events stand out and get remembered, which then form the core of the evaluation. The solution to this is twofold. First, aim to agree with your manager to make all goals SMART.[2] Making goals SMART makes it clear to anyone reading them what is to be expected by when. So, increase brand awareness by 20 per cent compared to today. Second, consider a 360 evaluation if it concerns your performance at work. A 360-performance review can be a survey with questions about your behaviours and performance, which is sent to various stakeholders you engage with inside and outside of work (e.g. peer, manager, customer, supplier). This way you can collect different evaluations, which are more rounded than just a management review.

Breaks promises – 'Unfortunately, I can't give you your promotion yet.'

Too often promises are broken and new promises are made to reconcile past agreements. You might hear, 'We just came out of the pandemic and I can't give anyone raises at this moment, but if you do well in the coming year, I will definitely take it into consideration.' This kind of vagueness is a serious red flag because there is no intention at all to stick to a firm commitment. Promises that are made verbally are easier to break and it is important to put in writing what you will get in the near future and which performance is expected to achieve that reward. Remember your future performance is linked to future expectations. Organizational culture plays a huge role in how well managers keep their promises. Some work cultures almost dictate that you have to sacrifice future rewards and benefits to be part of the organization, saying, 'We have to lose some to win some.' What you can do to minimize the impact of false promises is again twofold. First, whatever you agree to at work in terms of performance and reward, make sure that agreements are put in writing, either by your manager or by yourself in an email as a follow-up to the meeting. When you have your agreements in writing, you can always go back to them and make them aware of what was agreed to (by whom and when). But even then, managers might still not deliver on the promise (for legitimate or non-legitimate reasons). Having agreements in writing is always better than just a verbal agreement. Second, make sure to have alternatives to a possible reward. If not financial rewards, consider non-financial rewards, such as a new position, time off, more remote-work possibilities or education. Make sure to choose alternatives that you would be happy getting if the money option is not on the table anymore. If they promise to give a promotion next year instead, make sure a clear plan is in place to show how you will get it (with milestones).

Changes targets halfway – 'We have to increase our targets for Q3 and Q4 by 20 per cent.'

It can be very irritating if your manager halfway through the year changes the annual targets. It can feel very unfair to have to accept new targets, especially when you were close to achieving your goals. This can happen for various reasons. Sometimes, targets are adjusted downwards because the market is performing lower than expected. Unexpected events affecting the industry is a valid reason to lower targets. This helps you stay motivated when things are not going well. The opposite is true as well. When things improve, sales targets can be adjusted upwards. However, adjusting targets upwards that are not commensurate with your previous objectives can make you less motivated to achieve your numbers and feel like the company does not want to compensate you in a fair manner or is tricking you out of paying what they agreed upon for you reaching your targets. The latter is something you hope not to be true but, depending on the work culture or your manager's behaviours, could be a possibility. It is also possible that your manager is bad at planning and didn't carefully set targets for the year. It is therefore important to work closely with your manager to figure out why targets are being adjusted and to find ways to agree to new terms you feel comfortable with. Consider being paid for the targets you did achieve to date and re-negotiate compensation for achieving new targets. If target adjustments happen frequently in your organization or in your line of business, then make sure to discuss alternative scenarios in advance with your manager to be better prepared for the future.

Creates unachievable goals – 'We have to be profitable by next year. I know this is a stretch, but I am sure you can do it!'

If your manager creates unrealistic goals, then it can be very hard to stay motivated on the job. The moment you don't believe that you can achieve your commercial targets is the moment you feel that you have lost control. As humans, we need to feel in control of our environment to feel safe and productive. Losing a sense of control can make you less interested in working towards goal achievement. Managers might say that setting higher than usual targets will push you to go further. Setting stretch goals does increase motivation, but if targets are unrealistic, then it does the complete opposite. However, the question you need to ask yourself is, 'Are the goals truly impossible to achieve?' Is it a real problem or a perceived problem? If it is real, then the question to ask is, 'Why is my manager setting such ridiculous goals?' Time to challenge the rationale behind the goal-setting decisions. If the problem is a perceived issue, then it could indicate that with some skill training or coaching on the job, you could change your perception of the goals. It is important to become aware of what is in your control (and what is not) and what you can achieve.

> Not all bonus schemes that companies design motivate people in the right way. Sometimes creating aggressive targets or one-sided incentive plans can motivate bad behaviour. In the case of Enron, an American energy company that went bankrupt because of a massive accounting scandal, their reward scheme focused mainly on short-term gains, which contributed to employees gaming the system internally and creating a dysfunctional work culture, leading to all kinds of unethical behaviour. Money motivates people, but sometimes in the wrong way.

Bosses who keep moving the goal posts – what's the drama?

Setting goals has a strong motivational component to it. Goals help you to stay focused on the task at hand and evaluate how well you are doing in achieving your goals. Goals can be short-term or long-term orientated, which can influence the decisions you make in the moment or the behaviours you display over time. Goals also activate and energize behaviour, as we feel a sense of accomplishment and pride when we are able to reach our objectives at work and in life. Workplace targets and objectives are used to keep people focused on the task and motivated at work. However, sometimes goal setting at work can have adverse effects, especially when objectives are vague, hard to achieve or changed in the moment. Managers have the habit of changing financial objectives midway when they see that numbers are easily reached, increasing existing targets. Or a supervisor might promise to promote you if you reach a certain outcome at the end of the year and then not follow through. Changing the goal posts, which some do continuously, kills trust, motivation and employee morale. It's like breaking a promise and is just bad management. Adjusting one-off targets due to corporate necessity, fine, it happens, but making it a habit is not fine and should be avoided.

It's a **red flag** if:
- Your manager regularly changes the goal posts, making it hard to achieve targets and killing employee morale.
- Your manager sets unrealistic or vague goals, which are hard to achieve or interpret.
- Your manager bases your (bi-)annual performance review on mere incidents (often things that just happened) to evaluate your overall performance. They don't evaluate you on your overall performance.
- Your manager uses 'management discretion' to decide a large part of your bonus.

It's a **green flag** if:

- As a manager, you understand how to motivate employees intrinsically and extrinsically.
- Your manager sets challenging, yet inspiring and achievable, goals to help you stay motivated and grow.
- As an employee, you make sure to have your targets and bonus plans put in writing.
- You take an active approach to counter fake promises at work by documenting made promises and ensuring goals are made SMART.

Things to consider when deciding if you want in or out

If you have been subjected to fake promises at work and had the goal posts changed frequently, then there is a high chance that you have lost trust in your manager and maybe even in the organization. The question then is: do you want to remain in a company that can't keep promises or follow through on verbal agreements? Is it something that happens seldomly and are there legitimate reasons why the company needs to change the company objectives suddenly? Or has this way of managing the business become a common practice in the organization to maximize productivity while minimizing costs? Time to decide if you want to continue working for an organization that unremittingly keeps moving the goal posts.

Willingness to stay

- You understand that the company is going through some serious changes, which require a re-evaluation of the existing goals and strategies.

- You have a good relationship with your manager and are happy to go along with the changes.
- You are intrinsically motivated to do your job. The changing of goal posts regularly is irritating, but nothing that personally bothers you.
- You understand the importance of negotiations and are willing to accept the new financial targets only if it means increasing the rewards as well.

Time to leave

- You have had enough of not being able to reach your targets because they have been changed midway.
- Your goals are not made SMART and are kept vague intentionally.
- Your manager regularly breaks promises, which is impacting your motivation and trust.
- Your manager intentionally moves the goal posts as a way to harass you.

Dating

Red flags in dating

The dating scene is more active than ever before. The rise of online dating and dating apps has transformed what was once considered a fun and effortful activity done in social settings outside to an effortless endeavour done from the comfort of your sofa. Today, we also have more dating options than we did in the past. Plus, we don't have to ask difficult questions to get to know the other person. Online personal bios provide you with all the info you need to know what people like and are looking for. Do they prefer cats or dogs, do they like it hard or soft and are they looking for a George Clooney silver fox or do they prefer a career woman who knows what she wants? Easy access and countless options must mean that we are living in a modern-day dating scene renaissance, right? Unfortunately, the modern dating world has become super ambiguous, challenging to navigate and even toxic. Some people refer to it as a snake pit. If you are looking to date someone for the long term, then it is important to know what you are looking for. Not everyone in today's world is looking for love or romance. Modern dating has given rise to new forms of intimate relationships, such as fuck buddies, friends with benefits and situationships, each with its advantages and drawbacks, and definitely not an option if you are looking for something more exclusive or long-lasting. And with online dating being so easy, some people think it is OK to play games when dating, giving rise to all kinds of toxic behaviours, such as ghosting, breadcrumbing, cookie jarring and orbiting. Modern dating looks like it is more 'practising for divorce' than it is 'practising for marriage'. Being able to identify red and green flags in dating is super important, as it helps you to evaluate if someone is a good match for you or not. Today, more than ever, it is important to be able to identify healthy and unhealthy behaviours in dating as it can help you focus on people that do matter and prevent a lot of headaches down the road. Dating apps, unfortunately, do not yet come with a bullshit filter, so you will need to up your game to weed out what is not good for you. But, let's face it, no one is perfect and we all have some red flags inside of us. Especially when we start dating, obstructive thinking and behaviours caused by past traumas might surface. Do we run away at the sight of the first red flag or do we acknowledge that unsupportive behaviours might show up in a romantic setting? That we could be the partners to help each other grow through past pains using shared love, understanding and commitment? The coming six chapters about red and green flags in dating will help you untangle the complex jungle of modern dating and dating behaviours to find the right match and create something more sustainable over time.

Red Flag 13 'I just don't feel like dating!'
Choosing to stay single

'Our greatest weakness lies in giving up.'
Thomas Edison

Losing interest to date

Do you feel like dating has become cumbersome? Putting so much effort into getting to know someone but getting nowhere with them? Or do you feel scared to get too attached to someone out of fear of getting hurt again? Reminiscing on those horrible fights and the cheating, saying to yourself, 'Never again, I'd rather be alone.' Or have you just entered your bad boy or bad girl era, ready to break some hearts of your own? You got hurt by the F-boy, now it's time to retaliate and become the F-girl. If any of this sounds familiar, then most likely you are on a solo trip and dating will be the last thing on your mind.

But there are many other reasons why people are giving up on dating besides the heartbreak and the soul-searching. Some believe social media has made people less willing to date, others point to dating apps as a major cause, while others blame it on changing social norms and the loss of emotional and social connection. Focusing on yourself is a good thing at times, but feeling too scared or unwilling to meet new people or connect at a deeper level with someone could mean something else is at play. Whatever the reason, it is important to identify where your lack of romantic interest in others comes from.

We are social beings by nature and our mental and physical well-being, including our cognitive performance and the functioning of our immune systems, depends heavily on human connection. In this chapter, we will dive into the psychology of why people date less nowadays and explore when choosing not to date is a green flag and when it is a red flag. We will also look at what people are doing as an alternative to pursuing romantic interests, and touch upon trends such as 'dating yourself' and 'falling in love with fictional characters'. Understanding what is driving people's choices not to date can provide interesting insights into what can bring people closer together in a modern dating world (when they are ready for it, of course).

Modern dating trends

According to various studies published in *The Journal of Personality and Social Psychology* and papers on the topic of relational success and human dynamics, there seems to be a modern trend not to date.[1] Data are showing that many people are opting to remain single for longer, postponing long-term relationships and family planning till later in life, if at all. The single life is also heavily promoted on social media, with videos like 'catch flights, not feelings'. Many people can feel socially pressured to date (even when they don't want to) because they believe society will view them as less if not in a relationship or married. These pressures don't only come from family and friends, but also from colleagues and even strangers you meet for the first time. When you tell people you are single, they often ask, while giving you a bombastic side-eye stare,[2] 'So why are you not married yet?' or 'Why have you been alone for so long?', implying that there must be something wrong with you if you remain single. There are legitimate reasons why you shouldn't date yet. However, people's biases hold them back from seeing an alternative perspective to marriage and traditional bonding in general (and especially being happily single challenges the married person's beliefs about happiness). There are plenty of reasons why people prefer to be by themselves. Though I can't address all the reasons, let's explore some of the most important ones relating to modern life and dating.

Past relationship experiences

One of the major reasons why people choose not to date and to focus more on themselves is due to bad dating experiences in the past. After being with a narcissist (see Red Flag 16 for more on narcissism) or in an abusive relationship (see Red Flag 22) or with a cheating partner (see Red Flag 23), the experience can leave you feeling insecure, vulnerable or traumatized, and even make you less trusting of others. When this happens, there is no bandwidth to be able to focus on someone else again. Focusing on yourself is the best thing to do. And even after recovering from bad relationship experiences, you might still not be interested in looking for a romantic partner, out of fear of encountering another rotten apple. Focusing on yourself and not allowing anyone in to hurt you again is probably the safest option. Especially, when you see so many other men and women on social media going through the same, it can feel comforting to know that you are not alone in choosing the single life. That being said, I don't think social media is that social, as it has this ability to unconsciously isolate people.

The modern-day checklist

When we look at life today, we are definitely more informed than in the past. Being better informed should help us to make better decisions, but having access to too much information can also be debilitating, with us overthinking and overanalyzing every situation. Our lives are also busier than ever, and we are consumed by the uncertainty of world events such as global pandemics, geopolitical unrest and rapid advancements in technology, like generative AI, which people are becoming increasingly fearful of due to possible job losses. Many people have a well-planned schedule[3] nowadays, making them less interested in pursuing romantic interests if they can't fit them into their schedule. A famous quote on TikTok is '10 hours of work, 2 hours of training and 8 hours of sleep. If I text you, you matter!' which reflects the mindset underlying this trend. A friend of mine once said, 'We all have a checklist nowadays. And with the internet and social media, that checklist has just become longer. There is always a good enough reason for me not to take things forward if people don't meet my needs.'

There is an unwillingness to compromise when considering whether or not to date or look for a long-term partner. Many people are single and feel happy that way. You fill your day with work, sports and social interactions. Your social needs can be fulfilled through short-lived encounters with friends online or in the real world. When the tensions are high and you feel like some honey, your regulars or dating app hook-ups provide the momentary intimate happiness you need. The digital space has made it easier to focus on yourself. Not surprisingly, consumer technology and apps in the West have been designed to augment individuality. Hence, the names iPhone, i-Reserve, iFormBuilder, Mercedes me and Myspace to reflect the importance of individuality. In East Asia, a more collectivistic view underlying human relationships exists, which is often reflected back in the name of apps like the Chinese companies WeChat and WePay.[4]

The IKEA effect

In the past, we spent more quality time face-to-face with other people to get to know them better and build stronger relationships. Effort was (and is) needed to make human relationships work. We also relied more on our close social network to get support and feel safe. Though we might have more virtual 'friends'[5] today, the number of true friendships (and one's overall satisfaction with friendships) is rapidly declining.[6] The pandemic, technology and social developments have changed the way we connect with friends in the modern world and how much quality time we are willing to invest in these friendships. This is the same for spending time with someone you are romantically invested in. The more effort you put into others, the more you value them. In psychology, this cognitive bias is often referred to as the *IKEA effect*.[7] People subjectively value things (or people) more when they put more effort into them. Hence, the success of the IKEA store. People love going to that store, spending money on pieces of wood (and, more often than not, on a bunch of other random homewares they definitely don't need . . .) that they then have to put together themselves . . .

like WHY? There's a sense of satisfaction in having DIY-ed the furniture rather than buying it ready-made, and the increased effort directly correlates to an increased valuation of the object. If we put less effort into building platonic or romantic relationships, we value them less. It is therefore not a surprise that the perceived value of human relationships in a digitized world is becoming less, instead fostering a stronger focus on self and one's needs.

You don't want to date because you are an 'Aro' or an 'Ace'

More intrinsic reasons why people don't want to date can be related to how attracted they naturally feel towards other people. It's a false belief that everyone feels romantically or sexually attracted to people. There are many people who don't feel any attraction at all, which is not linked to mental health issues or past traumas per se.[8] People who don't feel a romantic attraction to others are called 'aromantic' or Aro for short. Often people confuse aromantic people with being asexual, which is not the same. Asexual (or Ace) is someone who doesn't feel a sexual attraction towards someone. Someone who is Aro can feel sexually attracted to someone but doesn't connect this sexual energy to anything romantic. It is often believed that Aro people don't experience love, which is not true. They can love a friend or a parent. They just don't feel in love with someone romantically. Aro people can desire a romantic relationship with someone, just there is no actual romantic attraction. Aces can be in love with someone or feel romantically attracted to someone, however not sexually attracted or interested. Interestingly, some Ace people do have sex, they just don't really feel sexually attracted to the other person. People can be both Aro and Ace. These people often have little desire for romantic or sexual relationships with a person (and can even feel repulsed by the idea) and might even question if feeling sexually or romantically attracted to someone is more of a response to social pressures than actual desire.

When is not wanting to date a green flag?

It is absolutely fine if you don't want to date someone or be in a relationship, and you shouldn't feel as if anyone is forcing you to. Seeing close friends and colleagues in relationships can make you feel like you need to be in one as well, but it's definitely not a must. In today's world, choosing to live alone or to be by yourself is a lifestyle choice and becoming less of a taboo socially (also in many societies where marrying early in life is culturally enforced). Single people choosing to live alone and not date often cite 'choosing for my own peace', 'more freedom', 'focusing on my career' and 'need time to heal' as reasons why they don't want to be in anything that resembles long-term commitment.

People's lifestyles have adapted to the times. For example, more women are choosing career first over family and delaying relational commitments and having kids until well into their 30s and 40s. We live in a world that prioritizes self-development and mental health. Nowadays, many people demand that a potential partner work on themselves first before entering a relationship. Taking lessons from past relationships, reflecting on how to be a better partner to someone or learning how to heal past wounds and traumas before committing to someone is something I highly recommend. These are all green flags when it comes to choosing to focus on yourself and not to date.

When is not wanting to date a red flag?

Not wanting to date is a personal choice, but not all personal choices are good choices. Choosing to be alone, when it would be better to be together, is something worthy of deeper reflection. Being by yourself for too long can become so familiar that it becomes your default setting, making you push anyone away who comes close to you without carefully evaluating if it could work. Alternatively, you can be too demanding of what the other person should be for you (to fit into your lifestyle). Don't get me wrong, being self-reliant is a good thing, but blocking people out of your life because you don't want to adapt or feel too scared to meet others can hurt you in the long run.

A landmark study conducted by Harvard that followed a group of people for over 85 years sought to discover the factors that lead to a longer and happier life. We're all aware that eating healthily and staying active throughout your adult years is key to a long, happy life. And this is partially true. However, the study found that the number one factor that leads to longer life was having strong social connections.[9] It seems that no matter how well we eat or how regularly we exercise, having close bonds with other people was the most important factor for longevity. Modern-day dating and living in a way that is more short-term orientated prevents us from learning how to build lasting relationships in many areas of

our lives and, as a consequence, we're less able to establish
long-term connections, and at risk of experiencing a lower
quality of life over time.

Falling in love with fictional characters

When I lived in Japan in the early 2000s, I became familiar
with anime (Japanese cartoons) and manga (comic strips /
graphic novels). They were not just popular among teen-
agers, but among adults too. It was very common (and still
is) for grown men and women to be huge fans of anime or
manga characters. Even Hello Kitty has a huge adult fan-
base (Hello Kitty has become so popular globally that she
has even reached cult status[10]). It was the first time that I
had heard of people developing parasocial relationships
with fictional characters.[11] I remember the manga character
Salary Man Kintaro, a motorcycle gang member turned
businessman, who working-class Japanese could recognize
themselves in. A man who fought against corruption and
the unfairness many people experienced at work. Kintaro
was a mental escape for many real-life office workers from
the daily pressures and frustration in the workplace.[12] He
became a beacon of hope to many during the changing
times of globalization and recession in Japan.

In the last year, I have devoted some of my social media
content to the phenomenon of falling in love with fictional
characters (often referred to as fictoromance, fictosexuality
or fictophilia),[13] a trend I then saw gradually make its way to
the West, but I hardly ever saw anyone talking about it. People
fall in love with the protagonist of a story – often a person,
a superhero or a villain portrayed in a fictional or anime

story – and are very aware that their adoration is towards someone not real. It is easy to understand why people become so consumed by fictional characters with whom they can identify, and how one can fall in love with the story protagonist who is so relatable. People want an escape from the frustrations of real life. It can be a distraction from the constant battles you are experiencing at home, or you are just so sick and tired of being disappointed by people in real life that your fictional character provides you solace. Perhaps you're feeling lonely and the story's main character provides much-needed companionship. You know that whatever happens your fictional character will always be there for you, save you from distress, and will never hurt you (or you them). You won't feel rejected, and you know you are always in control of the parasocial relationship you have with your fictional character.

The videos I posted on this topic on different social media platforms quickly went viral and made me realize that people's love and infatuation for fictional characters in the West were bigger than I expected them to be but can be explained by the growing disappointments people have with human relationships, especially romantic ones. At first, this idea might seem strange, but fictophilia can be considered a natural evolution of romantic and sexual relationships in the modern-day world. It wouldn't surprise me if artificial intelligence (AI) becomes the new escape for many people, seeking to build connection with empathic AI chatbots, robots and other human-like automata.

Identifying with the hero or villain of the story happens because the protagonist is so perfect (better than any human being could be) in the eyes of the reader, or because they like the villain character they portray (or the life they live), even if the villain kills and destroys. Eren Yeager from the famous Japanese anime *Attack on Titan* is a fictional character that many people adore but is definitely not your role-model good guy. Interestingly, people also fall in love with villains in the real world. In Mexico, for example, the *narco cultura* (Mexican drug world) is highly idolized and romanticized by many Mexicans. The Sinaloa Cartel is the largest cartel in Mexico (and according to US intelligence agencies, the largest in the world) and a family that many people admire. Not because of the family's illegal activities per se, but more because of their lavish lifestyle.[14] Street culture, fashion and even music are inspired by these mighty drug lords. It is easy to imagine why people idealize the thug life, especially when you see that your good behaviours don't always give you the upper hand.

The fact that many people nowadays are giving up on dating due to bad experiences and difficulties finding a suitable partner can make focusing on yourself seem like the best option. But who to fall in love with if you've given up trying to find a real-life someone? If you fall in love with fictional characters, then don't worry . . . you're not crazy, it's totally fine![15] There are many people who have this experience, though it can feel embarrassing to admit. However, fictophilia can be a problem if you are dating someone in the real world and you find yourself more attracted to, or in love with, your fictional character than with your real-life partner. Time to be open about it with your human partner.

DID YOU KNOW?
New dating trend: dating yourself

Because of today's *i-* and *me-*movement, people are choosing to date themselves. But what does it mean to date yourself? Dating yourself is devoting time and energy to nurturing your relationship with yourself, as you would hope an ideal date would. You treat yourself to lavish dinners alone, go on holiday alone, have Netflix nights with candles and snacks alone or go on a solo cinema date. Everywhere you go, you bring your trusted mobile phone with you to stay socially connected and snap some pics of your experiences, but you have intentionally chosen to be by yourself. Besides enjoying the time by yourself (or the self-pampering experience), dating yourself can also be therapeutic. It provides you with the environment to control how the date goes (you can say 'yes' and 'no' to things) to help you navigate interpersonal dates when they do happen. Sadly, because of our reliance on technology to facilitate interpersonal relationships, many people are finding it hard to engage in small talk, speak to strangers or express emotions. People need to learn how to date again (especially, if you haven't done it for a long time).

In Japan, there are restaurants that cater to those who want to dine alone, providing cubicles to eat by yourself and that require no social interaction with even the staff if you don't want it.[16] I wouldn't be surprised if, in the future, travel and hospitality services start catering more to the solo dater. In June 2023, Rosanna Ramos, a 36-year-old New Yorker, got virtually married to Eren Kartal,[17] an AI-powered chatbot she created herself in the app Replika.[18] Talk about moulding the ideal partner and creating opportunities for enhanced narcissism! Personally, I am not a big fan of promoting too much alone time. The health consequences of loneliness are well documented[19] and we need to remember that we are social by nature. We need others to survive (even when we have all the technology in the world to live independently).

Choosing to stay single – what's the drama?

Choosing not to date is an option, either a healthy or unhealthy one. There are many reasons why people choose not to date and to remain single nowadays. However, not all of these reasons are healthy. Are you choosing to remain single because you want to focus on your career or are you choosing not to date because you first want to heal from negative dating experiences in the past? Choosing to be single for the right reasons can be psychologically enriching and thus a valid reason not to date. Or you might find that your life has become too planned out or that you have been single for so long that you can't find the energy or interest to adjust your life to anyone else's. Maybe you don't date because you feel zero attraction to other people. And again, maybe you don't date because you think you are too old, have low self-esteem or because of the horror stories you hear about dating on social media. This could be a moment to reflect on whether you are actually making the right choices in life when it comes to romance. It is important to become more aware of why you are choosing to remain by yourself. Studies show that living a life of solitude can be good for a while but can also hurt you in the long run. The more aware you are of your choices, the more intentionally you can live your (single) life. This chapter is mainly about identifying red and green flags in yourself.

It's a **red flag** if:
- You have been too long alone and are too stuck in your ways. There is no compromise and you want others to adjust to your lifestyle (but not the other way around).
- You become aware that after years of not dating, you feel too scared to date or pursue romantic interests. Maybe it's time to speak to someone about your fears or feelings of insecurity.
- You can't handle relationship challenges and disputes. Conflict is an inescapable part of any relationship and swiping right or ghosting someone at the first sight of trouble is a huge red flag. Learning how to deal with challenges has multiple psychological and health benefits.
- You become so obsessed with a fictional character or AI chatbot that you refuse to date or fall in love with a human again.

It's a **green flag** if:
- You are purposefully prioritizing your career and you know it doesn't make sense to date for the long term so as not to break any hearts when you have to stay focused to achieve your career goals.
- You are on a healing journey, and you want to work on yourself first before being with someone

romantically. You choose this because you want to heal past traumas or improve your personal effectiveness so as to be able to set boundaries for yourself and express your needs more effectively.

- You are a F-boy or F-girl (or a person who knows they have a tendency to treat love partners badly) and you know you will break someone's heart if you date them. You choose to focus on hook-ups and not impact other people's lives through manipulation tactics (as much as possible) until you have reached a stage in your life when you feel that you want to, and can, change (remember, you can always change!).
- You are still figuring out who you are and what you truly desire. For now, exploring and experimenting is your main objective. Dating will naturally evolve when it feels right.

Things to consider when deciding if you want to change your single status

The modern world is making it easier to live by yourself and be more self-reliant. Choosing to remain single is a lifestyle choice and many people are opting for the single life. However, the single life doesn't come without its consequences. Being single for too long can be bad for your health and your overall well-being. Living too long by yourself can make you less comfortable interacting with people in real life and less likely to change your lifestyle to be able to live with someone or form a relationship. And stigma still exists for people who choose to be single for too long or at a certain age. However, choosing to be with someone is not easy either. It requires commitment, effort, adjustment and sacrifice. Not only that, negative dating experiences can also hold you back from wanting to date. This means you will have to trust again and be confronted with your own development areas and those of your partner. Do you think you are ready for it or is it too soon and you would prefer to stay single for a while? Here are some considerations to help you make that decision.

Better to stay single

- You are mentally and physically not ready to be with someone. Then don't! Stay focused on yourself, your career, your healing journey or your purpose in life.
- You enjoy your peace and being by yourself (without feeling lonely). Being single feels empowering and gives you more control over your life. To be a good partner you need to prove to yourself that you can also be content being alone. If you are still discovering if you can be by yourself, then be by yourself first. This will be beneficial to both you and your future relationship.
- You feel asexual and/or aromantic. If you have a hard time finding someone similar or who is willing to accept you for who you are, then better to stay single until you do find the right person. Don't compromise on your values and your feelings.

Time to date (again)

- The moment you feel that you want to let someone back in again. Don't dodge the bullet. Start dating.
- If you have given up on online dating but still desire to date, then keep on dating. Remember, there are

many ways to meet someone outside of a dating app: a friend's party, clubs and bars, events, sports clubs and even the supermarket. You will need to be able to strike up a conversation with someone though.

- Dating can help you discover what kind of partner you want to be and what not. It also helps you to develop a quality-over-quantity mindset if you are choosing to date one person.

Red Flag 14 'I prefer not to label it yet'
The situationship

'I know I am but summer to your heart, and not the
full four seasons of the year.'
'Sonnet XXVII', Edna St Vincent Millay

Situationships

Have you ever found yourself in the situation where you've
been seeing someone for months yet you've never reached
the point of defining what you both actually are to each
other? Either you are too scared to have the conversation or
your partner refuses to label it. If this is you, then you might
be in a situationship. A situationship can be defined as a
casual relationship that hasn't been labelled as such by either
of the partners. People can remain in a situationship for
years believing it's a relationship, but always conscious that
nothing has been defined and there are no explicit agreements in place about commitment or seeing other people.
This can be very confusing and even frustrating, asking yourself why after so many months the topic of labelling the
bond as a 'relationship' has not come up. You worry if what
you have with your partner will last and if you should invest
more time into it.

Situationships can come about as a result of manipulative
behaviour on your partner's side, but it can also be a form

of connection you both desire. Let's face it, in a world with so many options, not defining what you have gives you the freedom and flexibility to enjoy life without tying yourself down with one person. Situationships can lead to longer-term relationships, but you will need to put the effort in to get the ball rolling. And don't be disappointed if it doesn't work out. Understanding more about the psychology behind situationships, why people desire them, and how to navigate situationships in today's dating landscape will put you in a better position to make more empowered decisions going forward, especially in a dating world that is rapidly changing and where there are more forms of romantic connections than there traditionally have been. If you are in a situationship right now, then it's time to decide what to do with it!

Why have situationships become such a thing in today's dating world?

Before diving into the psychology of situationships, let's first explain where the term comes from and explore the reasons why this relationship status has become so popular in recent years. According to online dictionary WordSense,[1] the term 'situationship' appeared in literature works as early as 2014. However, several sources on Google indicate that the term 'situationship' was first dropped in the public space by free-lance writer Carina Hsieh in 2017 when dating apps started to boom. In the same year, Tinder mentioned situationships in their annual report as a valid relationship status.

Online dating apps have had a major influence on how people date and how they view 'hook-ups' and 'dates'. At the touch of a button, you have access to a plethora of potential

mates, including their personal information and sexual preferences, which you can swipe left or right on.[2] Not only that,
you also have algorithms working in the background trying
to keep you on the app as long as possible, pushing for more
connections and potentially more hook-ups. This is great if
you are going through a 'fuck phase' in your life, but challenging if you are looking to date one person more regularly. It's
like an addictive hook, pulling you back to the quick and easy
option for any instant gratification, not wanting to invest too
much in one person. Or when things are not going well,
dating apps create the illusion that you don't need to deal
with drama and emotions, and you can easily find someone
else. 'Bye bitch, next!' is the attitude people have, because
they know they can find another 'option' in the next five
minutes.

As a consequence, dating culture has changed drastically
in the past 20 years, and many people across all generations
criticize it for being 'toxic', 'emotionless' and for how it
'treats people like options'. Before the digital revolution, you
would have to go out to find someone and meet regularly
before you knew more about them. Effort was needed to
meet people and dating was the norm. Nowadays, hooking
up and having easy access and multiple options are the norm,
while dating or anything that requires more diligence feels
cumbersome or even unusual (especially for those growing
up in this dating culture). This is why traditional concepts of
romantic relationships and monogamy are becoming diluted,
and why many people are not opting for steady relationships
as much. Are you single and looking for NSA (no strings
attached)? Or are you partnered? Are you low-key seeing
someone regularly but still want to meet up with other girls
or guys, and everything in between? There are so many

options to choose from, which is a major factor in why situationships have become so popular.

Different forms of romantic connections

Not long ago, you were either 'single' or 'partnered' (e.g. in a short- or long-term relationship, registered partnership or married) and if you were anything outside of the traditional relationship status, it would have most likely been 'it's complicated'. Even scientific research mostly categorizes relationships along this binary. Digital technology, social media and shifting norms about relationships have made the dating playing field confusing and difficult to navigate. Not to mention the different types of dating and relationship statuses you can choose from. The dating world today has its own '50 Shades of Grey' in terms of dating and relationship status options, which is definitely more inclusive but also very confusing. Let's take a closer look at the different ways people can label their bond with someone, which can be categorized on the basis of the level of emotional connection and the level of sexual engagement.

Companionship

A companionship is defined as a bond where two people spend lots of time with each other (e.g. going out, visiting places, having dinners) and find comfort in each other (mainly emotionally). Companionships are largely platonic bonds with high levels of closeness involved. The difference between companionships and friendships is that friends normally spend less time with each other than companions. Besides humans, pets can also provide companionship.

Booty call

A booty call is a hook-up with someone for a *quick shag* (British English for a *quick fuck*). The level of sexual engagement for booty calls is high, but the level of emotional connection is usually low. But that's not to say intimacy is lacking in booty-call relationships.[3] To see someone on an occasional basis for a quick hook-up, even if it's just to fulfil physical needs, requires some level of intimacy.

Fuck buddies

Fuck buddies go one step further than booty calls. Fuck buddies are two people who meet up regularly for sex. Some friendship can be involved, but it is a very minimal aspect of the situation. The level of sexual engagement is high and the level of emotional connection low to medium. Both parties know that the main goal of being buddies is for sex (and nothing else).

Friends with benefits (FWB)

FWB goes one step further than fuck buddies. FWB is when both parties are mainly interested in sex with each other and occasionally hang out together (or with a group of friends) for a drink or dinner. The level of sexual engagement is high to medium and the level of emotional connection medium to low.

Situationship

A situationship is somewhat similar to friends with benefits but with the added complication that it has never been labelled as friends with benefits, or a relationship for that matter. Because things are undefined in a situationship, it can happen that one of the two partners develops more romantic feelings towards the other and wants to pursue an exclusive relationship (while the other doesn't). Because of the ambiguity around situationships and the stress it often causes, I prefer to call them 'shituationships'. The level of sexual engagement is high to medium and the level of emotional connection medium to high.

Consensual Non-monogamous Relationships (CNM relationships)

CNMs are non-exclusive relationships (also referred to as 'open relationships' or 'non-exclusive relationships'). Both partners are happy being in an open relationship and can decide to meet other people for sex together or separately, or a combination of both. The levels of sexual engagement and emotional connection are both high.

Relationships

Lastly, the traditional relationship is a romantic relationship in which both partners choose to be in a monogamous relationship together, which can vary in duration. Level of sexual engagement is medium to high and the level of emotional connection is high.

What is the psychology behind situationships?

There is no one single theory or psychological principle that can explain why people want to be in a situationship. There are various reasons why people choose a situationship and there are many more reasons why people choose to remain in one. Let's review the psychology for both sides.

Psychological reasons for choosing a situationship

- **Multiple/better options**
  A person can choose a situationship to purposefully keep things unclear with a specific individual, so that they can date other people (or eventually move to someone better). People feel more powerful with more options as it gives them a sense of control over their lives. The fear of missing out or loss aversion can also drive people to want multiple partners. Especially in a world that feels unpredictable and uncertain, people can feel the need to maximize their options as a way of survival (basic instinct). However, survival is not always the primary reason behind why people choose to have multiple options. It can also come down to personality or an individual's commitment issues. Ill intent and manipulation can also be the reason behind wanting multiple options or creating a situationship.

- **Temporary investment**
  A person can choose to have a situationship because they are only planning to stay in a specific place for a short period of time, knowing that they will move away later due to work or family commitments, or better opportunities elsewhere. Having a temporary partner without committing fully can help fulfil emotional and physical needs, while lowering the burden of breaking up when the time comes. Aside from breaking up, not getting too involved with someone makes it easier to stay focused on your personal and professional goals. Yet temporary

investments can also be manipulative, especially if your partner isn't forthcoming about their intention to leave in the near future or that they are only invested for the short term.

- **Less responsibility**

  A person can choose a situationship because they don't want the responsibility of a committed relationship. This can be due to personal concerns or a lack of desire to become more involved. They want emotional connection and sexual engagement but in a compartmentalized way. Not wanting the responsibility that comes with a more committed relationship status can also be a result of feeling they don't have full control over their lives. This can happen when your environment (e.g. family, culture) dictates who you will eventually marry.

Choosing to remain in a situationship

- **Fear of rejection**

  A person can choose to stay in a situationship because they are too scared to bring up the topic of how to label it moving forward, fearing that such a conversation might create tension and potentially end the situationship. This is often linked to a fear of rejection, which can be triggered by various factors, such as past experiences, people-pleasing tendencies, anxious attachment style, poor self-esteem, self-criticism and/or anxiety among others. Staying with someone who doesn't respect your emotional needs or who purposely uses your insecurities to keep you in a situationship is not healthy and you will do yourself more damage by staying than by leaving.

- **Dealing with social pressure**

  A person can choose to stay in a situationship because they don't feel the need to conform to social pressures to marry or be in a relationship. Situationships offer an opportunity to showcase that you are seeing someone while keeping your freedom in a discrete manner. People can also choose situationships because they have romantic interests their environment might not socially accept (e.g. dating someone from another culture or religion or dating someone of the same sex). Not fully committing to someone gives you the freedom to explore your desires without having to disclose them to anyone. In some cultures, you are expected to behave 'appropriately' in the public space, and as long as you do that, you can do what you want in the private space. This sounds harsh and unfair, but it is more common than you think. That being said, situationships are also created because one of the partners is cheating on another person. Never a good thing! Situationships kept intact because of social pressure or fear often lead to relational distress, so consider carefully if it is worth it to continue.

- **Ease of use**

  A person can choose to stay in a situationship because they enjoy the emotional connection and physical intimacy it offers without the commitment and depth of a monogamous relationship. Situationships provide companionship and a sense of security, and can even give you time to heal from the impact of a previous relationship. If both partners are OK with the situationship and are not looking for something too serious, then situationships can be ideal. It's like designing your own relationship based on your desires and needs without feeling tied down. Enjoying the moment has its benefits and not having to deal with relationship drama just makes it so much easier to be with someone nowadays. Situationships are definitely easier to find too. Just make sure you are intentional and happy about remaining in one.

DID YOU KNOW?
Have you been 'friend zoned'?
Being 'friend zoned' is quite a common term in the dating world. It refers to someone wanting to pursue romantic or sexual interests with another person (often a friend or acquaintance) and then being rejected (e.g. 'Jake wanted to date Jenny, but Jenny wasn't interested so she kept him in the friend zone.') You can also get friend zoned after having a couple of dates with someone. This can happen because the person you were dating either lost interest in you, found someone else, didn't enjoy the sex with you or just didn't feel a strong enough connection with you to pursue romantic interests further. They still might like you as a friend, so instead of ghosting you, they friend zone you.

In which situations can situationships be beneficial?

As mentioned, situationships don't always have to be something bad. People choose to be in a situationship because it allows them to enjoy the benefits of being in a relationship (the emotional connection, intimacy and/or companionship), while also enjoying the single life. It allows you time to get to know each other and test the waters. Who says you can't have your cake and eat it too? There could be other valid reasons for keeping things unclear. Maybe both partners have other objectives or interests in life and fear that committing to one another might jeopardize other life opportunities. Or it could be that both partners are not capable of investing further due to a lack of emotional availability or emotional immaturity. Situationships offer a playground to discover and find connection, but with the flexibility of exploring other options. Leaving things undefined doesn't always mean something malicious is involved. It could simply mean a person is scared of building a deeper connection at this point in time, or they feel pressured by today's rapidly changing world and feel life is fleeting. 'I am here for a good time, not for a long time' is the motto I hear many of my clients and students say nowadays. 'With so many options in this world, how do I know for sure what I want or if this is right for me?'

Another example of a positive situationship is the 'mutually exclusive situationship' – a new term that has popped up on social media recently and which refers to a situationship where both partners enjoy being with each other, are allowed to sleep with other people but are 'sexclusive'.[4] When your partner holds values or beliefs that don't align with yours you can choose to keep them away from your situationship without bad feelings. What all positive situationships have in common is that open communication and respect help keep people happy and sane within their bond. Not labelling what you are can serve a purpose and in a dating world full of uncertainty perhaps it's a way to define your own love story.

How do I know if I am in a situationship?

You're probably asking yourself, 'How do I know if I am in a situationship?' This is a necessary question to ask yourself if you are unsure about your relationship and desire more clarity. Here is a checklist to see if you are currently in a situationship. Do you identify with four or more of these statements?

1. You've been dating someone for 6 months or longer and you are not sure if you can call what you have a relationship.
2. Every time you bring up the topic of wanting to label the relationship as a 'relationship', your partner gives excuses for not wanting to label it yet, avoids the discussion or gets upset.
3. You have been given false promises for a long period of time about becoming more serious or exclusive.
4. You have developed emotions for your partner but are too scared to discuss it with them because you fear that it might jeopardize what you have together.
5. You feel emotionally drained due to the uncertainty of your relationship.
6. You or your partner are still sleeping with other people.
7. Your partner says all the right things, but their actions don't add up.
8. Your partner says they are not sure if you are the right person for something more serious, even though you have been dating for more than 6 months.

How do I get out of a situationship?

If you find yourself in a situationship and you are not happy about it, then it's time to get out! The lack of clarity, boundaries and commitment, and the inconsistency of the situationship, can have a serious impact on your mental and physical health. Studies find that situationships can increase anxiety, loneliness, self-esteem issues and depression, which can lead to you feeling too scared to leave, believing no one else will want you or feeling trapped in a vicious circle you just can't get out of.[5,6] To prevent this from happening (or to take action if you are in such a situation when reading this), here are two things you can do to move out of your situationship:

Speak openly to your partner

Speak to your partner openly and respectfully about your needs and explain how the situationship is affecting you. If they dodge the discussion, don't care about your well-being or give you false hope, then it is time to move away from your partner. Remember you are in a situationship, so you haven't expressly committed to anything, and nor has your partner. Don't obsess over them or obsess about yourself. Sure, it feels scary to let them go, but remember that your fears stem from inside yourself. People are attracted to other people who are confident and take care of themselves. If you feel that your self-esteem is low and fear is holding you back from leaving, then it's time to work on yourself before committing to anyone (even temporarily). The situationship will have helped you to realize that even more.

Block them!

If you don't feel you can have that conversation with your partner, then keep it to a descriptive text message and say goodbye. It sounds cold, but if your mental health is on the line and you don't see any improvement, then there is a high probability that it won't improve. I always say that the best indicator of how someone will behave in the future is how they behave today. Get rid of them, but in a polite and detached manner.[7] If they become aggressive or try to put you in your place, then block them! You're probably thinking, 'Dr Fenwick, how can you say that?' But I have your best interests in mind, remember, and this is one specific circumstance I highly recommend cutting someone out of your life immediately.[8] It will save you a lot of headaches and costly therapy sessions.

Situationships – what's the drama?

A situationship in the dating world is a casual relationship that has not been clearly labelled with the intent to keep things vague. In situationships, clear expectations, dos and don'ts and future plans are not discussed, as one of the partners (or both) wants to keep things flexible. This is often intentionally, so there is an option to date other people while fulfilling emotional needs and enjoying other relationship benefits (e.g. companionship) from the person they are keeping in the dark. For the partner wanting more certainty about 'what we are' it can be very confusing. If this is happening to you, then realize that the ongoing confusion and uncertainty with time can cause havoc to your mental and physical health.

With the rise of dating apps, situationships and other forms of dating have become immensely popular. The desire to date in the traditional sense has diminished, and the prevalence of online dating has contributed towards a hook-up culture where the words 'commitment' and 'being exclusive' almost seem taboo. With so many online dating options at your disposal, why would you try to be with one person or even stay with them if they cause too much drama? It's also important to remember that if someone tells you they are not ready to commit, don't secretly hope they will. Creating false hope for yourself is just as bad as doing it to someone else. However, not all situationships are bad and they can serve a purpose. They can help you heal from a previous relationship and allow you time to start feeling for someone again. Situationships can also be positive if you like being with someone but you both are still exploring options and figuring out what you want. It goes without saying that honesty, respect and open communication are key to making situationships work. You never know, a situationship one day could turn into something with 'more clarity'.

It's a **red flag** if:
- Your partner 'acts' like they are dating you but does not show signs of commitment or they haven't labelled it as something more serious.
- You have been in a situationship for six months or longer and the topic of 'commitment' or 'relationship' has not been discussed, but it is something you want. This is a red flag for both of you!
- You are confused about what you are. Your partner avoids the conversation or gaslights you whenever

you want to talk about your dating/relationship status or your future together.

- Your partner says to you, 'You are currently my #5, but if things go well between us, you can potentially become my #1.' Get rid of them immediately!
- You are suffering mentally and/or physically because of the uncertainty your situationship is causing you.

It's a **green flag** if:
- Both you and your partner are in a situationship because you want to test the waters together and take your time to develop a stronger emotional connection.
- Both you and your partner are clear about your relationship status, and both want to enjoy the benefits of a relationship without being committed to each other.
- You are not sure what you want yet and want to discover what your interests are. Be sure to make this known to your partner though.
- You want to heal before getting into a more serious relationship with someone. Situationships are a good opportunity to do this. Again, make sure you communicate this to your partner. Maybe they can help with your healing.

Things to consider when deciding if you want in or out

If you think you are in a shitty relationship, ask yourself first, are you really in a relationship? If things have never been labelled as such, then maybe you are in a situationship. What do you do? Do you stay or do you leave? This can be a hard decision, especially if you have developed feelings for your partner. You also know by now that situations don't always have to be negative. Here are some suggestions to help decide what to do.

Willingness to stay

- You are still getting to know each other and taking time to test the waters.
- You both enjoy each other's company and want to explore options. You are not looking for anything serious and are happy to see where things go (you are even OK if the other partner moves on to someone else).
- You or your partner do not feel emotionally ready to commit (yet). If you are both OK with giving each other time without further commitment, enjoy the situationship. Your aim with the situationship should be to fulfil emotional and physical needs. Healing, attention, companionship, being with someone and spending quality time together are different emotional needs that can be fulfilled in a situationship without having to commit. You are intentionally engaging in a mutually beneficial emotional and physical exchange.

Time to leave

- When your partner continuously dodges the ball about what you are or what your future is together.
- You find out that your partner is already in a relationship with (or married to) someone else.

Don't settle for second best. If they have no respect for other people, they won't change soon. Run!

- Your partner gaslights you when you ask for more clarity, or they become aggressive or abusive. This is a clear red flag that you need to leave the situationship ASAP! Ask yourself as well, 'Why am I staying if I am being treated this way?' Always remember, the longer you stay in an abusive relationship, the worse it will get.

- Your mental and/or physical health is deteriorating due to the uncertainty you are experiencing in the situationship or due to your partner's behaviours.

Red Flag 15 'Sorry I didn't text you for the past nine months. I lost my charger but now I've found it. WYD tonight?'

The perils of modern dating

'The man who has once been bitten
by the snake fears every piece of rope.'
Chinese proverb

Modern dating behaviour

Modern dating is a mystery to many people, and often a huge disappointment for anyone looking for something serious. Online dating is often compared to a snake pit full of people playing games and showing toxic behaviours. Navigating online dating challenges many of the dating norms and behaviours we once knew to be true in the real world. The plethora of 'options' available through various dating apps creates the illusion that you can easily find, use and replace people, which is impacting how people treat each other. Despite people being more hooked to their devices to find love, the closeness they feel when engaging with other people online is diminishing compared to real-life interactions. Not to mention the impact algorithms have on people's dating behaviours, online and offline. These developments have given rise to new behavioural phenomena such as breadcrumbing, ghosting and orbiting, to name a few, and fewer people interested in committing to one person. Economical thinking stated once that, 'The more we have, the happier we will be.' But behavioural science has proven that 'The more we have, the more paralysed we become.' Diving into the psychology and technology of today's dating world can shed a lot of light on why people treat each other the way they do. These insights will not only help you understand your personal circumstances or explain what you see happening around you, but also provide suggestions on how to improve your chances of success in the dating field. Understanding modern dating trends and behaviours, and why they happen, can reduce the concerns many people hold at this moment around dating. Let's clear things up and reduce that overthinking.

Modern dating versus traditional dating

What are the differences between modern dating and traditional dating, you might wonder? Well, to answer this question, it is best to start by describing traditional dating approaches. Traditionally, people would meet each other at bars or clubs, through friends or family or maybe through dating ads in newspapers. The process of finding a suitable partner to date required time and effort. And once you found someone to meet up with, it would cost you time to get to know the other person. The beautiful thing about dating the 'traditional way' was that excitement you felt when you did meet someone. You would put in the extra effort to impress a potential partner, and also to make it work longer-term. One of the primary reasons for dating someone was to find a suitable person to be with for an extended period of time and to have sex with regularly. Sure, people cheated back in the day and yes, toxic relationships existed too, but because fewer options were available, and societal pressures were more focused on building strong family units, people felt more compelled to make it work (though sometimes at the detriment of one or both of the partners, it's important to add). A positive consequence of traditional dating was that many couples learnt how to become more resilient together. Leaving a relationship wasn't that easy back then (and still isn't today in many cultures) and this is a reason why, for many of us Millennials and Gen Xers, our parents are still together.

To be honest, modern dating is not that different from traditional dating; many people today still want to be loved, want someone to share their time with or want to get married. The big difference in today's dating world is that less effort is needed to find someone. Dating apps and social media platforms have lowered the barriers of having to find a potential partner or knowing more about them. A simple adjustment of the app's preference filter *et voilà* . . . you have found that hot seven-figure daddy, tattooed, bearded, hung, who secretly likes watching cat movies in his spare time and will make you breakfast in bed on Sundays (only when his wife is not in town). Or that cute 26-year-old law student who loves reading, travelling, partying with her friends, and is looking for something exclusive (and with the right person is open for some 'hentai'[1]). Whatever the type, ambitions or kinks you are looking for in a potential partner, you can find it on an app nowadays. And there are so many to choose from. Modern dating has made everything so accessible. You would think this to be a good thing, but unfortunately easy access and ease of use have proven to have major drawbacks to them.

Having so many options at your fingertips has changed how people value their mating options and mating strategies.

Finding a partner for (regular) sex is one of the core reasons why people date. However, the ease of use doesn't necessitate the requirement to find an exclusive partner to fulfil one's intimate needs. Engaging in casual meetups and one-night stands has also become more socially acceptable in many parts of the world. Dating in the traditional sense is less desired for this reason, which has given rise to 'hook-up' culture. Generally, men's mating strategies have been found to be more short-term orientated;[2] desiring more partners over time and requiring less time to consent to sex than women. This holds true across different cultures and socio-economic classes. However, women equally benefit from short-term mating strategies and thus engage in them as well. With the focus being more on the short term than the long term, how people treat each other in the romantic sense has changed a lot in recent years. People can view sex as more transactional than as an act that connects people emotionally at a deeper level. Besides less focus on finding a long-term partner, online dating has also given rise to more malicious behaviour, such as emotional and psychological abuse. Whereas in the past your social network could help you vet people you met, the online space gives you access to all kinds of people, including men and women who are (mentally) not in a good space to date or have bad intentions.[3] All factors combined, for many dating in today's world has become cumbersome and, in many situations, a very painful experience.

The psychology of online dating

To foster healthy and durable relationships, effort and dedication are required to make things work. Human thinking and behaviour are complex and often flawed (e.g. mental biases, misconceptions, single-mindedness) and refined social skills and emotional intelligence are required in order to engage effectively with people over an extended period of time. Not only that, but past traumas and life experiences can also lead to suboptimal behaviours later in life. When dating someone for the long term, not only do you have to deal with life's day-to-day stressors, but also your partner's behavioural and cognitive shortcomings. It's part of the package. Psychological concepts such as trust, commitment, forgiveness, sacrifice and support are important virtues to have if you want to make long-term human-to-human relationships work in any area of life.

However, when dating apps impact the social nature of dating and emphasize short-term mating strategies over long-term ones, many of these virtues become less needed. Not to mention the impact dating apps are having on dating culture in general.[4] To better understand the psychological impact the digital space has on dating behaviour, I have broken down the effects that:

1. easy access
2. ease of use
3. perceived distance

have on human behaviour.

Easy access (accessibility)

If something becomes scarce, we give it more value and put more effort into attaining it. In psychology, this is referred to as the *scarcity effect* and is a very powerful driver of human behaviour. Think of how Booking.com says on their website 'There is only 1 room left. Book now!' You are more likely to book than when that message is not there. Or when you're waiting outside in the freezing cold trying to get into an exclusive club in London. You wait because everyone wants to go there and there is limited space.[5] The opposite of scarcity is abundance and when something becomes easily available you tend to give it less importance. The abundance mindset in the dating scene can make you more focussed on instant gratification and less appreciative of deep human connection. You are more likely to view people as options than as human beings, treating them with less respect. Or, when difficult times arise, instead of trying to work things out, an abundance mindset can motivate you to find someone else, as it is less mentally tasking to do so. Over time, the perceived ease of access can make you less willing and capable of dealing with difficult situations in general (e.g. dealing with disagreements, telling the other person you are not interested, putting in the effort to engage with people outside of the bedroom).

Ease of use (usability)

The human brain is inherently lazy and doesn't like to think more than it has to, especially when it comes to tasking physical and mental activities. That's why we like things that are easy to use. Think of going to the supermarket – most of us default to buying the same products and brands. By sticking to the same brands, we don't need to think too much about making a choice and we also know what to expect in terms of quality. Things that are easy to do (and pleasurable) we are more likely to repeat, which eventually turn into unconscious habits, making you less aware of your own behaviours. However, seeing people as easy to use is not a good thing, especially in the dating world. If you know it is easy to court someone online, you put less effort into the process. This translates into fewer conversations before getting freaky; more focus on short-term dating strategies (less commitment, even when you like someone); dating and sex becoming more transactional (and therefore less emotional); and not having to adapt one's bad behaviours to be a better person (because that requires a lot of effort). If we look back to traditional dating, we can see that challenge and effort were key ingredients to make relationships and love lasting.

Perceived distance (proximity)

Proximity is an interesting concept when it comes to human psychology. Physical or perceived proximity influences how we experience things. When we perceive things to be close to us, we pay more attention to them. Proximity does not only relate to the physical distance between people but also to the time spent together.[6] Studies show that there is a positive correlation between time spent together and attraction. This also holds true for friendships and work relationships. You are more likely to become friends with someone who sits next to you in class or at work than someone sitting far away from you. And when things are perceived as far away from you, you feel less impacted or connected towards that thing or person. Take, for example, paying with a credit card. In behavioural science, there is something called the *pain of paying*,[7] which refers to the negative emotions you experience when departing from your hard-earned money to pay for something. The pain of paying is higher when you have to pay with cash than with an electronic payment method. When we pay with a credit card or debit card, it feels less painful and therefore easier to do. But this perceived distance is also the reason why people are more willing to be less ethical when selling you tokens that can be exchanged for money (e.g. cryptocurrencies, stocks, sub-prime mortgages – think Enron scandal). The same goes for online dating behaviour. If you treat someone badly online you feel less pain because they feel so far away. There is also more anonymity online and therefore you think less about the consequences of your behaviour. Not to mention people faking who they really are (just think of the 'Tinder Swindler').[8] Perceived distance tricks you into believing you can get away with it and is also the reason why people love to be hotshots on social media or in your DMs. However, when you meet them in person, they act completely different or even avoid you.

Modern dating trends

There is much to be said about the impact of technology on human behaviour. Dating apps and social networks have not only made mating easier, but they have definitely contributed to a more toxic hook-up and dating culture. Easy access, ease of use and perceived distance have only exacerbated toxic behaviours, motivating even non-toxic people to behave in toxic ways. Not surprisingly, modern dating trends that have emerged thanks to online dating are mostly negative and based on the psychological effects dating apps have on human behaviour. Here are seven dating trends that everyone is talking about nowadays and you need to know about. How many have you experienced (or done to other people)?

- **Breadcrumbing**
  Breadcrumbing is the act of sending flirtatious messages once in a while or making false promises about future meetups without following through on them. The

purpose of breadcrumbing can vary from pure mind games to sending messages just to keep you attached for future gain or fun.

- **Ghosting**

  Ghosting is when someone doesn't respond to your messages anymore and disappears out of your life. Ghosting can happen at different stages of engaging with someone and is especially hurtful after you have been seeing them for a long period of time. The best advice I can give to people being ghosted is to 'Respect the Dead!' – they were just not meant to be.

- **Orbiting**

  Orbiting is when someone doesn't respond to your text messages, DMs or calls, but does watch and/or like your posts and stories on social media. Orbiting happens for various reasons (e.g. normal texting is not flowing well, an ex might be watching you but not responding to your messages, because someone is just a creep) but can feel very off.

- **Pocketing (or stashing)**

  Pocketing is a common dating trend where someone keeps you hidden away from their close friends or family. When you have been pocketed or stashed, someone only wants to meet you in private places (e.g. home) and avoids meeting up in public spaces (e.g. restaurants). They are reluctant to introduce you to their inner circle, even though you may have been seeing each other for a while. People pocket you for many reasons, one of them being that they are already seeing someone.

- **Cookie Jarring**

  Cookie jarring is when someone is dating you but is not interested in pursuing anything serious with you because their main focus is someone else and you are only there as a safety net or backup plan. You stash the cookie for when it is needed, otherwise you leave it in the jar. People cookie jar others because they often doubt themselves, believing that their primary partner might leave them when they identify their flaws, or when they are unsure whether the other person likes them.

- **Being zombied**

  Being zombied is first ghosting someone and then months later reappearing. It refers to someone coming back from the dead to revisit you. Just think of someone sending you a text message at one in the morning, saying, 'Sorry, I didn't text you for the past nine months! I lost my charger but now I've found it. WYD tonight?'

- **Delicate dumping**

  Similar to quiet quitting in the workplace (see Red Flag 7 for more on quiet quitting), delicate dumping is finding ways to part from your partner in a non-confrontational way. Gradually minimizing your energy, involvement and contact with that person till the contact ceases altogether. Because breaking up can be difficult, many people are now choosing to delicately dump their partner instead of telling them that they are not a good match.

- **Catfishing and kittenfishing**

  Catfishing has been around since the rise of the internet. Catfishing is the act of luring someone into a romantic relationship by using a fake persona or picture, often with the goal of extracting money from their victim. Sending someone filtered pictures of yourself (or pictures from ten years ago) to lure someone into meeting you and hoping they will engage sexually with you once you meet in person is called kittenfishing.

DID YOU KNOW?
The (un)intended consequences of algorithms on dating behaviour

When app developers create new apps, they design them to be persuasive. The more persuasive, the more likely you are to use them for an extended period of time. They design their apps with a focus on accessibility, usability and frequency of use. The easier it is to use, the more you will enjoy it. And the more accessible it is, the more frequently you will use it. At least that is the thinking in the short term. However, they also apply more sinister techniques to keep you attached, like sending you unexpected notifications, matches, discounts and rewards; playing into your emotions; and even sending you personalized messages that will trigger a response. Various studies, including my own research, show that dating-app design plays a key role in why people are addicted to their service. Dating apps create a fear of missing out (FOMO). As the app keeps luring you back, it becomes hard to stay focused on one person (especially if someone is using an app like Pokémon GO, going around collecting people and matches on their phone more for self-validation than for actually finding someone). Swipe-based dating apps have been found to create more psychological discomfort.[9] In conclusion, mobile-app design has been purposefully created to keep users more engaged and attached. Dating apps have turned traditional dating into a numbers game. However, using dating apps too frequently can be detrimental to one's mental health and also contribute to negative behaviours towards others online. A better strategy is to not spend too much time trying to find someone, instead spending more time on becoming the person worth finding. Let's start creating a joy of missing out (JOMO).

Fleeting romances and quick hook-ups are not just from these times. Pablo Picasso, who was a famous Spanish painter from the early 1900s, was known for being a masterful seducer. Picasso's autobiography describes many of his escapades with women. He was known for his ambivalent behaviour towards his mistresses, treating them first like goddesses and then as trash, only to discard them later.[10]

The perils of modern dating – what's the drama?

Modern dating can seem like a maze at times. Dating apps and social media platforms are the digital infrastructure through which people meet nowadays. The digital environment has made dating easy, accessible and endless. You would think that finding someone online for something more serious than a hook-up would be easier than in the past. However, nothing is less true. The ease of use dating apps provide, and the endless flow of potential mates to meet, has actually had the reverse effects, exacerbating toxic behaviours and leaving people feeling defeated when it comes to dating. In recent years, new dating trends have emerged like catfishing, ghosting, breadcrumbing and cookie jarring, which are all negative and reflect how dating apps have made it easy to treat other people in a bad way. The lack of human-to-human connection creates the illusion that the faces you see on your dating app are just 'options', which you can easily use, abuse and lose. The way dating apps have been designed also negatively impacts people's dating behaviours, making it hard for users to let go of their apps even when they have found someone they like. Today's dating landscape is more geared towards hook-ups and other short-term mating strategies, which is leading to a growing number of people being less willing to form deeper connections, feeling lost and being less capable of dealing with difficult situations.[11] To date successfully in the modern world, time, effort, focus and perseverance are needed.

It's a **red flag** in online dating if:
- People show that they don't care about you, but they send you a text message or say something sweet once in a while just to keep you attached (for future use). This is called breadcrumbing.
- They don't respond to your text messages but stalk your socials or like what you are posting but don't further engage with you. This is called orbiting.
- They don't want to meet you in public or don't introduce you to their inner circle like close friends or family. This is called pocketing.
- They send you filtered or very dated pictures of themselves online and/or have an exaggerated profile description to try to lure you in for a hook-up or date. This is called kittenfishing.

It's a **green flag** in online dating if:
- You show interest in each other by keeping regular contact through texting and or calling.
- You show genuine interest in each other by getting to know the other person outside of the bedroom.
- You treat each other respectfully (e.g. no blocking, respect each other's boundaries, no ghosting or silent dumping).
- You both feel safe and capable of having a difficult conversation with each other.

Things to consider when deciding if you want in or out

Knowing how toxic modern dating can be, you need to have thick skin and a good BS radar to be able to find someone online who is suitable to date. This also includes knowing when you are the toxic one and what you need to change in your behaviour to be a good catch for someone else. Online dating is like a snake pit at times, and toxic behaviours can rub off on even the nicest of people. Treating each other poorly online is steadily becoming the norm, so don't be surprised if you have unconsciously adopted the behaviours or traits of others. Deciding if you are in or out is a hard call when it comes to dating online. It's hard to find someone who is interested in something serious. Here are some indicators to help you decide:

Willingness to date

- If both of you show a keen interest to date, then date. Dating is not the main priority for many in today's dating world. Hook-ups and other short-term mating options are.

- Do you see compatibility? If you agree with many of your partner's views on relationships, dos and don'ts and life in general, then this could be a sign to pursue things further.
- You feel you are ready to date and willing to invest time in finding the right person. Knowing that extra effort will be needed from your side to search and that you are up for the challenge, start swiping mindfully!

Time to stay single

- You don't have the patience to date and/or you find yourself engaging in toxic online behaviours. Maybe it's time to focus on yourself before considering being with someone else (see Red Flag 13 for more on choosing to stay single).
- You are being mistreated by your partner or experiencing any of the red flags during your exploration phase. Time to leave.
- The other person doesn't show much interest in pursuing things further with you (even after discussing the possibility together), while you are interested. Don't chase an illusion.[12]

Red Flag 16 'I know it's only our second date, but I love you!'

Love bombing

'What's Love Got to Do with It?'
Tina Turner

Love bombing

Going on dates can be exciting. You just love the thrill of meeting someone new. Then one day you meet this special person. They look good, smell good . . . and damn, they even *feel* good too. They know exactly what to say and how to make you feel good. They shower you with compliments and go out of their way to make you feel special. It seems too good to be true, but you are really digging this new person and you're open to seeing where things could go. At the same time, you're worried about falling head over heels for this person as you've been through some bad romances in the past and don't want to make the same mistakes again. You say to yourself, 'How will I know for sure if their feelings are genuine? I don't want to lose my heart again to someone who is toxic, but I really feel a connection this time.'

It's not unusual to be blinded by infatuation, especially during the early stages of dating. Sometimes you are so smitten that you can't see the warning signs, even when they are right in front of your eyes. These feelings of infatuation can be intensified by different manipulation tactics, such as love bombing and false future projections. Unfortunately, not everyone is capable of loving people in a healthy way, and it's important to be able to distinguish those who can from those who cannot. The ability to identify red flags and green flags in the early dating stages can help you make better decisions and save you a lot of drama down the road. I often hear people around me lament, 'If I'd just paid better attention to those early warning signs, I could have avoided so much pain.' In this chapter, you'll learn how to spot red flags and green flags when meeting someone for the first time in the early stages of dating. We'll explore love-bombing behaviours, and the psychology behind them, along with learning how to build longer-lasting relationships.

Meeting someone for the first time

Though dating can feel laborious at times, it's still the best way to get to know someone if you are looking for something more serious than a casual hook-up. Getting to know someone gradually can help you discover how compatible you are physically, emotionally and mentally. An important part of this process is not only appreciating the positive things about someone you like but also getting to know their less desirable side. Do they get emotional or do they pull back and isolate themselves? Understanding how someone reacts when they're not their best and brightest can be very telling of how well they deal with conflict. The same goes for you. Let's face it, conflict is an inescapable part of any human relationship, be it romantic or platonic. Being able to solve difficult situations together is a key indicator of relationship success. Remember, no one is perfect, not even yourself. So, learning what triggers you and your potential partner is important to figure out before things get serious.

When things go too fast

Everything feels right. You're enjoying your dating partner's company, they make you feel special, shower you with compliments (and maybe gifts) and the sex is amazing. However, when things go too fast, you might question what to do. Maybe you ask yourself, why not just go with the flow? People nowadays won't even text you for a second date, let alone give you proper attention. Perhaps hearing 'I love you' after the second date is a bit weird, and they might be a little too protective after the third date, but the attention feels good, and you eventually decide to go along with it. Everyone around you seems to be in a relationship and you'd also like someone next to you. But two months in, your partner snaps at you in a way you haven't seen before, or they become completely cold and distant. You feel puzzled – usually they are so attentive and warm – but you're unwilling to lose them. So, you try your best to understand what is happening and to accommodate their needs as much as possible. They remain cold for a while, then out of nowhere they're back to their old, loving self. But only after you have given your all to get them back. A month later, the cycle repeats itself and you do the same thing over again. As the relationship progresses, you find yourself walking on eggshells, unsure when the next outburst will be and doubting yourself as your partner makes you feel like you are the one to blame.

If this has ever happened to you, it's likely that you've been *love bombed*. Love bombing is a manipulative tactic that often occurs during the early stages of a romantic endeavour and is characterized by the formation of a rapid connection through excessive communication (e.g. showering a person with attention, kind words, gifts) with the goal of obtaining control and power over someone. The love bomber gains power by making their victim reliant on their displays of affection and then intentionally deciding how much affection to show as a way to control or coerce behaviour.[1] The beginning stages of love bombing can feel amazing if you are on the receiving end. The special attention you receive, the roses, the gifts ... it just seems too good to be true. But eventually the pleasant behaviours stop, and the exchange turns into a psychological trap fuelled by a 'push away and pull back' strategy. During the push away phase, your love-bombing partner might stonewall you or disappear,[2] breadcrumb you[3] or even get aggressive with you.[4] During the pull back phase, the love bomber comes back and tries to befriend you again, saying all the right things to win you back. If you are on the receiving end of love bombing and you don't feel very secure about yourself or have previously been in bad relationships, you might be more likely to fall prey to this abusive cycle.[5] The impact of love bombing on the recipient can be huge, ranging from feelings of shame and low self-esteem to depression and PTSD. In 2023, the UK Crown Prosecution Service officially recognized love bombing as an act of abuse, which has made it easier for law enforcement officers to arrest and charge people love bombing their victims.[6] Sadly, acknowledging love bombing as a punishable act by law is not a common practice across the globe. But why do people love bomb people who they say they love? And what is the psychology behind this strange behaviour?

Why do partners love bomb?

Let's start by saying that anyone can love bomb a romantic partner. It's not exclusive to gender, age, race or sexuality. Men are often portrayed as the perpetrators, but women can equally be love bombers. Love bombing is often linked to a combination of underlying psychological factors. In one of the first studies published about love bombing,[7] researchers found that people who suffer from a combination of low self-esteem, insecure attachment style and narcissism are more likely to have love-bombing tendencies, though love bombing is not exclusive to narcissists. The core of the problem lies in one's attachment style.[8] If during one's childhood years someone had a disruptive or unstable relationship with their parents or caregivers, this could lead to a weak attachment style, seeing oneself as less worthy and not able to trust other people. Lack of self-worth and insecure attachment styles (e.g. anxious, avoidant) can lead to narcissistic tendencies later in life as a way to mask one's self-esteem issues, leading to grandiosity, self-entitlement and a disregard for the needs of others.[9] According to the authors of the paper, narcissists often use love bombing as a tactic to manipulate and control the other person for personal gain or self-enhancement.[10]

The deeper psychological reason behind love bombing can be linked to a need for survival. If the love bomber grew up feeling neglected and in need of affirmation, love bombing becomes a survival strategy to establish a deep emotional connection with someone fast. The love bomber's subconscious programming might be saying, 'I need you to stay with me, don't abandon me!', hence the heavy dose of affection and attention during the beginning stages. However, over time once the connection has been established, other manipulative behaviours can emerge that are more intentional and malicious, such as gaslighting, isolating and abuse. The sad part of the story is that the narcissistic love bomber is not actually in love with you but has fallen in love with an idealized version of you in their mind. Once something happens in the relationship that shatters this image of you in their head (which often happens in the first couple of months of being together[11]), the coercive behaviour, manipulation and gaslighting kick in. Think about it – if you shatter a mirror (aside from the seven years' bad luck), you can't put it back together like it once was, so you will start to devalue it. Also, the mirror won't look as shiny as it once did, so hoping to fully fix it is futile and could even cost you your sanity and physical health. Eventually, the narcissistic love bomber will discard or replace you, especially when they feel they are losing control over you. It's a common pattern for narcissists in romantic relationships to:

1. love bomb
2. devalue and, finally . . .
3. discard.[12]

Why do people fall for love bombing?

There are many reasons why you can fall for love bombing, even if you consider yourself an emotionally astute person or immune to sweet talk. The tactics that love bombers use are psychologically very powerful, and being showered with attention, compliments and gifts from someone you like can be very captivating. Let's face it, who doesn't want to feel like they are being desired? It's human nature. If you are sensitive or vulnerable to these displays of attention, you can easily fall for it and believe that the person you met is truly different and maybe even the 'one', especially if you are someone who is emotionally needy or has had partners in the past who haven't given you the attention you deserve. The tsunami of kind words and intense emotions during the love-bombing phase can be hypnotizing and even become addictive over time. This can make you emotionally and psychologically dependent, making it hard for you to leave if the relationship becomes controlling or abusive. You live in hope that the next love bomb will drop soon, waiting for that next dopamine hit, so you can experience what you did in the beginning.

The reason why being love bombed puts power and control into the hands of the abuser is that it creates an imbalance and dependency in the person being love bombed. The imbalance is created by giving you lots of attention and saying all the right things, which makes you feel like you want to reciprocate (even though it feels off in the beginning). You can reciprocate not only by giving attention and compliments back, but you can also be more willing to let your guard down (which is naturally present when meeting people in the beginning) and develop feelings faster. Letting your guard down too soon, especially when your intuition tells you that something is off, invalidates your own emotional awareness, which can make you more vulnerable to further attacks. Learn how to distance yourself physically and emotionally from the love bombing so that you can collect your thoughts and make better judgements about evaluating how authentic and healthy the connection is.

So, how to tell the difference between love bombing and someone showing genuine interest in you? The answer is excessiveness. If something feels too much, too fast or overwhelming, most likely it is. Also, if it feels too good to be true, it probably is as well. It's a red flag when this happens, but keep in mind that it's also a red flag if you give in too quickly (for whatever reason) to excessive displays of affection. It may be a sign to take a step back and reflect. Many narcissistic love bombers target people who are vulnerable. Vulnerable doesn't only mean emotionally weak or gullible, but can also include strong individuals who have recently come out of a contentious relationship or marriage and are in need of affection, or people who have a history of bad relationships and are accustomed to misbehaviour. It takes time for a healthy relationship to develop. People slowly open up to each other and if there is interest from both sides to pursue it further, you normally do so gradually, with balanced gives and takes.

Other factors to watch out for when dating someone new

When getting to know someone, it is important to look for qualities that represent long-term potential: behaviours such as being supportive, showing interest, putting in the effort, being respectful of you and others, the ability to actively listen, to reflect on one's own behaviours, to resolve difficult situations effectively and equal reciprocation, to name a few. Here are some examples of what these green flags sound like:

Green flags to look out for:

- **Considerate**
  'I can see how hard you are trying to achieve that goal, is there anything I can help you with?'

- **Reciprocal**
  'Please, let me get the bill this time.'
- **Active listening**
  'I guess you are also saying that you would prefer to spend more time together at home instead of partying every weekend?'
- **Resolving conflict**
  'I can see you are upset. Let's try to defuse the emotions and revisit what just happened. I think we just had different viewpoints about this situation. Help me understand how you interpreted what happened so that I can understand what you saw.'
- **Reflective and able to apologize**
  'I thought carefully about what happened yesterday and I realized that I could have said that differently. Thank you for pointing that out. I will be more mindful next time.'

It's equally important to look for behaviours during the early stages of dating that could be possible red flags. Severe red flags are easy to spot and most of the time will make you run. However, many people with ill intent (e.g. master manipulators) are good at concealing their bad behaviours. Don't be fooled by overt displays of emotional intelligence. For example, if a guy says he is in touch with his emotions or is very spiritual, or a girl says she has done extensive inner work. This doesn't automatically mean they are good partners and free of toxicity. It could be said intentionally as a way to conceal. Remember, it's normal for anyone to put their best foot forward, especially when getting to know people. It can be hard to see the bad in someone when we really like them. However, no one can conceal their true behaviours for very long or control their every behaviour. That's why it's important to pay attention to the subtle behaviours people show. How people behave or what they say during unexpected and stressful situations can be very revealing. For example, how does someone make you feel when you are in an argument with them (do they make you feel unsafe)? How controlling are they (do you feel that they are dominating the conversation or the decisions you make together)? Or do they talk down to you (do they belittle you)? Here are some examples of how red flags can sound, from the very subtle to the more obvious:

Red flags to watch out for:

- **Subtly creating insecurities**
  'Wow, that's very interesting. You're definitely smarter than you look.'
- **Not accepting blame**
  'Really, it's unbelievable. Not sure why it always happens to me. I tell you . . . all my exes were crazy!'
- **Deferring responsibility**
  'I'm sorry I messed up. I really can't help it. It's my past making me do this!'
- **Criticizing**
  'Why do you live that way?' 'Do you always make noises while you eat?' 'Why do you get up so late?' 'I don't like your sister.'
- **Generalization**
  'Wow, I can't believe you said something like that. Wow, wow, wow! Such a disappointment, you are exactly like the others.'
- **Triangulation**
  'There you go again, thinking I would do something like

that. Seriously, you need to get your head checked. I told my friends what you did, and WE all agree that you're crazy.'

Besides blaming and criticizing others, there are also more sinister red flags to watch out for when meeting someone new. At first, these words can sound very flattering, but they could fool you into believing the other person really feels something for you when they don't. Malicious people use persuasive communication tactics intentionally, so it's important to be alert when you hear them and to evaluate over a longer period of time if what they say truly has teeth. Manipulative communication strategies to be mindful of:

Special girl/guy syndrome: 'I've never met a girl like you before.' 'I think I have found my soulmate.' 'Nobody understands me like you do.'

> **Explanation:** Yes, it could very well be that you are that special girl or guy they had never met before. If the feeling is mutual and your experiences together over a period of time do justice to such a statement, then that is such a beautiful thing to hear, so embrace it. But if this statement is said too quickly or something inside of you says it's not right, then don't fall for it. If you really are that special, then the person who said that to you will have no problem waiting for their needs to be met.

False future projections: 'Imagine us getting married and having kids together.' 'Imagine us sipping cocktails on a beach in Bali together.'

Explanation: This could be a great prospect to have with your partner, especially someone you have been with for a while. Taking your relationship to the next level and getting more serious about each other is amazing. But for someone to say this to you after a couple of dates could mean that they are just trying to trick you. Playing into your hopes and dreams is a very manipulative tactic to convince you to do something or to make you develop feelings or to trust faster. Watch out!

The right approach to get to know someone

Though there are no exact rules to dating the right way, there are some basic principles you can apply to make sure you get to know the other person with more rigour. Dating apps make it easy to know a lot about people, but who says that their profile information is always correct? According to various studies, people tend to lie more when communicating via an online medium or a phone than in person, and lie to a partner on average six times a day.[13,14] Even if people send you dirty pics through Snapchat or DM you every day short 'good morning' videos, you still don't know who the person really is. So, how to get to know people more personally? Here are three principles you should apply when dating in the offline world:

Everything takes time

The first step in dating with more certainty is to take your time. Don't rush into things. Go on multiple dates and get to know the other person. Take it slow and pay special attention to the behaviours you find important. Especially, the small (unexpected) behaviours that can tell you a lot about a person. Do you enjoy their company in different situations (or just in bed)? Are they supportive and considerate to you? And do they treat you and other people around them with respect? These questions you can only truly answer once you get to know them.

Learn what someone's love language is

The concept of *love languages* has been a massive trend on social media recently. Everyone is talking about the different ways people express their love to others. Spending time to get to know someone's love language can be a great way to get close to someone. Some people use physical touch and express their love by touching their partner (e.g. hugs, kisses, cuddling and public displays of affection). Others show love through words of affirmation (words of encouragement or showing appreciation), giving gifts (e.g. buying stuff for someone), acts of service (e.g. thoughtful actions such as lending a hand or being supportive in various tasks) or spending quality time with someone (e.g. dedicated, uninterrupted time together). People express their love in different ways, and it can take time to understand someone's love language and find compatibility with it. Tune into how you express love and how your partner likes to express love. This will help you become more aware of each other's displays of affection (and why that is). Personally, I love exploring love languages when getting to know someone in the romantic sense. I like to express my love to someone through a combination of physical touch and spending quality time. And finding someone who appreciates that is an important ingredient to developing something more lasting.[15]

Develop closeness

In 1997, psychologist Dr Arthur Aron and his colleagues at the State University of New York at Stony Brook investigated if they could make strangers fall in love with each other by answering a set of 36 questions. The purpose of these questions was to help strangers dating fast-track the process of becoming more personal and intimate with each other.[16] As you progress through the questions, they become more inquisitive and personal, allowing partners to reveal more about themselves and eventually bringing people closer together. Various sources claim that people have found love and even got married thanks to using the 36 questions. On my social media, TikToks and Instagram Reels, the 36 questions have gone completely viral, being viewed and liked by millions. This also inspired me to come up with my own questions to help people develop a stronger bond with others and maybe even find love (see my 25 red and green flag questions to build a deeper connection with someone at the end of the book). A plausible reason behind why people want to find more closeness in their relationships is that so many people feel that real human-to-human connection is fleeting in today's world, due to social media, dating apps, etc. Regardless of which strategy you use to become more connected, finding ways to build emotional and psychological closeness is absolutely vital to any successful relationship.

DID YOU KNOW?
You're dickmatized! Watch out for the sex trap!

Men and women differ in chemical pathways when it comes to sex.[17] Studies seem to indicate that women are more emotionally impacted by great sex than men. This has to do with the chemicals that are released during sex. Women release more oxytocin when having sex, a bonding hormone that establishes a deeper emotional attachment and trust with their partners. Men, on the other hand, are more affected by a hormone called vasopressin when having sex, which is more connected to being adaptive and linked to the positive feelings of overcoming challenges or achieving certain goals. You could say that men therefore are neurologically more focused on engaging in sex and climaxing than bonding through sex.[18] Nevertheless, sex with a narcissist can feel very different. Narcissists can be very assertive, passionate and voracious lovers,[19] especially at the beginning of a relationship. Together with the charm and abundance of love that regularly comes with narcissistic love bombing, things can feel more intense than usual. The sexual intensity can lead to a strong emotional attachment, mistaking good sex for love. Women, in particular, can become more emotionally attached through mind-blowing sex with a narcissistic male partner, due to the role oxytocin plays in the sex-to-bonding process.[20] The strong sexual connection can explain why some women choose to remain in an unstable relationship (among other emotional and psychological reasons) longer than they should.[21] Being aware of this can help break the cycle. A quote I like to use, using the red flag analogy, to make people more aware of the sex

RED FLAGS, GREEN FLAGS

trap is, 'Just because it is red in bed, doesn't mean it's good for your head'. So, how is man-to-man attraction explained through bonding hormones? Interestingly, a study found how oxytocin impacts homosexual men differently than heterosexual men in terms of social approach tendencies.[22] Oxytocin increased ratings of evaluations of male attractiveness and approachability. Some evidence suggests that bonding hormones together with sexual hormones, like oestrogen and testosterone, are potential mechanisms underlying sexual orientation.[23,24]

When Julia Fox started dating Kanye West, Kanye (or Ye as he is now known) was quick to shower her with gifts. According to the *New York Post*, Kanye had a hotel suite full of clothes to give to Julia after their first official date.[25] Though Julia didn't see it as love bombing, showering people with lavish gifts early on in the dating process to create the idea of being the ideal partner or having the ideal partner could be a sign.

Love bombing – what's the drama?

Love bombing is a manipulative technique to psychologically control and emotionally abuse a romantic partner. People who love bomb shower you with attention, kind words and gifts during the early stages of dating. This excessive display of attention and affection is a powerful way to create emotional and psychological attachment fast. Because of the intensity, you might even believe that you found your soulmate. However, love bombers don't really fall in love with you and can suddenly become distant or lose interest, leaving you confused and empty, and wanting the same level of attention and intimacy again. This creates a push and pull effect, which can develop into a vicious cycle, leading to the acceptance of mistreatment and bad behaviours from an abusive partner. Love bombing can be unintentional (and can differ in intensity) and it is common for people with narcissistic personality disorder (including other personality disorders) to engage in it. Deeper psychological reasons why people love bomb range from emotional neediness and fear of abandonment (often due to childhood trauma – see Red Flag 2 for more on how parenting styles can impact behaviour later in life) to insecurity and malicious attempts to control or abuse. Besides love bombing, it is important to be aware of other red flags when getting to know someone new. Identifying red flags early on in the honeymoon phase can save you a lot of headaches down the road. Also, try to be mindful when meeting new people which of your behaviours are triggered, as these can be red flags.

It's a **red flag** if:
- They say 'I love you' or 'you are my soulmate' after the second date. Run!
- They create subtle insecurities by saying things like, 'You are smarter than you look.' Over time, these comments can impact your confidence. Remember it's a manipulation tactic.
- They say, 'All my exes are crazy', which indicates that they don't take responsibility for their actions and will always blame the other person. Run even faster now!

- You are currently emotionally vulnerable and feel susceptible to attention. Letting down your guard too quickly could make you more susceptible to controlling or abusive behaviour.
- You ignore the red flags because you think you can 'fix' or 'save' them.
- You ignore the red flags because you like a bit of drama in your life or you think 'Damn, that's hot!' You're just asking for trouble.

It's a **green flag** if:
- Your interactions with someone new feel positive, supportive and balanced. Getting to know someone should happen in a reciprocal way.
- They make you feel safe, even during disagreements.
- They take the time to get to know you and don't rush into things.
- You can communicate your needs and what you are looking for in a partner. You can also clearly communicate your boundaries and what behaviours you find acceptable or not.
- You identify that the other person has similar values as you and you both complement each other in a positive way.

Things to consider when deciding if you want in or out

Many narcissistic love bombers are actually very charming, social and great in bed. If you enjoy some temporary intense fun (and you are up for a challenge), why not learn how to entertain a love bomber? Enjoy the admiration, the attention, the gifts and the great sex. But be vigilant and pay attention to the signs when the happy phase starts to turn into an awkward phase (it happens eventually). The moment that things go south, don't hesitate, break it off immediately, and run. And if the love bomber contacts you, just say 'Thanks for the fun time. Ciao!' For the love bomber, not having control over you is the worst thing. They might try to get you back (e.g. to boost their ego), but best to stay away.

Willingness to stay

- You're up for the challenge and find the love bombing entertaining (or amusing at best).
- You're only interested in the sex and promise yourself to not get emotionally attached.
- You're writing a book and you want to collect some juicy material first-hand about narcissists or love bombing.

Time to leave

- Immediately when you notice the most common red flags about love bombing.
- The moment the love bomber pulls back or shows sudden negative changes in their behaviour.
- The moment they try to control you or become abusive.

Red Flag 17 'Why do I like my partners with more mileage?'

Dating older or younger

'Age is just a number. It's totally irrelevant unless,
of course, you happen to be a bottle of wine.'
Joan Collins

Searching for a mature partner

Beauty is in the eye of the beholder. Who you find attractive depends on so many different factors. You might find someone attractive based on how they look, their personality, their height or build and/or their age. We find these characteristics attractive because they signal something to us. And interestingly enough, we try to change these physical features (where possible) to make ourselves more attractive. One of the most intriguing factors of attraction is age. There are many associations we have with age and our attraction to older or younger men or women can also change with time. Beauty is often associated with youthfulness, indicating that your younger years of adulthood are your most beautiful. When you are young, you are full of life, energetic and at your best to procreate. However, not everyone finds younger more attractive. Many people are attracted to partners who are older and have more life experience.

You might think that this is purely due to mummy or daddy

issues or ulterior motives, but there are many more intriguing reasons why people feel more attracted to older than younger, and these differences can differ depending on which sex you are attracted to. With the rise of the internet, online dating sites and social media, it has become very easy to get into contact with people you're interested in. As easy as it is to send someone a WhatsApp message, a DM on Instagram or a Facebook message saying, 'Hey Daddy! I love your vibe. We should meet for coffee sometime', dating outside your age group can be difficult, socially challenging and full of drama at times. Not to mention the plethora of research available on this topic, which at times gives conflicting results. Unravelling the psychology behind age attraction and the opportunities and challenges of dating younger or older can help you to succeed in your dating efforts. Age is just a number, but what should you do if the age gap is too big? And what are the red and green flags to watch out for when dating someone with more or less mileage on their life meter?

What influences age-disparate relationships beyond sexual desires?

Age difference, or age disparity as it is often referred to, in romantic relationships has evolved over centuries and is very culturally dependent. Societies around the world have differing views about age differences within dating and relationships, and evaluating whether it is socially acceptable or not should always be viewed through a socio-cultural lens. However, the prevalence of age-disparate relationships in certain communities or environments not only depends on societal norms or sexual preferences, but also on mate availability, mating strategies and gender roles. In recent years, women are choosing to pursue professional careers and to postpone marriage and/or having kids until later in life. Moreover, the belief that men should be the sole provider for a family is also steadily changing (especially in Western societies), allowing for more women to take on the role of provider (within the family) or to date more assertively. In a global context, age-disparate dating and relationships can also be influenced by megatrends (e.g. having children at a later age), economic factors (e.g. job market, inflation) and uncertainty (e.g. pandemic, war, aliens . . . yes you read that correctly[1]). For example, many Gen Z young adults[2] feel more comfortable dating older people, stating that preferences for older partners are influenced by a need for stability and security.[3]

Can love work when you date older/younger?

The scientific literature on age-disparate romantic relationships is plentiful. A lot of research looking into relationship success conducted in different parts of the world shows similar results when it comes to dating someone around your own age and relational satisfaction. Generally, small age differences (up to three years between partners – usually men being the older partner) provide for the best relationship satisfaction in long-term heterosexual relationships and married couples.[4] Specifically in the early stages of a long-term relationship, relational satisfaction seems to be the highest for couples in the same age range. In most countries the age difference between partners in a long-term relationship is between one to three years on average.[5] Countries in Africa have the highest age disparity in relationships in the world.[6]

One evolutionary explanation for why the age disparity is higher in Africa than, let's say, in Europe or the US is due to the parasite-stress theory. The idea is that having more children with more people creates more diversified genes, and therefore a greater chance of your gene line surviving if you live in an environment where you are likely to die from pathogens. This has resulted in the acceptance of polygeny[7] in some areas and if fewer women are available for marriage, then competition becomes fierce for men to marry, driving up the age of men marrying younger women because they have the means to sustain a household with multiple wives. The parasite-stress theory also explains why, in more economically developed countries, age disparity is lower in relationships (less disease and more mates available).[8]

There is also research that shows that couples with a larger age difference than three years can have high relational satisfaction. Couples in long-term relationships where the age gap is larger than five years experience high relational satisfaction during the early stages of their union, and older men and women who have a relationship with a younger partner seem to be happier than when they have a partner of their own age.[9] In Western societies, 8 per cent of heterosexual relationships have a large age gap (ten years or more).[10] For same-sex couples, the percentage of large-age-gap relationships varies between 15 per cent (women-women relationships) to 25 per cent (men-men relationships).[11] Age-disparate relationships are more prevalent in same-sex relationships than in heterosexual relationships,[12] which is often attributed to a limited dating pool (though other socio-economic or psychological reasons could be at play, similar to those of heterosexual couples).

However, the research on age differences in romantic and

sexual relationships also shows a gloomy side. Age-disparate relationships compared to similar-age relationships experience more negative relationship outcomes,[13] such as a faster decline of marital satisfaction over time (especially as the age gap widens between partners), an increased likelihood of getting divorced and, according to one Korean study,[14] a higher occurrence of mental health issues, such as depression. I know this might sound discouraging, but don't despair, as not all research outcomes are consistent. Some can even be contradictory. A 2008 study in the *Psychology of Women Quarterly*[15] found that woman-older relationships, compared to woman-younger relationships, were the most satisfying. One reason for this difference is that woman-older relationships experience more trust and commitment, and experience less jealousy, compared to woman-younger relationships. However, it should be mentioned that no matter how large the age difference is, social dismissal by peers, family and/or friends of one's relationship can quickly damage one's romantic happiness.

Age compatibility – it's more complex than you think!

When it comes to age, 'what is compatible?' you might wonder. Most people don't look or think further than one's chronological age. This means most people seek partners in a similar age category. And this is normal, as we spend most of our time with peers in our own age category from school all the way into our senior years. We share similar life experiences, world views, expectations and interests with people who are of the same age or generation. We naturally gravitate towards what feels familiar. The chance of being attracted to someone your own age is therefore bigger. However, attraction is not only facilitated by the time you spend with other people. You can also be attracted to people older or younger, and people you don't normally engage with. Hence, age compatibility is a big concept and more complex than most people think. We humans not only have a physical age (e.g. muscle tone, skin firmness, mobility), but also an emotional and psychological age (e.g. emotional stability, sense of humour, agreeableness, nurturing, intelligence, wisdom, maturity), and a sexual age (e.g. stamina, sexual desire, sexual openness, fertility). These age categories can be compatible across different chronological age groups. For example, you can feel mentally more mature than your peers and therefore be more attracted to someone older. The opposite is also true; you might still be a kid at heart and physically very fit and feel someone younger[16] than you would be a better fit than someone your own age.

When you want to date, or are dating, someone in a different age category than yourself, you might be concerned about others' opinions of you or your relationship. In many communities and cultures, a large age gap between partners is often frowned upon. People might believe that your relationship is not really based on love, but more on ulterior motives. Facing ridicule or social stigma is not uncommon for couples in mixed-age relationships. You might ask yourself, 'What is a socially acceptable age difference between partners?'[17] Though there is no perfect answer to this question, there is a rule of thumb you can use to calculate the maximum age difference between a couple deemed socially acceptable. This is the 'half-your-age-plus-7' rule.[18] So, if you are 40, then according to the rule: 27 years (40/2 + 7 = 27) would be the youngest age to date someone to be socially acceptable. This rule is not a given, but a helpful way to make a quick judgement about what is more acceptable in the eyes of others.[19]

What's the psychology behind dating older or younger?

There are various reasons why people prefer someone older or younger than themselves. Let's dive into the psychological drivers of mate preferences for both age groups.

When dating older

Generally, younger men and women who choose an older partner, regardless of sexual orientation, are driven by a need for safety and security, which can be emotional, physical or financial. These psychological needs are not just socially driven, but also evolutionary based. A man who is capable of showing status or being able to provide at an older age must be someone with 'better genes' compared to a younger counterpart, who might be showing off his worth as a short-term mating strategy. (Just think of all those bling bling posts on Instagram, Snapchat or Tinder with guys snapping a pic of themselves in front of a Ferrari or a Lamborghini; nine times out of ten, they don't even own the car.)

Biologically, a woman's fertility decreases with age and, from a reproduction perspective, can't explain a younger male's choice of an older woman. However, there is a different evolutionary reason that can explain why younger men are attracted to older women. Older women allow younger men to grow in a more rounded way than younger women can.[20] Also, as women are pursuing careers and choosing to have children later in life (or not at all), this makes them more financially stable, which younger men also find attractive. Power and survival, it seems, drive a desire to date older for both genders.

Finally, being attracted to older partners can also come down to mummy and daddy issues, which is a common catchphrase referring to psychological issues caused by a problematic parent–child relationship (e.g. abuse, neglect, absence), which then manifests itself in partner attraction later in life. Mummy and daddy issues often result in complex and/or dysfunctional relationships with older romantic partners.

When dating younger

The psychological reasons why older men and women choose a younger partner also have strong social and evolutionary bases. Psychologically, an older man choosing a younger woman can be related to a desire to reproduce, to feel more youthful or less stressed, to boost their self-esteem or a desire to be more in control. Older women often prefer younger men because they signal more stamina, youthfulness and less baggage. Older women who live an active lifestyle can especially feel attracted to physically fit and more youthful men (remember physical age compatibility). Also, it can be argued that younger men have better communication skills than older men, in terms of being able to express emotions and one's state of mind. Younger men today are more open and can communicate in a more diverse way (e.g. talking, texting, using GIFs, images, videos) than their older counterparts to express themselves and their inner feelings. Younger men are also more willing to experiment, which some older women feel increasingly open to later in life, not to mention being able to better express their sexual assertiveness. Changing beauty standards and life priorities, and accessibility to potential mates through online dating sites, are increasing older women's self-confidence, resulting in higher levels of sexual satisfaction. Dating younger also gives women the possibility to reverse gender roles in the relationship, giving women more power in the relationship and the ability to be the provider. There are so many benefits to dating younger, which older women should embrace.

DID YOU KNOW?
Fascinating truths about dating behaviours according to dating apps
According to a study conducted by dating app OkCupid,[21] women in their early to mid-twenties are most in demand in heterosexual dating. After the age of 26, men can expect more dates than women of the same age. By the age of 48, the data shows that men are almost two times more sought after than women (many middle-aged men still preferring to date women in their twenties). Meanwhile, women seem to look for partners with a similar age profile. When it comes to women being attracted to older men, there doesn't seem to be such a distinct pattern as with men. Younger women do find older men more attractive, but this attraction continues as women age, which is different than older men's preferences for women. However, after 40, women do tend to look for younger men according to OkCupid's data. Interestingly, when older women message men through the app first, they are more likely to get a response from a 26-year-old man (60 per cent reply rate) than a 55-year-old man (36

per cent reply rate).[22] A 30-year-old man was the most likely age group to answer a 50-year-old woman. It seems that female assertiveness can reverse the age-gap gender norm in online dating.

The unfairness of age disparity acceptance across genders

Across cultures, older men receive less scrutiny if they choose to have a younger partner. In many societies, people herald an older man for having a younger partner (or even multiple partners. For example, sexual prowess is a sign of tolerated *machismo* behaviour in many Hispanic cultures.)[23] However, it's a completely different story for women. Older women interested in younger men are often labelled 'cougars' and made to believe that their motives for seeking younger men as partners are more sinister than that of their male counterparts in a similar age group. This perception is often reinforced through popular movies and TV series. Just think of Stifler's Mom from the movie *American Pie* or Samantha Jones from *Sex and the City*. Not only that, but in many cultures women above a certain age who are still single or divorced and looking for love are viewed differently. This is especially true for countries with cultural dimensions scoring highly on masculinity and power distance.[24] In these countries, patriarchal norms and traditional views of gender roles are still very much alive, giving rise to gender stereotypes and misogyny (compared to more feminine and egalitarian countries like Finland, Denmark and the

Netherlands). In China, if you are not married past your late twenties, you are considered to be a 剩女 (pronounced *sheng nu*) or 'leftover woman', making it hard to find a mate later in life. Dating older men is socially accepted in China, but for many 30+ year old women their dating options are limited to younger mates as older men prefer younger women. In Japan, similar trends can be seen. For many years, women in Japan who were not married past the age of 25 were often referred to as クリスマスケーキ (pronounced *kurisumasu keeki*) or 'old Christmas cake' (meaning that no one buys a Christmas cake after 25 December as it is spoiled). Although more women in Japan and other Asian countries are prioritizing their career over serious dating and relationships in today's environment, these slurs and limiting gender beliefs still prevail in certain cultures.

In recent years, however, global attitudes towards traditional gender roles have been shifting and people have become more accepting of woman-older couples. Celebrities like Priyanka Chopra and Nick Jonas, who differ 11 years in age, and Ellen DeGeneres and her wife Portia de Rossi, who differ 15 years in age, are challenging stereotypes and positively influencing the public perception of age-hypogamous relationships.[25]

Challenges when dating older or younger

Dating outside your age category can be very exciting, but also quite challenging. Most challenges age-disparate partners face will relate to problems centring around:

1. Misalignment of life goals, experience and maturity

2. Health, energy levels and sexual desire
3. Stigma and social disapproval
4. Misbehaviours

Though some of these topics have already been discussed in this chapter, I want to focus on some of the more unexpected surprises you could experience when dating someone older or younger than yourself.

When older doesn't always mean more mature

If you are looking to be with someone older than yourself, then you are probably interested in being with a person who is emotionally stable and mature. There is a higher probability of finding a more mature partner if you go for someone older. However, being older doesn't always indicate that they will be emotionally or mentally mature or stable. Some older people can be intellectually aged, but emotionally still stuck in their childhood, responding to daily drama in the same way they did when they were kids. Past traumas or personality issues that have not been dealt with effectively can persist into adulthood. Older people can also carry a lot of baggage with them, which makes it difficult for them to love or be emotionally available. Moreover, as people get older, they can also become more manipulative if such behavioural traits served them well in previous relationships or life situations. Dating a younger partner can give the older man or woman the feeling that because their partners are more naïve, they can get away with misbehaving or acting like a child in the relationship. It is therefore important to carefully evaluate who you are dating and how your older partner treats you.

Older men and women can be more controlling – power imbalance

When the age gap is big between people it can also influence the partner dynamics, often leading to the older man or woman taking on a more controlling and directive role in the relationship. Some younger partners might like this or even find it attractive, but healthy relationships are based on a mutual exchange of support, communication, respect and trust. When the power shifts to one side, the daily exchanges between partners become unbalanced, resulting often in the dismissal of the ideas or voice of the younger partner because of their age. These power struggles in age-disparate relationships can lead to impulsive and even abusive behaviour over time.

Younger partners are not always looking for love and growth in the traditional sense

The reasons why younger people in general seek out an older person to date is not only down to looks and maturity. Financial stability and status are also driving factors behind why younger people prefer to date older people. Popular culture even promotes looking for a 'sugar daddy' or 'sugar mama' to pay your bills and buy you first-class tickets and expensive Louis Vuitton bags. 'My Sugar Daddy buys me Prada', as sung by Qveen Herby, and 'Pay my tuition just to kiss me on this wet-ass pussy', from the song 'WAP' by Cardi B featuring Megan Thee Stallion, are typical lyrics of many pop artists. So, how do you know for sure that the younger person you are with is really interested in you for who you are and not only for what you have?[26] The (unfortunate) truth about dating in today's world is that most young people (specifically Gen Z and late Millennials[27]) are not looking for a long-term relationship. I remember a 21-year-old a couple of years ago telling me with confidence during an interview for a marketing study, 'I have relationships because I want something from someone. Once I have it, I don't need the relationship anymore.' This surprised me at first, but later I realized that young adults growing up in a rapidly changing and uncertain world just want to advance and survive. Friendships and romantic partners are becoming more 'exchange commodities' (that you quickly make and let go of) rather than 'people' you invest in for the long run. When you ask someone on social media, 'What do you think about unconditional love?', many will say, 'It doesn't exist! Everything is conditional.' This made me also realize that the way a 23-year-old defines what 'love' or a 'relationship' is can differ significantly from how a 40-year-old would define these words, leading to all kinds of misunderstandings and false expectations.[28] If you are looking for something more serious with a younger partner, be explicit about your needs and expectations and see if you can find common ground together to create something more long term. A successful relationship requires a higher level of engagement and deeper connection than just simple tradeoffs for physical intimacy.

Dating older or younger – what's the drama?

Dating someone older or younger than yourself is nothing new. Stories of age-disparate relationships have been documented for centuries, often portraying older men dating or marrying a much younger woman. Research shows that men and women are generally attracted to people their own age, but that the number of people in age-disparate relationships is growing.

In same-sex relationships, bigger age gaps are more common compared to heterosexual relationships. When it comes to attraction, younger women are often attracted to older men because they provide them with a sense of security and safety in the long term. Younger men are often attracted to older women because they can help them grow in a more rounded way. In recent years, woman-older relationships have become more popular thanks to changing gender norms, social media and online dating apps; however, women face more backlash than men for dating a younger partner.

Age-disparate relationships in general face many challenges due to problems relating to misalignment of life goals, social stigma and a mismatch in energy levels and sexual desires. Also, the bigger the age difference between partners, the more likely relational dissatisfaction is to occur over time compared to similar-aged couples. A socially acceptable age difference between partners is the 'half-your-age-plus-7' rule. The most important things to consider when dating someone older or younger is whether you can make it work in the long run and what the underlying reasons are for being together. Exploring these points while dating can help you navigate the excitement into something more serious.

It's a **red flag** if:
- You are dating someone older due to ulterior motives (e.g. financial resources, revenge) without

your partner knowing about it. If you are looking
for a sugar daddy or mama, make sure both of you
are on the same page.

- You are subconsciously dating older because you
  have mummy/daddy issues. You believe by dating
  older you can solve issues from the past, but
  instead you find yourself in a vicious circle or toxic
  relationship.
- Your older partner still acts like a kid (e.g. wants to
  party continuously, acts immaturely or behaves
  irresponsibly) and thinks that they can get away with
  their behaviour because you are younger.
- Your older partner chooses you because they know
  they can manipulate you easily (e.g. due to your lack
  of experience or maturity).
- Your values, beliefs, family needs and/or goals are
  not aligned due to the age gap.

It's a **green flag** if:
- You choose an older partner because you see long-
  term compatibility with them.
- Besides physical attraction, you are also emotionally
  and intellectually attracted to each other. You feel
  that being with each other is empowering and the
  age difference compliments instead of hinders the
  relationship.
- You both can communicate effectively together, and
  you can set clear expectations about potentially not
  experiencing certain life moments with each other if
  the age difference prevents them (e.g. partying,
  travelling, having kids).

- You and your partner are indifferent about what other people think about your age difference and you don't allow external pressures to negatively affect your relationship.

Things to consider when deciding if you want in or out

Dating across different age categories can be very exciting and rewarding, but also very challenging. You need to weigh the benefits and disadvantages of being with someone much older or younger than yourself. If the age difference brings you both benefits and you complement each other, then that's great. Go for it! However, if the age difference creates unmanageable struggles or discomfort, or facilitates mistreatment, then maybe it's time to leave. Here are some key considerations to evaluate if dating someone older or younger is for you:

Willingness to date

- You are both enjoying the moment and not looking for anything too serious.
- You appreciate the feeling or experience your older or younger partner gives you.
- If you both want to take it a step further, you understand and have discussed possible limitations that a big age difference might have on a long-term relationship.
- You both feel emotionally, intellectually and/or physically compatible with each other.

Time to leave

- One of the partners is using the other for emotional, physical or economic gain.
- Your partner mistreats you and thinks they can get away with it due to the age difference.
- You are sensitive to what others think about you and can't deal with public or social disapproval of big age differences in dating or relationships.

Red Flag 18 'I think I found the right person, but I don't feel anything!'

When there are no emotions

'If we just wanted positive emotions, our species
would have died out a long time ago.'
Martin Seligman

When you don't feel anything

One of the most beautiful moments in life is the moment when you fall in love. It is an experience that can be best described as engulfing and positively overwhelming. Your feelings are everywhere, you have butterflies in your stomach, you only have happy thoughts about your partner and your only desire is to be together and build a happy future. These feelings can be so intense and so positive that you lose your sense of time (and sometimes even your appetite), praying that this moment will last for ever. Some people only fall in love once or twice in their lives, others multiple times, and some never at all. It's a human experience often depicted in movies and literature, and together with heartbreak, it's the theme for many songs across the world, from Spanish serenades to Arabic love songs and Bollywood soundtracks.

Yet many people complain nowadays that they don't feel anything at all, even when they think they have found the right person. In the modern dating world, people seem to prioritize sexual chemistry over emotional connection, making love something best expressed as an emoji. But are only dating apps to blame for the lack of emotions people feel towards each other? How is modern life impacting on how much emotional connection we are willing to have? And when is not feeling anything at all a sign of a more serious underlying issue?

Approaching emotional detachment from a behavioural perspective can help you better understand why you might be feeling less than you should and, more importantly, what you can do about it. Humans are emotional beings programmed for deep social connection. Living in a world that heralds self-reliance above collaboration and human attachment can have serious negative consequences. Not only to yourself but also to your love life and society at large. That's why it's important to know when emotional detachment is a green flag and when it is a red flag.

Is it normal not to feel anything?

You're probably wondering if it is normal not to feel anything, ever or in specific situations or times of your life. It is perfectly normal to not feel anything at times. Feeling stressed out over an upcoming exam, working too much to meet year-end targets, overthinking breaking up with your girlfriend or boyfriend and being hyperfocused on your gym routine are very common reasons why people emotionally feel less sometimes, or are not able to conjure up emotions for others when needed. You might find it strange not to feel anything, especially in moments when you know you should feel something, like during birthdays, graduation, weddings and funerals. You observe people around you feeling intense emotions of excitement, happiness or even sadness. However, you don't seem to feel the same. Emotional numbness comes in all shapes and sizes and could reflect experiencing less emotion than usual or feeling nothing at all.

Emotional numbness, or emotional blunting or reduced emotional reactivity as it's also referred to, can also make you feel disconnected, not really caring about other people (and sometimes not even about yourself) and like you are going through the motions. There are various reasons why you could be feeling less than you should, especially when you are not feeling anything when you've met someone you like.

Psychological reasons

Reading one's own emotions can be difficult at times, especially when you are going through a rough patch. Disassociating yourself as a coping mechanism is a normal human response when under stress or in survival mode, making it hard to not only read one's emotional state but also that of others. If you were hurt in the past or disappointed by an ex, you could go through a period of emotional numbness. This is often an automatic reaction of the body to the anxiety, stress, grief or trauma you are experiencing (or have experienced) or in some cases could be a conscious choice as a means of self-protection. Emotional detachment can be a choice for personal or social reasons. It's common for people to want to numb negative emotions instead of dealing with them, and they do this by binge watching TV, spending hours on social media, throwing themselves into work, overeating, drinking alcohol or taking drugs.[1]

However, purposefully blocking out emotions is not always

by personal choice. Emotional suppression can be due to societal norms or cultural rearing. You might hear people saying, 'As a man, you are not supposed to cry', 'Don't show weakness in front of people' or 'You can't show anyone you like that person. It's not allowed!' Feeling pressured by your environment not to express what you truly feel can condition you to suppress your emotions. The unfortunate truth about numbing emotions is that it isn't selective. If you want to numb pain, you might also numb joy and excitement. There are also more serious psychological conditions linked to not feeling anything. Depression, Schizophrenia,[2] PTSD,[3] anxiety disorders, dissociative disorders[4] and borderline personality disorder[5] have often been linked to emotional numbing. Medication and drug usage have also been linked to feeling less.[6]

DID YOU KNOW?
Alexithymia

Alexithymia (Greek for 'no words for feelings')[7] is a personality dimension in which someone is not able to feel or read one's own emotions. The clinical literature does not view Alexithymia as a mental disorder in itself but does link it to a range of psychological disorders, such as depression and autism.[8] Alexithymia is also prevalent in people without mental health issues and is seen as a psychological trait that remains stable over a lifespan. According to the literature, alexithymia is prevalent in 10 per cent of the population, making it quite common. As someone who experiences emotions, it might be hard to imagine that you can't feel or read emotions. Just like colour-blindness, there is emotion-blindness.

People with alexithymia can still experience love, though they might not be able to express emotions or words of affection as most people do. This can be hard for the person on the receiving end (especially at the beginning) as the lack of emotional expression can make one feel invalidated. However, instead they might choose to act out their love for another person by doing things for them.

Sexual chemistry rules!

We live in a society where sexual chemistry is prioritized over emotional connection. Online dating and porn have made intimacy more transactional. When you feel the need, you can pursue it, no matter the time of day. No need to court someone and spend ample time with them to be intimate. Jump on your dating app or social media account and there is a high chance that you will soon find someone to jump into bed with.

In the past, more effort was needed to meet new people and get intimate (see Red Flag 15 for more on traditional dating versus modern dating). The easiest way was meeting people at a bar or club, but that at least would cost you a drink, and maybe even a dance, in terms of investment to get to second or third base. Before the internet, most people had to date first before they got intimate (unless you paid for it). If you dated, there was a chance that you would develop feelings for that person. Nowadays, there's less and less time given to developing an emotional connection, at least not a deep one. And because prioritizing sexual chemistry over emotional connection has become the norm in today's dating scene, people also get scared to emotionally connect out of fear of getting hurt.

This combination of regular casual sexual encounters and

lack of connection can make you emotionally numb. Not to mention, the constant exposure of (un)solicited 'dick pics', 'booby pics' and 'sexy video snaps', which can make you less excited about seeing people naked and having normal sex.[9] Some people can also experience having sex as a stressful event and therefore feel motivated to consume alcohol before having sex. This might be de-stressing in the short term but can be emotionally numbing in the long term.[10] Focusing too much on sex without connection can clearly impact how much you feel in the long run.

Note: If you have not been feeling anything for a while, it may be a good idea to figure out the root cause. It is more important to know why you are not feeling anything when other people do, when in the same situation. Consider having a chat with a licensed clinical therapist to help you get to the root cause.

Is it really love at first sight?

When I speak to couples, I sometimes hear them say, 'It was love at first sight.' But I question if it was really love. To fall in love with someone takes time, appreciating the person to their fullest and the way they make you feel. Love is a consequence of a chain of events in which positive emotions develop towards someone. Love at first sight is more attraction at first sight, or infatuation at first sight, which can leave a very powerful and lasting impression on someone. Just think of the duckling when it first sees its mother after hatching out of an egg. Ducks are hardwired to seek and remember the image of their caregiver to help them survive after birth.

And this imprinting remains for a very long time. This imprinting is not exclusive to ducks, but can be seen in other animals, insects, fish and mammals.[11]

In humans, similar cognitive mechanisms are at play, especially when we form first impressions of people. First impressions can influence how we evaluate and feel about people years later. It's a bias often referred to as 'thin slicing'. Various cognitive and social psychological studies have investigated the impact of first impressions on attitudes and beliefs. First impressions can be made based on one's personality, humour, energy, physical attractiveness and other personal attributes. First impressions can be as fast as a fifteenth of a second up to a couple of seconds or longer.[12] Now think again about attraction at first sight. How powerful the first seconds of seeing someone can be on how many feelings you develop for them (or are willing to develop for them). In today's 'swipe right' society, which often presents unrealistic (e.g. filtered) images and lives of people, these first impression biases can make us more judgemental of people or even hold us back from really getting to know someone in the real world (as they don't meet the criteria you find online). Inevitably, this leads to less emotional development and attachment.

The mere exposure effect

In the chapter Red Flag 17, 'Why do I like my partners with more mileage?', I mentioned that attraction often develops towards people your own age because of the time you spend with them at school, work, sports or in other social settings. In psychology, this is often referred to as the mere exposure effect.[13] Merely being exposed to people for long periods of time can lead to developing positive attitudes and emotions for someone. Interest, or attraction in this case, develops because it is something that has become familiar. And seeing as our brain is wired for survival, it generally likes things that feel familiar. If it becomes familiar, it becomes easier to process and positive emotions can develop towards something (or someone) your brain finds fluid and predictable.[14] The mere exposure effect also explains why we often gravitate towards similar types of people. The question is, what impacted that initial attraction to people in a romantic way and why do we find certain people more attractive than others? Hormones definitely play a role, but so does imprinting. Psychological and social imprinting by caregivers doesn't only impact the type of attachment style[15] you develop in your adult years but can also influence who you find sexually attractive[16] (I am pretty sure I've got Freud turning in his grave right now). What you find attractive later in life can be partially influenced by the imprinting of your caregivers as a child, looking for partners who share similar physical characteristics such as height,[17] eye colour,[18] hair colour,[19] hairiness[20] or similar personality or behavioural traits.[21] The psychological similarity helps to partially explain the attraction in interracial couples. Attraction, it seems, is a re-enactment. I am pretty sure that you are feeling a bit disgusted by now reading all this (especially if you were never aware of sexual imprinting before or just came to realize that your current or past partner does look or behave like one of your caregivers). But I am not saying you are sexually attracted to your parents or siblings, merely that the physical and psychological attributes your caregivers have can be unconsciously linked to attributes such as survival in your mind, which can influence who you find attractive today.[22] There is even research that claims that who you find attractive is also genetically influenced, linking it to partner choices our ancestors made.[23] The opposite is also true. People might be attracted to people who don't remind them of a difficult past or one's caregivers (e.g. a parent who was never present). However, some studies refute the broader impact caregiver imprinting has on who you find attractive later in life[24] and, for now, the research is inconclusive. As we learn more about the brain and human behaviour, we might find ways to resurrect Freud from the dead after all.

Can dating apps kill emotion?

Since the rise of dating apps and social media, people spend less time engaging with each other in real life, focus less on building strong emotional ties with people and are more willing to let people go. If falling in love requires time invested in a person, then dating apps definitely make this more difficult to achieve. Similar to any commercial mobile application on a digital platform, dating apps have been designed to keep you on the app for as long as possible. Studies show that one of the reasons people find it hard to let go of their dating app after finding a potential partner is the persuasive design of the technology[25] and excessive swiping (focusing more on collecting matches for instant gratification and self-worth validation than on making a connection).[26] App developers and designers intentionally apply behavioural psychology techniques to create habit-forming behaviours in their users.[27,28] The longer you swipe, match and comment, the more likely you are to continue to use the service. This benefits the app developer as it can make money through in-app purchases or through advertising. These techniques hack into your brain chemistry, creating short bursts of dopamine spikes that make you feel good or help relieve negative emotions temporarily. It is no surprise that people who are highly anxious, depressed or experiencing other kinds of psychological or emotional discomfort are more likely to use their mobile phone and mobile apps that apply habit-forming techniques. Unfortunately, mobile phone usage or social media consumption don't help you eradicate the negative emotions, they can actually make your problems worse.[29] The continuous dopamine hits and quick emotional fixes have also been found to numb people's emotions.[30] Dating apps don't care whether you find love or not, or that you experience trauma after being with someone you met online. They care about your being on their app as long as possible. More and more studies (including my own) are showing that the usage of modern-day technology is hurting human emotions and connection. It's time tech developers rethink why and how they design (dating) apps and focus more on using technology as a cornerstone to enhance human properties rather than damaging them.[31]

The me-Generation: the perils of self-reliance

There are moments in your life when you realize that focusing on yourself is much needed. Taking time off from work to rethink your life priorities and become more your authentic self is a great example. Another good reason to focus on yourself is when you realize that certain thinking patterns or behaviours are not serving you well, causing you problems in your love life or in your friendships. You need time to work on those self-limiting beliefs and tackle problem areas in your life – such as mindset, behaviour or health – before dating again. You might need time for yourself to develop some healthy lifestyle habits before venturing back into the wild again. Let's face it, modern life in many parts of the world has made it very easy for people to be more self-reliant. So much so, that focusing on self feels easier to do than trying to forge strong relationships (rationalizing it as self-protection). It's no surprise that today's generation is often referred to as the *me*-Generation.[32] The paradox of becoming too self-reliant is that you become less likely to work on yourself and less willing to adapt to other people. Why should you change if you can do everything by yourself how you like? Our brain is very lazy that way because it doesn't like to put too much effort into things that seem mentally tasking. And our technology usage also contributes to becoming more self-centred and merely interested in information that fits our world view. You could almost say that 'smart' devices are actually making us dumber – what a paradox!

The self-reliant and self-love movement creates this illusion that doing things by yourself is the ultimate goal and that asking for help is considered needy, which creates feelings of embarrassment.[33] The self-empowerment movement has contributed to increased loneliness. Loneliness has been linked to emotional numbness. If you suppress your emotions long enough because you are not sharing your problems with anyone, this could lead to emotional numbness, which in turn could make you feel lonelier.[34] It's clear that too much self-love becomes a vicious circle of self-sabotage.[35]

When you just focus on yourself, you lose your ability to think broadly and critically. It is a trend nowadays to label any behaviour you don't like as toxic, any person that doesn't give you enough attention as a narcissist and any problematic experience as trauma.[36,37] From a self-empowerment perspective, giving it a name without critical thought provides a false sense of control over reality and thus a mechanism towards self-protection and hence feeling less. However, there is a fine balance between being downright self-centred and unwilling to change and taking some time off to focus on yourself to become a better person. Balance is key, as is not getting too comfortable with one's self, especially when we live in a society that heralds self-reliance.

When there are no emotions – what's the drama?

Many people nowadays say they feel less when it comes to dating and romance. But the big question is why? There is no simple answer to this question. Human emotions are complex and there are many reasons why at times we feel less than we should or nothing at all. Feeling less doesn't have to mean that there is something wrong with you. It could be your mind's way of dealing with a stressful situation at work or being hyperfocused on a specific activity. However, in other situations, feeling emotionally detached could be the result of specific life choices or the consequence of excessive dating-app usage. In some cases, feeling emotionally numb could be a sign of a more serious underlying psychological issue, such as depression or PTSD. Our lives in recent years have been characterized by uncertainty, technological breakthroughs and rapid social developments, which have contributed in various ways to how we feel about ourselves and about human relationships, especially the romantic ones. Being aware of how your lifestyle choices impact your emotions and taking charge of your mental health are critical to staying emotionally grounded and romantically engaged in a rapidly changing world. Too much self-love can lead to self-sabotage, creating more loneliness and less connection.

It's a **red flag** if:

- You have not felt much in a while. If you can't find any apparent reason why you have become emotionless, maybe it's time to speak to a specialist.
- You have been too focused on self-love for too long after your last relationship. If you are less interested in establishing a loving connection with anyone besides your pet.
- You prioritize sexual chemistry over emotional connection when dating. This will not help you date successfully as you are sending out the wrong message.
- You are focused more on why you don't want to be with somebody (or want to break up with someone). Love is about commitment and building a lasting relationship.

It's a **green flag** if:

- You feel less due to manageable stressful events at work or in your private life.
- You feel less as a way to cope with grief (e.g. loss of a loved one). Not everyone feels emotional in the moment when someone passes.
- You choose to feel less as a way to stay focused on the task at hand. Once completed, you will go back to feeling more again.
- You feel less because you are tired. You know that when you take more rest, you feel more again.

Things to consider when deciding if you want in or out

Feeling less doesn't have to be something that just happens to you. In some cases, you can consciously choose to feel less. If you are dealing with a difficult situation, choosing to stay focused on the task could be your priority, switching emotions off as a temporary solution. However, excessive periods of emotionless living can become the default, making it hard or even scary to want to connect again. If you have been in a couple of bad relationships, you can feel completely turned off from emotionally connecting with someone again. You focus primarily on yourself, not allowing anyone in. It is also possible that you don't feel anything at all. It's a psychological trait you've always had or developed over time. However, you understand that your emotional blindness can be misinterpreted by a potential romantic partner as non-caring, and you are eager to engage in practices to help them feel validated by expressing your love in ways you are capable of. Here are some scenarios to help consider if it is time to change the way you feel:

Willingness to stay the same

- You know yourself well and understand that feeling less or nothing at all is a temporary issue that will pass.
- You realize that your lifestyle choices are impacting how you feel and you are ready to make some changes to those to start feeling more.
- You are learning to set boundaries for yourself and feeling less (e.g. guilt, shame) at this moment helps to set those boundaries.

Time to change

- Feeling less or nothing has been going on for some time and you cannot find a clear answer to your problem. You feel it is time to change and you want to do something about it.
- You can see that not feeling anything is hurting your personal relationships. We need human connection to survive and hence it's time to work on feeling again or recognizing how your emotional state is holding you back from engaging socially.
- You realize that feeling less is making you less empathetic and therefore less caring of others.

Romantic Relationships

Red flags in romance

Romantic relationships play an important role in our lives. They help us to understand who we truly are, elevate our self-esteem and are a source of purpose, connection and happiness. Investing time and effort into a love relationship serves a purpose as we humans naturally want to be emotionally and psychologically connected to others. However, when things don't go well in love relationships, it can severely impact one's mental and physical well-being. Being able to see warning signs early on in your love life is crucial to succeeding in relationships, and also to protecting yourself from unnecessary pain and suffering. Maintaining a healthy long-term relationship requires time, effort and sacrifice, but why put energy into something that doesn't feel right? Identifying red flags in relationships should create moments of pause and reflection, not only to decide if continuing a relationship makes sense, but also to acknowledge the severity of the red flag and the true source of the issue. Does your partner leave the dishes in the sink? Frustrating, yes, but a red flag? Probably not. Saying 'you are nobody without me' to put you down – red flag? Most likely yes! Some red flags are redder than others, and there are even some circumstances where *you* might be the red flag.

However, red flags don't only have to be warning signals indicating that the road ahead is out of service. They can also provide opportunities for growth and learning for both you and your partner. Sometimes we believe certain behaviours are warning signs when they are actually not. And in some

cases, people see not meeting relationship ideals and expectations as a red flag. Learning to understand why certain
behaviours trigger you can help you to become more aware
of the flaws in your thinking, how you react to others and
how best to deal with these issues and become a better partner. The red flags we believe we see in others are sometimes a
reflection of the red flag(s) in ourselves (though some of us
prefer to be selectively colour-blind when reflecting on our
own flaws). Being able to distinguish the true red flags in your
relationships from the false ones is crucial to the success of
your love life and even your mental health. Ultimately, though,
when you identify the red flags in a relationship, the most
important factor will be deciding what to do with, and how to
respond to, them. Do you take action, do you respond negatively or do you just turn a blind eye and do nothing at all?
The coming six chapters about red flags in relationships will
help you see the forest through the trees and enable you to
make better decisions about your love life.

Red Flag 19 'Stable relationships are boring!'

Seeing chaos as a sign of love

'Everyone thinks of changing the world,
but no one thinks of changing themselves.'
Leo Tolstoy

Relational boredom

Boredom and dullness in relationships happen a lot, especially when relationships become stable and develop a solid routine of daily activities. Your first reaction to relational boredom might be to think that the spark has gone out, or that your partner is not worth being with anymore. Let's be honest, romantic relationships are supposed to be fun, exciting and full of passion. And you might know many couples who have never experienced boredom in their relationships. However, studies show that relational boredom is very common and also a major reason why relational satisfaction declines over time.[1] The good news is that experiencing dullness in relationships can be beneficial, as long as you know how to give meaning to it and deal with it effectively. Learning how to navigate boring moments together is crucial to maintaining a successful, long-standing relationship. However, not addressing the boredom in your relationship early on can lead to more serious problems down the road and even to the end of the relationship.

So, what to do once the excitement thaws out and the relationship starts to wane? It's important to know that not all relational boredom is the same nor can it be fixed in the same way. A good first step in evaluating your change in mood is figuring out why you are feeling bored. Sometimes boredom isn't due to the monotony of your recurring lives together but to your need for change and stimulation, or an unconscious response to traumatic experiences from your childhood or past relationships. Maybe you feel bored because your partner doesn't challenge you anymore and only wants to meet your needs. Whatever the reason, identifying the cause of your boredom is a crucial first step in doing something about it. Only then can you tackle it head-on.

What if I am the red flag?

Taking a moment to reflect on why you feel bored in your relationship could make you realize that being bored with your partner is more a *me* problem than a *you* problem. This can be very confrontational at first and, in some cases, you might not want to admit it, but deep down inside you know that the boredom you are experiencing is a product of other processes at play. This awareness is truly a gift, but it also brings to light the need for change on your side. Before any change can happen, it is important to bring to light what mental processes are at play underlying your beliefs and emotional responses. You can achieve this by asking yourself reflective questions, such as 'What does feeling bored say about me?', 'What is so boring about being in a healthy and stable relationship?' or 'Am I able to find the excitement I am missing right now with

someone else, or will I face the same problem again later?'
Write the questions and answers down for yourself and take
time to reflect. Remember, it's easy to judge others, but it's
harder to be introspective and challenge the mechanisms at
play underlying your thinking. Finally, in evaluating your relational boredom from a *me* perspective, ask yourself which
emotional and psychological needs are currently not being
met and question if these needs can realistically be met by
your partner. This should help you gain perspective about
what you want to change about yourself and what discussions
you want to have with your partner about the relationship.
Even though it is a *me* problem, it is important to remember
that in a relationship there is always an *us* solution.

When stable relationships feel boring after being in an abusive relationship

Abusive relationships are often characterized by emotional
and physical pain, feelings of uncertainty and unpredictability, guilt, shame and lack of safety. If you have ever been in
an abusive relationship, then you know that the pain and
suffering don't stop when the relationship ends. Its emotional and psychological effects can linger on long after
the relationship has ended. Especially when forming new
romantic relationships, feelings of guilt, shame, disbelief
and mistrust often arise unexpectedly, leaving you caught in
survival mode.

In survival mode, you are more focused on making sure
your new surroundings are safe instead of focusing on creating a solid, healthy bond and environment with your partner.
In fact, the brain of a survivor of an abusive relationship has

a hard time switching off its alertness, leaving the important parts of relationship building untouched. Also, for many survivors of abuse, having a partner who makes them feel safe by itself can already feel like enough. However, not spending enough time early in the relationship setting clear boundaries and finding ways to communicate more effectively with each other can lead to issues down the road (which often arise once safety isn't a concern anymore). Not to mention, the problems that can arise from not addressing old patterns of thinking that helped the survival of abusive relationships in the past but are no longer conducive to a healthy relationship (e.g. being hypervigilant, non-trusting and seeing chaos in the relationship as a way of life[2]). We need dynamic moments in a relationship to bond and set boundaries to test our compatibility and find a common ground both sides are happy to continue with. If safety is all that you want, then it can feel very boring once this stage of your growth has been reached. However, it doesn't end there.

Once there is more stability in the relationship, it is not uncommon for survivors of abusive relationships to miss the chaos and unpredictability of their past relationship. This doesn't mean they miss the abuse, but rather that they have become so accustomed to the volatility of past relational distress that a healthy relationship doesn't feel interesting anymore.[3] Peace in the relationship makes them more aware of their inner chaos. The unpredictability of past relationships has an addictive component to it. It's like pulling on the handle of a slot machine, never knowing when you will get your three matching symbols. The abused brain becomes primed for excitement and stability definitely doesn't provide the hit it needs.

If you are a survivor of an abusive relationship and you recognize yourself in this, then it's important to realize that the boredom you are experiencing right now is not actual boredom from not doing something interesting, but a phase your brain needs to go through to find excitement in the secure bond you have with your partner. Interestingly, it happens that when people leave an abusive relationship they might look for high-intensity or adrenaline-filled experiences (e.g. racing or combat sports, parachute jumping) to relive the rush they experienced in their volatile relationship. The impact of unhealthy bonding either in childhood or adulthood can impact how you see yourself and how you form new relationships.

Are you addicted to toxicity?

Unfortunately, it happens a lot that survivors of abusive relationships end healthy relationships and re-enter abusive ones because the spark they are looking for is linked to the chaos they have become so accustomed to. Emotional outbursts are often seen as acts of love and there is a belief that if you don't argue, then you don't really love each other. Changing the mental programming of the abused survival brain requires conscious effort and patience from both partners. Even after being in a healthy relationship for many years, the mind of an abuse survivor can still find itself trapped in the mental programming of the past, impacting how they perceive and interact with their partner.

The Johnny Depp and Amber Heard case is a testimony to how toxic relationships can be. Regardless of whether you supported Johnny or Amber (or neither of them), it was clear from the live-streamed trial that the Hollywood duo were no role-model sweethearts. From a relationship perspective, their short-lived marriage radiated toxicity from all angles. Why would anyone in their right mind stay in such a relationship? The fact of the matter is, so many people do stay. You can be addicted to toxicity. Not because you enjoy getting hurt or want to hurt others per se, but because life without drama can feel 'boring', especially to those who have become accustomed to it. This strongly influences how you view toxicity and how much importance you give to it in your romantic affairs. If you were brought up in an unhealthy environment or experienced many unstable relationships, you could find yourself saying, 'Fighting regularly is absolutely fine, it's an act of love', whereas someone who was brought up believing that fights and disagreements happen but should be seen as an opportunity to learn more about each other, might say, 'Fights are an inescapable part of life and we should find ways to resolve them constructively and grow from them.' Consciously you might be saying that you don't like toxicity and that toxicity is bad, but unconsciously your mind can be attracting it more than you think. It's important to become aware of how you frame your experiences and what you are really attracting and accepting.[4]

DID YOU KNOW?
The neuroscience behind experiencing boredom
A great way to understand where the boredom is coming from is to understand what is happening under the hood. Let's look at what is happening in the brain when stability becomes a pain. The human brain is an evolutionary masterpiece. Over millions of years, our brains have evolved into a super-efficient computer capable of processing gigabytes of information, while allowing us to walk, talk, flirt and scroll our socials at the same time

(absolutely fascinating, if you think about it). Thanks to habits that turn daily, routine activities into unconscious effortless processes, the brain has mastered the ability to multitask and remain efficient. The moment daily activities become a habit is the moment the brain says, 'Let's automate this shit so that you can focus on more important things in your life.' The more it automates, the less energy is required. But the problem with this process is that it's not neurologically stimulating anymore. So, when you see your partner and you engage in the same thing over and over again, dopamine gets depleted, and you start to experience the onset of relationship dullness.

Is it boring when your partner meets all your needs?

Being addicted to toxicity is not the only reason why stable relationships can feel boring. Sometimes having a partner who always agrees with you and who doesn't argue can make you feel that your relationship is monotonous. You might also lose a sense of self if your independence is not asserted enough within your relationship. Arguments and conflicts are a natural occurrence in any relationship and if dealt with effectively can lead to a stronger and healthier bond. Not disagreeing with each other could mean one of two things. You have the ideal partner, one who meets all your needs (and it's you who needs to do something about how you feel about that), or there could be something wrong in your relationship. If your partner is trying to keep you happy at all costs, then alleviating boredom should not be your main priority. Instead, focus on the root cause of why your partner wants to please and accommodate you, if not purely out of love. If their pleasing behaviour happened after you both have been in the relationship for some time, then other emotions such as fear, guilt or relational unhappiness could be the reason for their recent change in behaviour. Whatever the reason, know when it is a *you* problem and when it is a *me* problem, but always try to find an *us* solution if you care about continuing the relationship. If there is no progression in solving the problem together, then it might be time to re-evaluate the purpose of being together.

When is boredom in a relationship a green flag?

Most relationships are fun and exciting in the beginning. During the first weeks and months of the relationship, you are getting to know each other and everything is new and exciting. Eventually, you feel closer to your partner and you know what to expect from each other. This is when things can start to wane, and excitement becomes less. So, is this a good thing? Well, in most cases it is. It means you and your partner feel comfortable with each other. Your relationship is stable, you have a routine and you know what to expect.[5] Studies show that boredom helps to unleash creative potential, which can explain why many people feel motivated to bring new experiences into their relationship.[6] When the boredom kicks in, it's the brain's way of saying 'time to stimulate the senses'. Especially in long-term relationships, you will experience boredom many times and in many different ways throughout all the areas of your relationship, from daily interactions all the way to the bedroom. As the boredom creeps in, it becomes more and more important to find new ways to learn how to deal with the dull moments in a relationship. Bringing some spice back into the relationship or your marriage helps you to re-focus your interest and energy on your partner.

Bringing some excitement into the relationship

If you feel your relationship is becoming monotonous and dull, then maybe it's time to inject some excitement back into it. You might be asking yourself what kind of excitement you should consider, and this is a great question. Excitement and fun activities can come in different forms and sizes, but not all kinds of uplifting experiences are beneficial to help deal with relational boredom. It is important to be intentional about the type of excitement you want to create. Excitement can mean different things to different people and not everyone is inter-ested in engaging in fun activities together when feeling bored.

What kinds of excitement exist, and which one should you focus on? There are two different types of excitement. There are predictable stimulating moments and growth stimulating moments. Predictable stimulating moments are moments of excitement that help you step away from your daily routine. Going out for dinners, seeing friends or watching a movie together. They are generally fun to do, and you both know what the outcome will be of such events. This kind of excite-ment, if both experience it as a positive, is good for the relationship but won't specifically put the spark back into things. These experiences feel familiar and maintain a sense of security in the relationship. Growth stimulating moments, on the other hand, are experiences that are both stimulating and new and provide an opportunity for exploration in the relationship. Examples of growth stimulating moments are travelling together to a far-away destination, doing a course together (or separately), finding new ways to solve issues in the relationship or exploring how to spice up your sex life. Growth stimulating moments are harder to work on as they cost more time and effort, and also require both partners to equally invest and participate in the activities. But growth stimulating experiences can reignite the flame in the relationship and strengthen the bond even further.

Things to do to spice up your relationship

If you feel that your relationship can use a boost, then don't sit down hoping things will magically change. Take charge of the excitement process! Besides love and care, bringing fun and excitement into the relationship should be high on every partner's priority list of things to do to sustain a long-lasting love. However, many of us forget to do this, let alone think strategically about spicing up the relationship when it's needed most. And this is a major reason why many couples eventually break up or continue in unhappy relationships. So, here are three practical strategies you can apply today to bring more pizazz to your existing love life:

Pleasant surprises

Everyone loves surprises, but are you always thoughtful about the types of surprises you introduce? Well, behavioural research shows that intentionally creating positive surprising moments can be beneficial in more ways than one.[7] Surprises are one of the few neurological mechanisms that can hack your brain and alter what you believe and how you see the world.[8] To bring this to light, we all remember the unexpected win of Saudi Arabia against Argentina during the 2022 FIFA World Cup in Qatar. No one expected Saudi Arabia to win, yet they did, which baffled everyone and created a sense of excitement and new interest in the team and the World Cup in general. Similarly, positive surprises in a relationship can become a catalyst to propel the relationship forward again with new energy and beliefs about each other. And if used intentionally, surprises can create magical moments and even create richer lives. So, how can you use surprises strategically in your relationship to reignite passion and purpose? One example is deciding to take care of a pet together. Especially when there are no kids involved, having a pet to care for can be a new way to bond with each other. It can help you see and experience your partner (and maybe even yourself) from a different perspective. Another example of a surprising moment in a relationship can be the way you communicate with each other, intentionally using more words of affirmation and support. Rethinking the way you communicate your love, adoration or commitment to your partner, especially during the dull moments, can be the unexpected trigger that creates excitement for each other again.

Create new traditions

When your relationship becomes monotonous, not only do daily activities often feel cumbersome, but you might also lose the significance of why you are together. Relational boredom can signal a lack of meaning about moments and each other. This is where traditions can help. Traditions help us live successfully together by providing moments of shared meaning, connection and direction. Think of how Christmas and other major events bring people together in unity. Successful long-standing love relationships utilize traditions to relive positive experiences, keep momentum and help get through difficult times. Examples of relationship traditions can be the renewal of your vows after many years of marriage or it could be a simple ritual like having a mobile-free Sunday to ensure you connect with each other without screens in between you. Whatever the tradition you create with each other, shared meaning and emotional connection should be at the core of your practice. When the dull moments eventually kick in, revisiting existing traditions can be a way to find renewed interest and purpose in being together.

Spice up the bedroom scene

Intimacy is an important foundation of any love relationship. A relationship without intimacy is hard to consider a love relationship. If your sexual life is in decline for whatever reason, you might lose interest in your partner, eventually seeing them more as a friend than someone you consider as your other half. Others might be content with limited bedroom action and prefer to focus more on other aspects of the relationship. The difference between being content or not content with the level of intimacy in the relationship depends on feeling passion and/ or compassion towards your partner. Also, people's interests and desires change over time, and it is important to address changing needs in a respectful way, regardless of how hard it may be. True compassion is when you can move away from personal needs alone and focus more on what is important to the other person. Combining your passionate needs with compassion to spice up your relationship is therefore a good strategy to focus on. Discussing and considering doing things differently in the bedroom could bring more excitement to what now seems a dull routine. And there are many ways to do this. Keeping something on (e.g. a piece of clothing or an accessory) in the bedroom can actually create excitement. You could also consider role play and unconventional date nights once in a while to explore ways to spice up your love life. If you are both interested in seeing other people (see Red Flag 21 for more on open relationships), then find ways to make this work within your relationship without risking an eventual break-up. In a *Black Mirror* episode called 'Striking Vipers' (Season 5, Episode 1), Danny Parker and his wife Theo decide that having a 'cheat' night once a year is a way to satisfy certain needs they both have as individuals without jeopardizing what their marriage stands for. Finding a balance between traditional values and modern-day relationships can be extremely beneficial when looking for ways to sustain love and commitment in today's zeitgeist.

Relational boredom – what's the drama?

It's normal to feel bored at times in a relationship. Every long-term relationship has its dull moments, especially when things become routine. Learning how to surprise each other or spice up the relationship can help to overcome the monotony couples experience at times. A nice way to look at relational boredom is to see it as an opportunity to do things differently for a while. Boredom can also kick in because the relationship has actually become very boring. No one is trying their best in the relationship to do things differently nor has any interest in improving the situation, instead staying in the relationship out of habit. On the other hand, sometimes you perceive your relationship as boring when in fact it is stable, safe and predictable, thinking there must be something wrong with your partner when in fact you might be the red flag. This can be especially true if you have been in abusive relationships in the past or have been brought up in a chaotic environment. Not experiencing volatility and unpredictability in the relationship can make you feel uncomfortable – confronting you with your inner chaos. Respect, stability and predictability are important characteristics of a healthy relationship. But for the person addicted to chaos, it can feel very boring and might even make them create some drama in the relationship to feel alive again. It is important to understand where the source of the boredom is coming from. Is it a 'you' problem or is it a 'me' problem? Whatever the situation, there should always be an 'us' solution.

It's a **red flag** if:
- You find your stable, safe and predictable relationship boring.
- You or your partner put no effort into addressing the boredom in the relationship.
- You or your partner are in a relationship out of habit. No one is putting in the effort to make things better.
- You don't find your partner interesting anymore. Time to think about why.

It's a **green flag** if:
- You or your partner find ways to break away from the routine of work, home or family to spend quality time together.

- You understand that people and interests change in a long-term relationship. When the boredom kicks in, you have an open dialogue about your evolving needs and how both people can accommodate each other to meet these new needs together.
- You find ways to spice up the bedroom action when the dull moments kick in.
- You acknowledge that your inner chaos might make stability in your love life feel boring, and actively try to find ways to address this with your partner.

Things to consider when deciding if you want in or out

Relational boredom can happen at any time in a relationship and for multiple reasons. Trying to figure out the cause of the boredom is important. Do you feel like you're going through the motions because your relationship feels too stable and predictable? Is the boredom just a temporary thing that you know will pass with time and some effort from your side? Have you become addicted to pornography and now your sex life feels boring because it doesn't compare? Or is your partner really boring and not willing to put any effort into the relationship, even after you've tried many times to turn things around? Addressing the problem at the core, and deciding if you are in or you are out, requires deep reflection and solid conversations with your partner.

Willingness to stay

- You acknowledge that the boredom is temporary, an inescapable part of any long-term relationship.

- You find ways to bring some excitement to the relationship from get-away trips and date nights to changing the existing routine and spicing things up in the bedroom.
- You realize that the boredom in your relationship might be a 'me' problem and you try to find ways to address it together with your partner.
- You or your partner are going through a rough patch, which makes it hard to demand change at the moment.

Time to leave

- You or your partner don't love each other anymore or have no interest in improving the relationship.
- You or your partner are with each other out of habit and are scared to break up.
- You realize that your inner chaos is preventing you from having a stable relationship with your partner. You want to work on yourself for a while.
- The relational boredom is killing, and you find yourself stuck. At this point, it's affecting your mental and physical health.

Red Flag 20 'You're out of my league!'
The insecure partner

'There are many things that we would throw away if
we were not afraid that others might pick them up.'
The Picture of Dorian Gray, Oscar Wilde

Insecure? Who? Me?

We have all felt insecure at some point in our lives, and many
of us today carry multiple insecurities that influence the choices
we make, the places we go to and even the people we choose
to be with. Believing that feelings of insecurity are only
reserved for the very few is incorrect. It's human nature to
doubt yourself. Insecurity reflects feelings of uncertainty and
inadequacy that shape our self-image and self-confidence.
Feelings of insecurity can make people anxious about dealing
with certain situations, taking action or forming relationships.
The source of one's insecurity is not always easy to decipher
and can stem from different areas of your life and development (e.g. upbringing, life experiences, change of routine,
trauma, cultural factors, technology usage, and even personality traits). Feelings of insecurity can manifest in different
ways in different people too, debilitating some while motivating others in a positive way. Not feeling sure how well you will
perform in your next presentation, not feeling comfortable
with how you look or losing confidence when you see others

do better than you? Life is full of opportunities that can make even the strongest person insecure. However, fear or insecurity doesn't always have to be a bad thing. In his 2003 book, *The Soul of a Butterfly*, the famous boxer Muhammad Ali said, 'We can't be brave without fear', indicating that the nerves he felt before getting into the ring were healthy and served a purpose. Learning to identify, and how to deal with, your insecurities is pivotal to your mental health and your relationship success.

Insecurity in relationships

Studies show that having high self-esteem has a positive effect on relationship satisfaction and the quality of the relationship.[1] Learning how to deal with insecurity and self-esteem issues in a relationship is important. If you are in a long-term relationship, then it is normal for both you and your partner to grow and change, together as well as independently of each other. These changes, which can be mindset or physical changes, can affect how you view yourself and your significant other. There are many reasons why you or your partner can become insecure in your relationship. You can develop insecurities over time as your body changes or as a consequence of ageing (and the beliefs you have towards these changes). You can also start to doubt yourself if your partner belittles you or makes negative remarks about your behaviour or appearance (see Red Flag 5 for why people belittle others in friendships). It is also possible for insecurities to develop due to reasons outside the relationship. It could be that you have always had low self-esteem (similar to personality traits, levels of self-esteem remain fairly stable over time). Insecurities can also develop as a result of losing a loved one or being fired from a job, which can leave you feeling less confident in your relationship or love life. Whatever the reason, it is crucial to talk about feelings of uncertainty or inadequacy with your partner and to find the space and time to allow this conversation to emerge.

What are some signs that your partner might be feeling insecure?

Picking up on people's insecurities is not always an easy task. Not everyone is comfortable showing their imperfections and being vulnerable, especially when trust is an issue in the relationship. Moreover, it is in fact quite common for people to display opposite behaviours as a way to cover up their actual insecurities and shortcomings. The following is an overview of some typical behaviours that can indicate your partner is dealing with self-doubt and insecurity:

Lack of self-esteem

Self-esteem reflects your beliefs about your abilities and your worth as a person. A lack of self-esteem can manifest in different ways. People who experience low self-esteem often look for validation and reassurance in their love relationships. An insecure partner might ask you, 'Do you still love me?' or 'Do you still find me attractive?' Though it is very normal for these types of questions to occasionally pop up in your relationship, continuous reassurance or extreme neediness is not and is often a red flag that your partner is dealing with insecurities. It is important to figure out why this is happening, if this didn't happen before in your relationship. Is it for personal reasons or because of the way you have been treating your partner, or is it due to how the relationship has been evolving recently? Another example of low self-esteem is negative self-talk. Partners suffering from low self-esteem might put themselves down frequently and trust themselves less, criticizing their own beliefs or abilities, and weighing more heavily on what other people think to inform their own decisions. They might say things like, 'I don't deserve you!' or 'I can't do anything right!'[2]

Jealousy

If your partner is often jealous, then this could be a sign that they are dealing with insecurities, especially when there is no legitimate reason for being jealous besides their own feelings of inadequacy. An insecure partner can show their jealousy in different ways. Examples of things jealous partners might say to you are, 'I don't like you meeting that one friend of yours', 'Show me on your phone who you just texted!' or 'I don't think you look so good in that outfit.' Jealousy can trigger your partner to be suspicious of you (fear of betrayal), criticize you or pull you down as a way to feel more in control, or downplay your achievements by not acknowledging you. Jealousy can be a relationship-killer and even motivate partners to actually engage in activities they are being falsely blamed for. This is better known as the self-fulfilling prophecy. Blame someone so much that they eventually give the jealous partner a reason to be jealous. A recipe for disaster.

Overreacting to criticism

It is also very common for insecure people to overreact to the slightest criticism. Any negative feedback or criticism is seen as a personal attack and can put them on the defensive. Not only does negative (or even constructive) feedback draw their attention to their own insecurities or negative beliefs about themselves, but it can also be seen as possible rejection from their partner.[3] Fear of rejection can be deeply rooted in a person, stemming from past trauma or insecure attachment styles. Things insecure people say when being criticized are, 'I'm sorry I'm not as perfect as you! Probably never will be!', 'Why are you always pointing out my mistakes?' or 'You're like everyone else, trying to make me feel small. If I am not good enough, go find someone else!'

Overly promiscuous

A less understood reason for feeling insecure, but a reflection of today's zeitgeist, is having a high body count (having many sexual partners). Today's dating scene is often characterized as a hook-up culture and many people have multiple partners in their lives. To put things into perspective, the average number of sexual partners men and women in the US have had is approximately seven and in Italy it is five.[4] Sleeping with multiple partners can have a negative impact on your psychological well-being,[5] leading to self-esteem issues (which can make you sleep around even more). From a behavioural perspective, having regular hook-ups generally exposes you to people who are equally, if not more, easygoing when it comes to casual sex. Meeting with someone who has higher standards or is considered a high-value individual (after you have lowered your standards too often) could make you feel insecure (seeing the other person as out of your league).

Finding yourself feeling insecure in your relationship or having an insecure partner puts responsibility into both of your hands to find ways to deal with these insecurities. If left unchecked, not feeling confident about yourself can negatively impact your relationship and the desire for each other. As the insecure person, you might even feel guilty about your insecurities, if your partner is very supportive, and leave a healthy relationship to be with someone who doesn't treat you right. The other problem with insecurities is that your partner, if malicious, can use your insecurities to control you. You might never think that the person who says they love you would do such a thing, but never forget that a relationship or marriage is always a partnership in which people are continuously negotiating and persuading each other. Sometimes, your insecurities become the leverage.

When insecurities stifle your relationship

Feelings of insecurity can hurt your relationship in various ways. Lack of confidence and self-doubt can hold you back from being yourself in your relationship or can make you very uncertain and jealous about your partner. Deeply rooted insecurities (e.g. fear of abandonment, insecure attachment styles) can unconsciously make you want to control, manipulate or even abuse the person you love and cherish. Being aware of how your insecurities influence your perceptions of your partner and behaviours towards them is a first step in addressing the problem. In the following, I will provide examples of how insecurities, either your own or those of your partner, can stifle your relationship:

When my partner uses my insecurities to control me

It is common for abusive people to withhold affection from their insecure partners or threaten to leave them to make them dependent. Your partner could also purposefully withhold affection or validation from you as a way to control you (knowing you seek validation from them). They do this by denying you affection, or emotional support when you are going through a hard time, or by not acknowledging your achievements.

When my partner tries to control and manipulate me due to their insecurities

Fear of abandonment can cause partners to pull you in and then push you away. This behaviour is often referred to as *hot and cold* behaviour. The heat and coldness in a relationship can make things feel very unpredictable and the back-and-forth behaviour can even become addictive. You are continuously treading on eggshells, trying not to upset the other person, and when your partner is upset, you are checking to see when they will warm up again.

When I get jealous of my partner because of my insecurities

Your own insecurities can make you less confident about your partner. This can make you jealous about the way they look or behave, the people they mingle with or how they spend their time. You might want constant reassurance that things are fine or want to know who they are meeting. These insecurities can make you blame your partner for things they haven't done, potentially pushing them to engage in the activities you are accusing them of. Your insecurities can also make you do things that you might regret or destroy the trust you have with each other (e.g. checking their phone, putting them down, cheating on them).

What to do if your partner feels insecure

Insecurities can be deeply rooted in people and addressing these feelings and beliefs can trigger people to become defensive and even aggressive. It's therefore important to approach your partner with empathy, open communication and a non-judgemental attitude, creating a safe and trusting environment first before trying to address the problem at its core. There are a few ways to do this. Try listening first and speaking last. Give your partner the feeling that you are hearing what they are saying and that you acknowledge their concerns. Clarify further if needed, but don't judge. Remember that people can react to past experiences in different ways and their reaction might be different than yours, so be respectful of their experience and reaction to that experience. Once past wounds have been discussed, make sure to reassure your partner that their experiences are valid and that you care about them. This can be a very vulnerable moment for them, so restating your understanding and commitment can be a pivotal moment in finding a way to resolve concerns. This is also the moment to be open and share your thoughts about your partner's insecurities and how you believe they are impacting your relationship. It is important at this stage to also explain that the goal of sharing your concerns is because you want to find a way to help your partner and improve (or save) the relationship. Again, providing reassurance at this stage of the conversation is important. Finally, find agreement on what needs to change to turn things around. What should you and your partner do, or not do anymore, moving forward? Take more self-care? Communicate more effectively? Speak to a friend or go into relationship counselling? Agree on what both of you will do together and create a plan to make it actionable. You can also agree to check in with each other at various intervals to see how things are progressing and to see if anything more needs to be changed. Virginia Satir once said, 'We get together on the basis of our similarities; we grow on the basis of our differences.' Learning how to grow in a relationship is what keeps people together in the long run.

How to build your confidence

Having worked a lot with high-performing people in business, education, government and sports throughout my life, I have learnt a lot about confidence and resilience. One of my key takeaways from working with high-performing individuals is that one's source of motivation and resilience doesn't always have to come from a positive place. Many high-performers have experienced some kind of trauma in their lives, which has become a source of inspiration and motivation instead of a limiting belief or psychological roadblock.[6] These individuals have found a way to see challenge as a potential stepping-stone to greatness. The way high-performers reframe negative experiences is key to understanding how they can turn a negative or a fear into something positive. Unfortunately, there is no simple way to become more confident overnight, but the good news is that there are techniques that you can apply to help you tackle your fears and reappraise past or appraise current experiences.

Here are ten things you can do to help reframe experiences and learn how to deal more effectively with your insecurities:[7]

1. Identify the negative thoughts you have about yourself and learn how to challenge them.

2. Learn to age gracefully and feel confident with your body.
3. Be flexible in your thinking – try to look at your experiences from someone else's shoes. Can you see a different viewpoint to the same experience?
4. Reflect on where you are to blame for past experiences and where not.
5. Try to see failure or setbacks as a natural process of learning.
6. Have a relationship goal you want to work towards.
7. Imagine how it would be to be more confident and visualize what that future might be like for you.
8. Try developing a positive or growth mindset through journaling or meditation.
9. Practise positive self-talk and focus on your strengths.
10. Find support from your network, like speaking to a friend or working on your insecurities with a therapist.

The insecure partner – what's the drama?

Self-doubt or being insecure are normal human behaviours. Everyone experiences these feelings at some point in their life and some more than others. Self-doubt triggers thoughts and emotions of insecurity, which can hold you back or motivate you to perform better. Too much insecurity is an issue though, as it can lead to other problems in your life. Being able to identify your insecurities (and where they come from) is a first step in learning how to deal with them. In relationships, inse-curities can cause you or your partner to behave in ways that are unhealthy and even damaging. However, it is not easy and, in some cases, may even be impossible to eradicate without proper attention from a relationship expert. It is important to decide how willing you are to work on your own insecurities or those of your partner if they are jeopardizing your relationship. Both partners should be responsible for dealing with insecurities in a relationship, not only to find ways to overcome feelings of inadequacy, but also to protect each other from the manipulation and abuse that can arise from leveraging insecurities to one's own benefit. Even when the relationship can't be saved, there is a lot to be gained from addressing these issues.

It's a **red flag** if:
- Your insecure partner
  - Tries to bring you down or belittles you to make you feel insecure due to their own insecurities.
  - Is cheating or misbehaving and blaming it on you because they believe you are doing the same.
  - Is always jealous of how you look, what you do or who you mingle with.
  - Is continuously checking up on you or looking for reassurance about, for example, your love, your commitment/faithfulness to them or your intent to meet people.
- You
  - Put your partner down or abuse them due to your own insecurities.
  - Don't fully open up emotionally and don't trust your partner due to your insecurities.
  - Are starting to feel insecure and less confident about yourself because of how your partner treats you.
  - Use your partner's insecurities to play with them or control them in the relationship.

It's a **green flag** if:
- Your insecure partner
  - Openly communicates with you about their insecurities.
  - Actively works on how they look at themselves through positive self-talk and practising reflection and mindfulness techniques.
  - Doesn't get jealous or upset with you even when they don't feel secure in themselves. Rather, they challenge their fears and insecurities as best they can to work on themselves and improve your relationship.
- You
  - Actively listen to your partner about their insecurities and find ways to address them without compromising your own needs and boundaries.
  - Show empathy to your partner and listen to them in a non-judgemental way.
  - Reassure your partner during discussions to improve your relationship and find ways to help them deal with their insecurities in a progressive manner. Be kind to the person, but tough on agreements and principles.

Things to consider when deciding if you want in or out

Dealing with insecurities in a relationship can be tough, but necessary if you want to maintain a sustainable and loving relationship. Feeling insecure is normal human behaviour, but the way we deal with insecurities differs from person to person, and the need for support in a relationship to deal with these insecurities can vary widely. How willing are you to support your partner in addressing their insecurities and improving your relationship? If you are the insecure one, how willing are you to work on your issues? When is enough, enough? Here are some situations to consider to decide if you are in or out.

Willingness to stay

- You want to work through things together.
- You can openly communicate with each other and find common ground and agreement.
- You see a future together and understand that dealing with personal insecurities and difficult situations is necessary to build a sustainable relationship.

Time to leave

- Your partner misbehaves or cheats on you because they believe you are doing the same.
- They try to put you down and control you repeatedly, playing into your insecurities instead of helping you out of them.
- They are continuously jealous of you, even after reassuring them that there is no need to be jealous.
- Your partner is extremely clingy, continuously needing reassurance, and getting upset when they don't get it.

Red Flag 21 'Let's open things up!'
When one is not enough

'Open Sesame.'
Aladdin

Open relationships
(also known as consensual non-monogamy)

So, what is an open relationship? Open relationships – or consensual non-monogamous relationships, as they are often referred to – are characterized as being intimate with other people besides your own partner. Couples in an open relationship can choose to have sex with other people either separately or strictly together. The idea of an open relationship scares or overwhelms many, and so it is not surprising that polyamory is often frowned upon in our society. Monogamy, which is a construct deeply rooted in many societies, cultures and religions, makes it hard to imagine sharing someone you love with someone else. There are also plenty of scientific research and spiritual teachings that favour the unity and the sacred bond two partners have with each other, above that of polyamory. However, open relationships are increasing in popularity across the world, and it could very well happen that one day your (future) partner will walk into the room and suggest that you open your relationship up. How do you react when something like this happens? Should you even consider this as a possibility? And what to do when you'd rather swim in a pool full of sharks than spell the words 'open relationship'? In this chapter, we will do a deep dive into the reasons why some couples decide to be in open relationships, as well as learn when these situations or partner behaviours are potential red flags or green flags. We will also discuss the psychological and societal motives behind why open relationships are becoming a trend and provide strategies on how best to navigate the, let's be frank, rather complicated discussion.

Why have open relationships become so popular?

In Western societies, the era of finding things 'for life' seems to be coming to an end. A job for life, a friend for life or a partner for life are all becoming rare occurrences. The modern world is rapidly changing and has become highly uncertain, making us feel like we are constantly operating under pressure with less and less time to experience life itself – creating a fear of long-term commitments. Social norms are also changing, making it easier to talk about different forms of relationships, such as open relationships. Besides changing attitudes towards relationships, not wanting to stick to one partner can also be motivated by today's abundance of options. With dating apps and social media platforms, people have more choice than ever before – you don't even have to leave the house to find your next date. The idea of becoming intimate with someone else can also seem like an easy fix to ongoing struggles in a relationship. It is very normal for couples to feel bored with each other as well as to feel attracted to other people. Still, many couples put in the effort to stay committed to each other and sacrifice their time and desires to build a stronger bond together. However, the concept of relationships is rapidly changing and not everyone feels the need to be in a long-term committed relationship, not to mention that the recognition of gender and sexual diversity in recent years challenges common beliefs about traditional monogamy. The intensity of today's world has even created a fear of long-term commitment, motivating many partnerships to open things up or to see each other on a 'non-exclusive' basis in the initial stages of dating. [1]

The stigma around open relationships

Various studies show that open relationships face stigma in society[2] – and no wonder. Open relationships are often perceived as unhealthy, risky, not serious and even short-lived. Other sources claim that people in open relationships, crazy as it may sound, are perceived as less likely to pay taxes and less likely to take their vitamins daily.[3] However, in recent years polyamory has become socially a bit more acceptable, especially among younger generations in Western countries. As polyamory and other forms of relationships become more and more popular, knowing how to deal with a request from your partner to open things up is increasingly important. Mostly for your own sanity, that is.

When to run away . . .

There are many reasons why people might like the idea of being in an open relationship. However, 'liking the idea' does not necessarily equal 'being a good idea'. A way to distinguish a behavioural green flag from a red flag is by understanding the motive behind wanting to shake things up. An open relationship can be a red flag if it means that one person is not getting the attention they need and deserve from their partner. Let's bring this to life with some examples. If your partner tells you that they are still exploring options before solidifying a stronger commitment to you, then it's clear that they see you more as an object to be replaced by something 'better' once it comes their way. Accepting to be in this position should also be considered a raging red flag. Not valuing yourself as someone worthy of love and commitment is a sign that you should focus on yourself first before getting serious with anyone at all. I remember a client of mine telling me she was her partner's 'number five' choice and how happy she was when, after four years of being in an open relationship, she became his number one. They broke up three months later. Another example of a red flag is when your partner tells you that they want to be in an open relationship because it gives them a 'free pass' to date other people without having to cheat, rationalizing that 'opening up' is better than having to find out later that someone is being unfaithful. Last, but not least, if for any reason at all you don't feel comfortable being in an open relationship (even after trying it), then guess what – going forth with it is a red flag.

. . . and when to possibly stay

If both of you feel comfortable opening up your relationship consider this a green flag, at least initially. The idea of being able to date other people while still being in a relationship can be exciting and there are many reasons why both of you may want to explore other options, together and consensually. One good reason to experiment with your current setup could be to overcome the boredom in the bedroom. If you both feel that an 'open plan' could spice up the relationship, then this might be a good reason to explore a different model. You can always decide to undo your choice if one of the partners does not feel comfortable with it anymore. Just be sure to have a safe return plan if in the end opening things up doesn't work for you.

What to do if you don't want to be in an open relationship (but your partner does)

If your partner wants to talk with you about opening up the relationship, you will need to decide how you want to approach this. If you're keen to try, go for it, but never, ever feel pressured to say yes. Here are some things you can do and say to reject such a proposal:

- **Be clear and direct from the beginning**
  Setting expectations from the beginning can minimize the chances of the conversation coming up again in the near future. Express what you are looking for in a relationship and which things you are open to and which things not. If polyamory is not a thing for you, then clearly state so early on in your relationship.
- **Be upfront about your reasons**
  It is important to also explain the reasons why you don't want to be in a polyamorous relationship. These reasons might include your fears, personal values and beliefs about love relationships and emotional needs, which

you find hard to fulfil if you are not in a monogamous relationship.

- **Engage with your partner in a learning conversation**

  Give your partner a chance to share their own thoughts and feelings about why they want to be in an open relationship. Also, listen to how they feel about your needs and reasoning for not wanting to be in an open relationship. Really try to understand their perspective without too much judgement.

- **Be open to compromise**

  If you and your partner have different ideas about being in an open relationship, then you may want to find a way to meet each other's needs. This might include taking a break by putting the relationship on hold for a while, finding ways to set boundaries or considering other ways to meet each other halfway. If you both can't find a way to make it work, then there is always the option to end the relationship.

- **The value of commitment**

  Explain that your desire to be in a monogamous relationship is your way of showing devotion to your partner. Being committed to each other requires sacrifice and dedication. These are not just behaviours, but also virtues that psychologically strengthen the unity between two people. Desiring another person can be interpreted as 'I am not enough for you'.

Relationships are like sailing the ocean – sometimes you sail to familiar places and at other times you find yourself in uncharted waters. Not everyone on board will agree on which direction to head, but hopefully together you can figure things out. Be respectful of each other's evolving needs, communicate openly, compromise at times, but always stay true to who you are. And remember – there is always an escape boat at the back for you to get on if the ship starts to sink.

Brad Pitt and Angelina Jolie allegedly had an open relationship for a while. Both partners don't believe in restricting each other nor do they believe that fidelity is an absolute requirement for a relationship.[4] The couple was together for 13 years before deciding to split in 2016. Open relationships are not easy to manage and are not always a solution to make marriages work.

When one is not enough – what's the drama?

In today's modern world, an increasing number of people are choosing not to be in a monogamous relationship. Modern life is making it hard to stay focused on one person. People are travelling more than ever before, dating apps provide unlimited options and people are less willing to deal with difficulties in relationships. It seems that today's formula for companionship requires a broader set of stimuli (e.g., people, experiences, learning) that help understand who we are in a rapidly changing world. There also seems to be an end to loyalty in all areas of life, from work to romance. 'Why should I just focus on one person?' is the mindset many people are starting to develop, and not just in the dating scene. Some people in long-term monogamous relationships are also opting to meet other people outside of the relationship, independently or as a couple. It can be quite a shock if your partner asks you to open up the relationship, especially if you have never considered being in an open relationship before. An open relationship is not for everyone (nor approved of in various cultures and communities), and you definitely don't have to feel pressured to be in one if you don't want to. However, an open relationship can work if both people want it and are clear about what 'open' means. Open relationships have both benefits and disadvantages connected with them, so if you are considering opening up the relationship and allowing other people to join in, make sure to explore how and set some clear ground rules (and a contingency plan) to make sure no one gets hurt. Talking about meeting other people outside your relationship is not something that happens overnight. It requires a lot of open discussion, trust and time. It is also a discussion many people might be offended by, so be ready also to lose your partner if you decide to bring up the option in conversation.

It's a **red flag** if:
- Your partner pressures you to be in an open relationship.
- Your partner wants you to be exclusive while they are meeting other people.
- Your partner proposes being in a polyamorous relationship after they have met someone else.
- Your partner disrespects the agreements you made about opening up the relationship.

It's a **green flag** if:
- You and your partner want to be in an open relationship.
- Your partner respects your desire not to be in an open relationship.
- Your partner reverts to a monogamous relationship after you tried being in an open relationship but asked to go back to being exclusive.
- You and your partner openly communicate about your needs in your relationship as needs can change with time.

Things to consider when deciding if you want in or out

It can be hard to decide if your partner asks you if you are open to meeting other people. It can make you feel very uncomfortable and even question why you are still together if they want to be with someone else. For many, monogamy is the only form of relationship they want. However, there is a growing interest in open relationships, which are socially still stigmatized in many cultures and communities, but slowly becoming more accepted. If you are unsure but open to the idea, then it is important to have a good conversation about what it means to be 'open' and how you could make it work. Meeting other people might spice things up in the bedroom but comes with unique challenges, which you will need to consider before deciding if it is worth being in an open relationship.

Willingness to stay

- You and your partner started the relationship as an open relationship.
- You are open to your partner's proposal to meet other people, independently or together.
- You are not willing to open up the relationship, which you communicate to your partner. Your partner respects your decision and doesn't open up the relationship.
- Your partner respects the rules of engagement you put in place when opening up the relationship.

Time to leave

- When an open relationship is not an option for you (for whatever reason).
- You don't want to be in an open relationship and your partner is being difficult about your choice.
- Your partner does things with others that you didn't agree to.
- Your partner won't revert to a monogamous relationship after you both decided to meet other people but now you want out.

Red Flag 22 'Why can't you realize it's your fault!'

When your partner gaslights you

'The search for a scapegoat is the easiest
of all hunting expeditions.'
Dwight D. Eisenhower

The blaming partner

Blaming is a normal psychological response when things go wrong. But why do we do it? It feels safe when we can point the finger and lay responsibility in someone's hands. Hopefully, the other person will reflect on what they did and learn from it moving forward. However, things don't always play out that way. The psychology of blaming is complex, involving different thought processes and emotions. For example, when someone points the finger at you, it is natural to feel shame. Feelings of shame can make you want to protect your self-image, which in turn triggers you to blame the other person (even when you know that you are in the wrong). Blaming in this case can help avoid these feelings of shame and shift the focus away from one's own mistakes. If you are being blamed by your partner for something that isn't clear to you, then it is important to know why. In some cases, blaming can become a compulsive behaviour or even a weapon of abuse.

Having a partner who continuously blames you for things that go wrong in your relationship is a red flag. People can develop a habit of blaming and become so used to this behaviour that they do it even unconsciously. Continuously being blamed for things can take a huge toll on your relationship, not to mention your mental health. Continuous blaming is also a red flag because it could be a sign that your partner doesn't want to accept responsibility for his or her actions, instead deferring responsibility and pointing the finger at you. Finally, in some cases, you really might be the one to blame, which should make you consider that it is you who is the red flag. Time to reflect and learn why you are creating problems in your relationship. Whatever the reason, learning about blaming and why people engage in this process will provide you with insights and strategies to help you strengthen your relationship with your partner or to prevent yourself from becoming (or remaining) the victim of antagonizing behaviours, such as gaslighting.

What is gaslighting?

The term 'gaslighting' has become immensely popular in recent years, especially in the dating world and in relationship circles. The *Oxford Dictionary of English* even shortlisted 'gaslighting' as one of the words of the year in 2018.[1] However, many people don't fully understand what gaslighting means or where the term came from. Gaslighting is a form of psychological manipulation with the intent to make you doubt yourself and question your own judgement. The aim of gaslighting is to control a person through false accusations, telling lies or twisting facts to distort someone's reality. Your reality, memories, feelings and experiences are being denied. Gaslighting is not only a psychological manipulation tactic, but also a power play to create power asymmetries between people (e.g. husband and wife, boss and employee, mother and daughter[2]). The term originated in the 1930s when a play (later turned into a movie) by Patrick Hamilton called *Gas Light* told the story of a man trying to convince his wife that she is going insane to have her placed in a mental institution and steal her inheritance.

People who gaslight generally try to convince you that your reality is not real or that your perception of truth is false (even when you have evidence of the truth) and find ways to turn the conversation around to make themselves out as the victim. A typical gaslighter might say, 'Ever consider why I cheated on you? You made me do this!' Gaslighters know exactly how to twist things around with words and make you feel like you are the one to blame. There are a variety of psychological reasons why abusers gaslight their partners, which can range from cruelty and the fear of abandonment to past abuse and personality disorders like narcissism.

What happens when you are being gaslighted?

People who are the target of gaslighting often report not believing in or knowing themselves anymore. They feel scared to address problems in their relationship and can suffer from confusion, anxiety, depression and/or overthinking.[3] It is not uncommon for people to have emotional regulation problems after being gaslighted for long periods of time. Having an emotional breakdown or becoming hysterical can happen if you start to lose faith in what you believe is true. People who eventually leave unhealthy relationships in which they have been gaslighted repeatedly can have difficulties forming new romantic relationships due to self-esteem issues and feelings of rejection.[4] It's easy to understand that if your reality is questioned regularly and you don't feel secure about yourself (anymore), you can easily lose yourself and remain a victim of abuse.

Gaslighting is a malicious form of emotional abuse, and it is important that you identify it when it happens and address it as best you can. Surrounding yourself with people who affirm your reality is vital to keep in touch with what is fact so that you don't lose your sanity. However, as gaslighting can be subtle at first, it can be hard to detect and, if you accept the falsehoods thrown at you, both you and your partner could find yourselves in a vicious circle of verbal and emotional abuse, which eventually can lead to domestic violence and mental health decline.

Are you gaslighting yourself?

After months and years of gaslighting, you can begin to gaslight yourself, meaning you invalidate your needs or believe that the person harming you is not doing it on purpose. The abuser has made you the abuser of yourself. So, why do people stay in a relationship when they are being gaslighted? Firstly, if you lose your sense of reality, you will not know what is true anymore. This can immobilize you emotionally and make you very insecure, keeping you trapped where you are. If you are a people pleaser, you will not want to question your partner's arguments and probably accept them to prevent further confrontation. Avoiding confrontation only makes the problem worse when it comes to gaslighting. It is also common for people to seek approval and validation from people who hurt them, which keeps the abused in the relationship hoping to be loved or to be able to save their partner from wrongdoing. Gaslighting is a 'mutual participation', meaning that you as the abusee (the one being abused) also play a role in allowing yourself to be gaslighted.[5] It is important to become aware of your agency and to take charge if you want gaslighting to stop. Gaslighting and being gaslighted can easily become a vicious circle if you don't feel confident enough to address the problem in your relationship or if you are looking for love in the wrong places.

Common gaslighting tactics and behaviours?

There are various mind-manipulation strategies and behaviours linked to gaslighting. A form of interpersonal manipulation, gaslighting aims to invalidate you, discredit you, create doubt, undermine your confidence and distort your reality. Gaslighting tactics can be sorted into four specific categories:

- **Constant lying**
  People who gaslight often use lies to distort your memories, beliefs and experiences. Common things abusers say to distort your reality are, 'That never happened!', 'You only believe what your friends tell you!' and 'You're clearly not seeing things straight!' If done repeatedly, distortion can make you doubt not only your experiences but also your memories of past events.

- **Trivializing**

Trivializing is a gaslighting tactic used to make you feel small and unimportant. Your needs and experiences are undermined, and you are continuously being told that you're 'Crazy!', 'Too sensitive!' or 'Why would anyone listen to a person like you?'

- **Scapegoating**

Scapegoating is continuously blaming the other person to change the topic and escape responsibility for one's own wrongdoing. The abuser will try to put the focus on the abusee so that the other person is only focused on defending themselves and not focused on the actual problem to start with. An example of scapegoating is, 'You're always nagging, no wonder I am always away from home. Why don't you look at your behaviours first before coming at me!'

- **Coercion**

Coercion is a form of gaslighting that seeks to isolate someone, have someone do things they don't want to do or make someone feel bad for things they may have done. People can be coerced through charm and positive affect, but in gaslighting most often it is done through verbal or physical abuse. Examples of coercion are, 'I am not going to talk to you for a week because of what you've done' and 'I am going to block you! I will unblock you once you admit I am right.'

What to do if your partner starts to gaslight you

If you find yourself in a relationship where you suspect or know your partner (or maybe a family member or co-worker

309

for that matter) is gaslighting you, then it is time to do something about this. Not addressing gaslighting head-on can have severe repercussions, even if you think it is 'acceptable' behaviour today. At the point of reading this book, you might think, 'I am already so deep into an unhealthy relationship, I can't change anything anymore. I accept things how they are.' This is a very common thought pattern for people who have experienced any kind of abuse in their relationship for sustained periods of time. What I want you to realize is that your own mind and feelings of insecurity are trapping you in the moment. Let's consider the following to regain your sanity and take back control of what you know is real and what is good for you:

- **Build (self-)awareness**
  Become aware of your personal situation by asking yourself some self-reflective questions: 'Do you find yourself in an unhealthy relationship?', 'What makes your relationship unhealthy?', 'Can you remember a time when things were different?', 'If so, what made it different and how were you different?' Ask yourself why you are accepting remaining in an unhealthy relationship and challenge yourself to consider one thing you can do today to make a change to your current situation, no matter how small.

- **Identify gaslighting (document it)**
  After reflecting on your own situation, it's time to focus on your partner's behaviours. Ask yourself simply, 'Does my partner gaslight me?' To help you with this question, see if you say 'yes' to any of the following eight statements:
  ○ My partner makes me question my reality by telling me that my observations are not true.

- My partner doesn't take responsibility for their mistakes. Instead, my partner finds ways to blame me.
- When I confront my partner's bad behaviours, they tell me I am the reason why they behave that way.
- When I confront my partner about their misconduct, they quickly redirect the conversation so that the topic doesn't get addressed.
- My partner plays the victim when I catch them doing something wrong or inappropriate.
- My partner gets angry with me when I point out that they did something wrong.
- My partner often lies and when I catch them lying they attack my character, telling me I am 'delusional' or 'crazy'.
- My partner tries to discredit me by gossiping about me to other people or trying to ruin my reputation (as a way to protect themselves).

- **Regain trust in yourself**
  If you recognize any of these behaviours, then maybe it's time to do something about it. Protecting yourself is key, as being subjected to continuous blaming or gaslighting can have a severe toll on your sense of reality and mental health. If you have been subjected to gaslighting for a long time, then you might feel helpless or too scared to do anything about it and believe that whatever you do won't help. Always remember that you have the right to be treated with respect and that your voice and reality matter. Also, consider consulting a close friend who can help restore confidence in yourself by affirming your beliefs.

- **Time to push back[6]**
  When you feel confident to speak up, write down different things you can say to defend your position or your observations. Here are some examples of what you can say:
  - 'I've realized that you get upset / blame me / call me crazy / change the topic when I point out your misbehaviours. This is your way of deflecting from taking responsibility for what you have done. I am not accepting this behaviour anymore.'
  - 'Blaming me for your wrongdoings is unacceptable. You chose to do what you did. I won't allow you to gaslight me anymore.'
  - 'I have caught you lying to me multiple times. You tell me different stories or turn facts around. We can't remain in a trustworthy relationship if you keep on behaving like this.'
  - 'Whenever I address you about your misconduct, you go to others to rally support and talk bad about me. This is unacceptable. If you think you can continue to behave this way, then I don't see a future between us.'

- **Practise, practise, practise**
  You might feel very uncomfortable at first to push back, but remember, your brain is not used to this new way of behaving. You might even feel guilty for trying to defend your position or yourself. If you do feel guilty, just remember that it's your default brain trying to keep you trapped in old thinking patterns. See the feelings of guilt as a positive sign of change as your brain is trying to develop new emotional responses to feeling comfortable with pushing back. Feelings of guilt will disappear the more you practise standing up for yourself and your

reality. It's time to reconnect with yourself and to validate your experiences.

- **The bark back**

  Once you start standing your ground, it is very common
  for your partner to retaliate or dismiss your behaviours.
  Remember that this is normal and that the only way people
  will start treating you better is when you stay true to your
  position and values. If you find it hard to deal with the
  bark back, then you can always reach out to someone for
  support. Asking for help is not weak. It actually shows
  strength and conviction towards your goals.

Gaslighting happens in various ways. Shimon Hayut,
better known as the 'Tinder Swindler', was a master
manipulator and gaslighted his victims into believing he
was the son of a billionaire.[7] His gaslighting tactics,
ranging from manipulating reality to coercion, were so
effective that he was able to convince women he met on
the dating app Tinder to give him money, which he used
to fund his lavish lifestyle.

When your partner gaslights you – what's the drama?

The psychology of blaming is intriguing and complex at the
same time. While blaming can serve a purpose in the short
term, continuous, habitual blaming or gaslighting is definitely pure drama in any relationship. If you are in a relationship
where blaming is used as a mind-manipulation tactic, then

it's time to become aware of it and to address it. Always remember that blaming people to manipulate them, distort their sense of reality or gain control over them is abuse. And abuse can go unnoticed, especially in the early stages. Being gaslighted can lead to feeling trapped and insecure about yourself and you might feel you can't get away from your partner. Remember that you can and that it's important to seek help when you do, either from a friend or a relationship specialist. Being abused is never OK, so you shouldn't allow it, no matter how much you love someone.

It's a **red flag** if:
- Your partner always blames you (and you are accepting the blame).
- Your partner uses blaming as a way to distract from their own shortcomings or wrongdoings (gaslighting).
- You are the one blaming or gaslighting your partner to gain power or hurt them.
- You accept being gaslighted because you believe you can fix your partner.

It's a **green flag** if:
- Your partner blames you for something you did that you shouldn't have done, and you acknowledge that what you are being blamed for is your mistake. You see the blaming as a moment for reflection and for improving your behaviour.
- You refrain from using blaming as a tool to manipulate your partner. Instead, you work on your issues and acknowledge that no one is perfect.

ROMANTIC RELATIONSHIPS

- You debate issues with each other or behaviours you are not happy about. Instead of blaming, you focus on the issue at hand without making it personal.
- You tackle gaslighting head-on when it happens. You don't allow your reality to be questioned.

Things to consider when deciding if you want in or out

If you are at the receiving end of blaming or gaslighting, it's time to start thinking about how to move away from it. Most likely you are in an abusive relationship. You might rationalize that your partner is not doing it on purpose or that they have been through rough times in their life, and that's why it's OK to be treated the way they are treating you. Nothing is further from the truth. Accepting abuse can be a response to being abused or it can be related to how you value yourself. Whatever the reason, it's not healthy and it's important to move away from the relationship or renegotiate how both of you should continue in a healthier way. I understand that this is not that easy, so don't do this alone if you feel stuck. Reach out to a friend or a counsellor who can help you deal with abusive partners. If you want to maintain the relationship and you believe it still has a future, decide which behaviours you are willing to accept and which not. Also, think about what consequences there should be if certain agreements are not honoured. At what point do you say goodbye? Be clear about where your boundaries are in your relationship and also with yourself. Finally, consider your personal and cultural circumstances when deciding if you want in or out. How easy is it for you to leave if you want to?

315

What are you giving up if you leave? Is it really worth the drama to stay?

Willingness to stay

- Your partner has a tendency to point the finger a lot, but never in a bad way.
- Your partner has gaslighted you in the past, but now acknowledges their behaviour thanks to deep introspection and/or counselling.
- You have kids and leaving your partner is not an easy option to follow. You both go for counselling before deciding to break up.
- You understand that being blamed for things actually could mean that you are doing things in a wrong or hurtful way. Time to have an open conversation about what is going wrong.

Time to leave

- You realize that you are in a verbally abusive relationship.
- Your partner regularly gaslights you to make you question your reality.
- Your mental health is deteriorating because of your partner's misbehaviour. Time to leave or make some distance.
- You find yourself accepting bad treatment due to low self-esteem.

Red Flag 23 'I never meant to hurt you!'
The unfaithful partner

'I'm not upset that you lied to me, I'm upset that
from now on I can't believe you.'
Friedrich Nietzsche

Infidelity . . . what do you mean?

Being cheated on is a terrible experience, and a very common
one. The fact that your partner had sex with someone else is
an uncomfortable realization. Not only because it happened,
but also because you are likely to question yourself about it.
The repercussions of infidelity go way beyond the deed
itself. It can negatively impact your self-worth, destabilize
your family, affect your desire to socialize with others and, in
some settings and cultures, impact your reputation. So why
do people cheat and what is there to gain from being promis-
cuous? And what's considered cheating in the era of social
media? Is liking someone else's picture on Instagram borderline cheating? What about installing a dating app, flirting or
even sexting?

The psychology of cheating helps to explain why people
feel the need to give themselves to others physically or emotionally when already in a relationship, and how people justify
their cheating behaviours. This is a fascinating topic, which
this chapter explores and explains in a contemporary way

and which might challenge some of your existing assumptions about cheating.

Defining what infidelity means in a modern world

Cheating or infidelity is defined as 'the act of having a romantic or sexual relationship with someone other than one's husband, wife or partner'.[1] This definition of cheating clearly indicates that being intimate (e.g. intercourse, kissing) with another person besides your partner is a non-consensual act taking place within a monogamous relationship. This relates more to physical cheating. However, what Webster's definition of infidelity lacks is the consideration of emotional cheating, which can be more than just physical. Emotional infidelity can happen when your partner develops a close emotional bond with someone outside of your relationship, to an extent that it undermines the trust and intimacy you have with each other. Emotional infidelity can be as damaging as physical infidelity and can ruin marriages. Both men and women find being emotionally cheated on terrible, and in many cases worse than being physically cheated on. What's interesting about emotional affairs is that most courts don't consider it adultery, which makes it harder to pursue a divorce within our legal system.

Additionally, with the rise of social media and dating apps, there is now also digital infidelity. Digital infidelity is when your partner engages in a cyber relationship with someone or sends romantic/sexual text messages or DMs to someone (who they have never met in person) online. Digital infidelity can also be considered to be in evidence if your partner keeps in contact with their exes or people who they know they could engage with in a sexual or romantic way (again). This can be hard to decipher. However, one rule I use to decide if it is digital infidelity is if your partner keeps their contact with other people a secret (e.g. doesn't tell you about specific contacts, uses fake names for people, deletes messages from these contacts). Some people consider a partner liking specific pictures on Instagram or Facebook of people they could be attracted to as digital infidelity.

Though some of these behaviours can seem harmless, digital infidelity can lead to major relational distress and eventually to other forms of infidelity. Digital infidelity can be considered a form of emotional infidelity. However, with the rise of erotic games, virtual reality and even robots, it can also become a cyber-physical form of cheating, which I call 'Sci-fi cheating'.[2] Not to mention how easy the digital realm has made it for people to discover new sexual desires and kinks. My own investigation into mobile apps and infidelity shows that persuasive design techniques used in most digital platforms and aimed to keep users hooked contribute to keeping digital infidelity intact. Interestingly, a study in *Computers in Human Behavior* found that approximately 21 per cent of Tinder users are in a committed relationship, citing mobile phone addiction and swiping as some of the reasons why people continue to use dating apps even when in a relationship.[3]

With the rise of the internet and the ongoing digitization of our lives, I believe that the definition of what cheating means in today's world needs to be revisited. And if you think liking people's pictures online or 'sexting' is being unfaithful, then it is important to express to your partner what you consider acceptable behaviour within a relationship. For some, these behaviours are completely harmless, while for others, they are totally unacceptable. A 2022 study in *The Journal of*

Sex Research found that women's judgements of unfaithful behaviour are stricter than men's judgements, which could prove problematic when trying to find common ground.[4]

However, the behavioural scientist in me forces me to warn people about the 'slippery slope', where one small behaviour can lead to a huge problem down the road if not tackled immediately, especially if tech design creates habits and propagates unconscious behaviours.

Why do partners cheat?

There are many reasons why people cheat, and these reasons are not only because they feel bored or unhappy about their relationship or fall in love with someone else. Cheating can be triggered by feelings of insecurity or low self-esteem and therefore cheating is a way for you or your partner to feel validated or to boost one's ego. Many people also cheat because they can't control their impulses or resist temptation. And others might cheat because they enjoy the thrill of doing something bad and seeing if they can get away with it. These psychological reasons behind cheating are the hardest to address as they are deeply rooted in the psyche of a person. Besides psychological reasons, there might be one-off situational causes, circumstantial reasons or socially driven factors why your partner might cheat on you. A common circumstantial reason is revenge.[5] Your partner might feel attacked or mistreated by you, for which they take revenge by cheating on you. Two wrongs don't make a right, but unfortunately this type of cheating happens a lot. Finally, socially driven cheating is when different cultures, communities or groups of people have different attitudes towards fidelity. In some cultures, men are praised (or seen as macho) for having affairs outside of their marriage. In others, people marry to fulfil parental obligations or traditions within their culture (e.g. arranged or forced marriage), occasionally limiting how deeply connected partners feel towards each other and affecting their attitudes towards cheating.[6] Cheating is a complex behavioural phenomenon and can happen for many reasons, so it is important to understand why your partner is cheating as it can help you to remain level-headed in dealing with this problem in your relationship.[7] What's important to realize is that with cheating, your biggest competition is not other women or men – it is your partner's values, insecurities and past traumas that you should be most concerned about. Also, if you don't take your partner's cheating behaviour personally, then being able to distance yourself from the problem can help you to not blame yourself for any of your partner's wrongdoings. It is very common for people to feel blame or guilt when their partners cheat on them and in most cases these reasons are invalid. Whatever the reason, there is no excuse for cheating on someone and no reason why you should accept being cheated on either.

Who cheats more: men or women?

This is a very popular question and a question many studies are trying to answer. Especially with changing gender norms, one would expect shifts to take place. Instinctively, you would say men cheat more. However, there are various forms of cheating, cheating can happen at different stages of your life and cheating can be more frequent in certain communities or cultures than others. Also, one's definition of cheating (or one's rationalization of what constitutes cheating behaviours) can impact who cheats more. If a woman avoids responsibility and tries to rationalize sleeping with someone else from a victimhood or blaming mindset – 'My man doesn't give me enough attention' – then she could very well deny seeing her behaviour as cheating.[8] For men equally the same. A more nuanced answer to the question 'Who cheats more?' is required.

When it comes to physical cheating, it seems that men cheat more.[9] The US *General Social Survey* by the Institute for Family Studies, investigating infidelity among heterosexual married couples in the US, found that on average 20 per cent of men cheat physically, while for women that number was 13 per cent.[10,11] Two interesting findings in their study are that married women in the age category 18–29 cheat slightly more than men do (men 10 per cent vs women 11 per cent) and infidelity rates among men reach their highest point between the ages of 70–79 (26 per cent). Although there are various explanations to be given for these findings, based on these results I like to say for women it is 'try before you commit' and for men it is 'try before you die'. Infidelity within the LGBTQI+ community is not well studied or documented, but research shows that infidelity in gay monogamous relationships occurs frequently,[12] and both gay men and women are less negatively affected than heterosexual couples by physical infidelity.[13] When it comes to emotional infidelity, the *General Social Survey* cites that women are more likely than men to cheat emotionally. Interestingly, women are also more likely to be negatively impacted by emotional affairs than men.

When is cheating a green flag? Wait, what?

Can cheating ever be a green flag? Some people find cheating unforgivable, while others can forgive it but not accept it. A clear red flag for any relationship you might say! Why would anyone accept to be cheated on? The truth of the matter is that for some, infidelity can be seen as a green flag. Surprisingly, according to the *World Population Review*, less than 50 per cent of Finnish and French people think that cheating is always wrong.[14] And many other Europeans second this belief. Reasons for believing infidelity can also be seen as a green flag are that it keeps your primary relationship fun and (sexually) interesting, helps you to deal with relationship problems and lack of intimacy without ending the relationship and allows you to have sexual experiences you can't have with your primary partner. Due to changing norms about marriage and sexuality globally, the latter is becoming more prevalent. Someone might allow their partner to actualize their sexual fantasies, believing that people's interests change over time and that giving more freedom in the relationship is what keeps people together. Inevitably, seeing any kind of infidelity as a green flag is a personal choice.[15]

Red flags indicating your partner might be cheating on you

How to tell if your partner is cheating on you? There are various signs to look out for that might indicate that your partner is physically, emotionally or digitally cheating on you. Here are some common indicators that your partner is cheating:

- **Change in routine**

  We are creatures of habit and after being in a relationship for a while, you clearly know your partner's daily routines. When there is a sudden change in routine, like spending long hours at work, travelling more, paying more attention to physical appearance, unusual spending, wearing different clothes or perfume or going out more frequently, this could be an indicator that your partner is spending more time with someone else. Sometimes new moves in the bedroom could also be an indicator.

- **Being unusually secretive**

  If your partner is being more protective of their computer or mobile phone (e.g. new password, more texting than usual, deleting messages, suddenly turning the phone upside down while in your presence), then this could be an indication that your partner is being secretive about someone or something. They might also feel less need to disclose details with you about their day or time away from home.

- **Becoming distant**

  If your partner is less intimate with you, physically or emotionally, then this could be a sign that your partner is losing interest in you (e.g. due to relational problems) or is getting their needs met somewhere else. There could be other reasons for lack of intimacy in a relationship (e.g. stress, past traumas, feelings of rejection, death of a parent or close friend), so try to find out why your partner doesn't feel like being intimate with you.

- **Drastic change in attitude**

  If your partner gradually changes their attitude towards you or the relationship, then this could be an indicator that your partner is losing interest in you or is dissatisfied with the relationship. It is common for cheating partners to be more critical towards you, putting you down, blaming you more or gaslighting you to make you question your reality (see Red Flag 22 for more on gaslighting). Other changes in behaviours can be giving you more gifts than usual, which can be caused by feelings of guilt.

During his marriage with Jennifer Garner, Ben Affleck supposedly had an affair with 28-year-old nanny Christine Ouzounian.[16] Shortly after, the Hollywood couple got divorced. Infidelity can happen to anyone and being super pretty (think Adriana Lima) or super famous (think Will Smith) doesn't make you immune to extramarital affairs.

The unfaithful partner – what's the drama?

Cheating in relationships happens a lot. One in five people will be cheated on at some point in their life. It is a terrible experience to be cheated on. Not only is it very hurtful, but it can have severe repercussions for the people around you as well. When people think of cheating, they only think of physical cheating (being physically intimate with someone outside your relationship). However, cheating comes in various forms and sizes. People can also emotionally cheat on others, which can be just as painful as physical cheating to the person being cheated on. And with the rise of social media and dating apps, digital cheating has now also become a phenomenon. When you ask the question 'Who cheats more: men or women?' you would naturally think men, but depending on the form of cheating, it can be just as much women. There are various reasons why people cheat, such as boredom, self-esteem issues, the need for validation, revenge or even situational circumstances. People also differ in their attitudes towards cheating and how much they tolerate being cheated on. Some people do not see infidelity as an issue in a relationship or marriage. What are your beliefs about cheating?

It's a **red flag** if:
- Your partner is emotionally or physically intimate with someone without you knowing about it.
- You blame your partner for cheating when you are the one actually cheating.
- You are having intimate conversations or sexting with people you met online while you are in a relationship.
- You accept being cheated on because you are scared of losing your partner or don't believe you deserve better.

It's a **green flag** if:
- You both are OK being with other people.
- You can clearly articulate to your partner how you feel about physical, emotional and cyber infidelity.
- You choose not to be in a monogamous relationship because you don't feel you can be faithful to someone (yet).
- Your partner doesn't engage in cyber flirting.

Things to consider when deciding if you want in or out

If your partner cheats on you, you will need to decide if you're in or you're out. Choosing to be out is easy. Believing simply 'once a cheat, always a cheat', you will decide in a heartbeat to leave the relationship. However, there are many factors that could prevent someone from ending the relationship after being cheated on (e.g. family, varying attitudes about infidelity, interest in seeing other people as well, not having a good enough discussion about what kind of relationship you are in and if sleeping with other people is considered cheating). Are you the forgiving type and do you believe people can change? Or should you walk away when your partner cheats on you? There is no magic formula to tell you to leave or not. It will depend on your personal values and also on the context of why and how the cheating happened. What would you do if your partner cheated on you?

Willingness to stay

- If you haven't set clear boundaries yet in your relationship about seeing other people.
- You don't think infidelity is an issue in a relationship.
- Your partner has cheated on you but is now going to therapy about it to find ways to change their behaviour.
- Your partner cheated on you, but you're willing to open up the relationship to give yourself the opportunity to meet others as well.

Time to leave

- You don't accept any form of cheating. Once a cheater, always a cheater!
- Your partner's cheating behaviour has impacted you and your family severely.
- Your partner is addicted to sex and, even though you are both in a relationship, can't stop being intimate with others.
- You rationalize your cheating behaviour to the point that you don't see it as cheating anymore or as unacceptable behaviour. Time to reflect deeply on your behaviour before stepping into a relationship again.

Red Flag 24 'When the situationship ghosted me, but at least I got over my damn ex'

The rebound

'Every new beginning comes from
some other beginning's end'
Lucius Annaeus Seneca

The rebound

Falling in love with someone is amazing, especially when you start feeling those butterflies in your stomach. Everything feels exciting – until your partner starts bringing up their ex. You know they broke up two months ago and they haven't had any contact since. So why is their name popping up so frequently? Or maybe your partner continuously makes comparisons between you and their ex. If this is happening to you, then there's a high possibility that you are in a rebound relationship. A rebound relationship (often referred to as 'on the rebound') is a romantic relationship that is formed either unconsciously or intentionally by one of the two partners not long after ending a previous relationship.[1] The reason for forming this new relationship is related to contending issues from a previous relationship.[2] The term rebound in sports means to regain possession of a missed shot or ball after hitting a hard surface. Similarly, rebound partners form new relationships as a way to deal with the pain or distress from a previous relationship and often move on or go back to their ex. Being on the receiving end and realizing that your partner is not mentally and/or emotionally invested in you can be painful, especially if you are invested in them and were expecting more. Popular culture would have us believe that rebound relationships are bad and that it's important to take your time before moving on to a new relationship. However, it doesn't always have to be a bad thing and there is scientific research on this topic that actually confirms that it can have more positive than negative effects. If done correctly, it can benefit both partners and, in some cases, lead to a long-standing relationship. Learning about the psychology behind rebound relationships, and how to identify if you are in one, can help you navigate the complexities of dealing with past relationship distress and rebound relationships.

The psychology and neuroscience of wanting a rebound relationship

Break-ups can be very stressful and wreak havoc on your self-esteem and mental well-being. They can even severely impact your physical body and health. Especially if the relationship ended abruptly or on bad terms, the psychological and physical impact can be huge. Research also suggests that men rebound more often than women due to their ability to fall in love more easily than women and experience more discomfort after breaking up.[3] Rebounding partners don't always look for new love straight away because of selfish reasons. The motivations to re-partner after a relationship has just ended can be broad and complex, and even unconscious.

Let's dive into some of the most common psychological and bodily reasons behind the need to rebound, some of which are interconnected at different levels.

Coping strategy: rebound to recover from break-up distress

As mentioned, breaking up can be stressful, fearful and painful. Finding someone new can be a coping technique to help buffer or deal with negative feelings and resolve the distress.[4] Especially when a new partner closely resembles the previous one, this process of re-attachment can happen fluidly and unconsciously. Becoming involved again shortly after a break-up can also be influenced by loss of benefits (e.g. financial support) or support (e.g. care). In this case, rebounding can be a response to feeling a need for personal security or the fear of having lost it due to the break-up.[5] A less common example of dealing with ill feelings is revenge. Being with someone new can be a way to retaliate and punish the ex-partner.

Fear of being alone: minimize the time being single

It can be a shock breaking up with someone, especially when you don't see the break-up coming or when the past relationship was very intense emotionally or sexually. The psychological impact of splitting up can be huge, regardless of which side you are on. Not to mention the physical pain associated with breaking up.[6] Sadness, anger, guilt and/or shame are common emotions people feel after breaking up with a partner. And for those divorcing, financial hardships and issues concerning child custody and relocation also contribute to the distress. It's very normal to feel scared being without a partner, fearing you might remain alone for ever. This can drive some people to look for a new lover quickly, purely to fill the void and as a replacement for lost love.

Self-identity: loss of self when breaking up

Ever wondered why you feel lost and empty and that a part of you is missing after splitting from a romantic partner, especially one you have been very involved with for many years? The answer is that your concept of yourself has been shattered.[7] Your sense of self can be destroyed in many ways. Your understanding of who you are could be deeply intertwined with who 'we' were. Your self-identity is a dynamic construct, always evolving and taking on new norms, values, beliefs and behaviours, depending on the people or social groups you strongly associate with.[8] Having a strong person in your life or someone you really care about, relate to or look up to can help you understand who you are more than when you are alone. When the relationship ends, it can feel like a part of you is missing,[9] and you need to rediscover this part of your self-identity again. This loss of self can be very distressing, driving some – especially people with an anxious attachment style[10] – to find a partner as soon as possible to feel complete again, or to rekindle a relationship with a past ex.[11]

Chemical impact of break-ups: the role of hormones in relationships and break-ups

Humans seek social connection and acceptance from others. When you find attraction to, and build attachment with, someone you like, your body releases all kinds of hormones. From sexual arousal hormones, like oestrogen and testosterone, to oxytocin (better known as the 'cuddle hormone' as it relates to physical touch and feelings of attachment) and dopamine (better known as the 'happy hormone', related to attraction). However, break-ups have the opposite effect. They create stress and pain, which cause the body to produce cortisol, the 'stress hormone'. Cortisol is important for human life and helps your body to deal with stressful situations. However, heartbreaks can last for a long time, exposing your body to high levels of cortisol for extended periods, which can cause all kinds of complications, like sleeping issues, headaches, tensing of the muscles, especially in the chest area, high blood pressure, compromised immune function and digestive problems.[12] Some break-ups are so severe for some that they have what doctors call *broken heart syndrome*, a physical sensation mimicking a heart attack. Break-ups can literally make you love-sick, driving people to look for someone they can be with again as a way to relieve the pain and heal.

The primary goal of a partner on the rebound is often not to form a deep and healthy emotional connection. Rather, the focus initially is superficial, concerned with healing from past wounds and buffering negative emotions from the break-up. A partner who is deeply invested in forming a committed relationship with someone on the rebound can be devastated to find out that their partner doesn't share the same invested interests. However, learning about the psychology of rebound relationships and becoming more aware of why they happen can be a stepping-stone to a more sustainable bond together.

Can a rebound be positive?

'Is jumping into a new relationship right after a previous relationship a bad thing to do?' The predictable response would be, 'Of course it is! Rebounds are a major red flag.' There is a stigma in society that moving too fast into something new is bad, and your friends will likely encourage you to work on yourself first before trying again. However, I don't think this advice is entirely valid. There are both pros and cons associated with being in a rebound relationship. Generally, I find that rebounds can actually be positive and even healthy, and in some cases can be just as sustainable as normal romantic relationships. The key thing to consider here is both parties' motivations behind entering into a rebound relationship, making sure intentions are clear, and for both partners to consciously examine their feelings. To better understand what I mean, let's explore the positives and negatives of a rebound relationship from the perspective of both partners:

The rebounder (the person forming a new
relationship just after ending a previous one)

- Pros of being in a rebound relationship:[13,14]
  - Getting back into a relationship quickly can help boost your confidence and self-esteem. Feeling like you're still in the game (one's date-ability) and attractive can help deal with insecurities related to the break-up.
  - It can help you detach effectively from a previous relationship (easier than for those who remain single). It helps to buffer pain and deal with lingering emotions from a previous partner.

- ○ Forming a relationship quickly after one has ended has been shown to lead to greater relational well-being (e.g. potentially due to receiving emotional and social support from both partners).
- ○ In some cases, the ability to re-partner shows adjustability and higher attachment security (e.g. emotionally stable, feel safe bonding and being intimate with someone, more trusting).
- Cons of being in a rebound relationship:[15]
  - ○ Still have feelings for the previous partner.
  - ○ Staying in contact more frequently with an ex-partner.
  - ○ Comparing the new partner with the previous partner.
  - ○ Not being completely emotionally or mentally invested (or being on the rebound without conscious examination of why).

The receiver (the person entering the relationship with the rebounder with no lingering issues from a previous ex)

- Pros of being in a rebound relationship:
  - ○ It can be nurturing and healthy if both partners have come from a previous break-up and now know more about what they want. They share the same experience, which can provide common ground to grow from.
  - ○ If you feel that your needs are being met in the dynamic of the rebound relationship.
  - ○ In the rebound relationship, your partner is willing and able to emotionally connect, then it is worth exploring a deeper connection beyond the 'rebound status.

- Cons of being in a rebound relationship:
  - Being on the receiving end, you might experience (for a short or long period of time) that your partner forms less of an authentic and emotional connection with you (maybe even less likely to commit).
  - The rebound partner is avoiding emotional work after the break-up and similar behavioural issues might persist in the new relationship.
  - Rebound relationships are temporary distractions and often short-lived (more rebound-dating than actual relationships).

DID YOU KNOW?

Getting married again after dissolving a previous marriage shows no rebound effect in terms of the longevity of the relationship.[16] It seems that matrimony creates a more sustainable mindset. So far, breaking up has been portrayed as something negative. However, break-ups can also be positive. We learn things about ourselves, have the opportunity to change unhealthy behaviours and ways of thinking, and focus on self-development.

What are signs that you are the rebound?

Identifying if you are in a rebound relationship can be difficult, especially in the early stages of the relationship when you feel in love and infatuated by your new partner, commonly referred to as 'the honeymoon phase'. It's hard to see red flags when both of you are on your best behaviour and emotions may be clouding your judgement. To help identify if your partner is on the rebound (or yourself for that matter), here are some common behaviours that could be possible signs:

1. Your partner talks a lot about their ex – 'My ex never complains about stuff like that.'
2. Your partner often talks with their ex – 'Hey you, just checking up with you to see how everything is going.'
3. Your partner compares you a lot to their ex – 'My ex dressed better than you do.'
4. Your get-together is mainly at home and your partner doesn't introduce you to their friends or family as they don't expect the relationship to last – 'I prefer we keep our relationship to ourselves.'
5. Your partner mainly contacts you when they are down and need comforting – 'Bae, can we meet today? I am not feeling that great and need to be with you.'
6. Your partner hardly discusses future goals or plans with you – 'I want us to focus on now and not tomorrow.'
7. Your partner often says 'I' instead of 'we' when they speak about recent developments or the relationship.

If you believe you are in a rebound relationship, then it is important to have a neutral conversation about this. In your communication, make sure to inquire first and listen carefully to what your partner is saying before stating your observations and concerns. If you want to remain in the relationship, then explain to your partner that you are not upset about being in a rebound relationship (if this is the case) and discuss what you both would like to get out of being together. Knowing that rebound relationships can actually become long-term relationships, aiming to transition from 'rebound status' to 'sustainable' is a goal you can both try to work on. Exploring what is needed to achieve this transition is what you should discuss together, as this can vary from person to person. However, some fundamental qualities I can assure you that you will need to have in your relationship are open communication, trust, space and time to heal, and clear expectations.

With any relationship, you don't only get the person, but you also get the baggage, unresolved feelings and past trauma of that person. Relationships are a mutual exchange and learning how to deal with and resolve issues in the relationship is key for it to be sustainable over time.

The rebound – what's the drama?

Rebound relationships are relationships formed after one or both of the two partners have just ended a previous relationship and got into a new relationship as a way to deal with past pains or discontent. The connection a partner on the rebound looks for is often superficial, as their primary focus for the new relationship is to resolve psychological distress, buffer negative emotions and/or heal. Rebound relationships are often short-lived but can sometimes turn into long-term relationships if managed effectively. The science also confirms that rebound relationships can be more beneficial than we originally thought to be true. Understanding the psychology of rebound relationships, the conscious and unconscious drivers that motivate people to re-partner after just ending a relationship, and the benefits and disadvantages of being in a rebound relationship can be very empowering. These insights can provide pathways to transforming a 'rebound status' into something more sustainable.

It's a **red flag** if:
- Your rebounding partner continuously compares you to their ex.
- Your rebounding partner uses you purely to resolve past pains and gives nothing in return (socially, physically, emotionally).
- Your rebounding partner is not interested in a future with you nor is willing to discuss their true intentions for being with you (especially after you have asked them).
- You are emotionally invested in your rebounding partner, but you are not willing to address the topic of being on the rebound out of fear of losing them or doubting your self-worth.

It's a **green flag** if:
- You both are happy with the dynamics of the relationship (investing in the relationship as it progresses and happy to part ways if it doesn't work out).
- You can have an open conversation with your partner about being on the rebound. Explore the reasons, discuss the psychology and show mutual understanding with the aim of creating something

more sustainable once the 'rebound status' has passed.

- Both partners have come from a previous break-up and now know more about what they want. They share the same experience, which can be a common ground to grow from.
- You might enjoy the physical, emotional, intellectual or financial benefits you receive from being with your rebound. The benefits outweigh the possibility that the rebound goes back to their ex.

Things to consider when deciding if you want in or out

It can be quite unsettling to find out that your partner is on the rebound (or to realize the true reasons why you are re-partnering so soon). Deciding to stay or go can be a difficult decision, especially if you are developing emotions towards each other. As the rebounder, you might not yet be emotionally ready to welcome someone new into your life. And being on the receiving end, you might not want to get hurt or risk rejection. A tough choice to make for someone you really like. The general belief most people have about rebound relationships is that they are bad, but the science shows that they can be mutually beneficial if managed correctly. Here are some key points to consider when deciding whether you are in or out:

Willingness to stay

- You are both willing to communicate your needs and expectations about the rebound relationship. Both of you agree to gradually invest emotionally in the relationship, giving each other space and time to heal.

- Don't treat your relationship as a rebound. See it more as casual dating where both of you are happy to leave if it doesn't work out. It was fun while it lasted!
- Your partner shows that they are capable of deep emotional connection and interested in discussing future goals and plans.

Time to leave

- To keep things in the sport's analogy, your partner is in it for the sprint and not for the marathon. They also continuously compare you to their ex in a negative way and maintain regular contact with them.
- Your partner has a one-sided interest in the relationship. They only care about themselves and their needs. They also don't engage you with their close friends or family.
- Your partner holds resentment towards their ex and takes it out on you.

Concluding thoughts
Becoming the best version of you

'The happiness of your life depends upon
the quality of your thoughts.'
Marcus Aurelius

Becoming your best version yet

As you've now come to the end of the book, I don't want to
let you go without leaving you with some final thoughts. I
hope that reading this book has provided you with many
insights about yourself and others; insights that help explain
the inner workings of the human psyche, human behaviour,
and about modern-day life and its impact on human relationships, as well as the importance of human relationships
in various domains of life and how important (but also challenging) it is to keep relationships intact. It is wonderful to
learn new things and gain new perspectives on how you see
the world. However, knowledge without action is just an
empty shell, and won't make you a better person per se. If
you want to improve the way you think, respond differently
to specific situations and build better and more sustainable
relationships in your life, then you have to turn thoughts
and words into action! Reading alone is not going to improve
behaviour.

*Improve your thinking by activating
your reflective mindset*

Throughout this book, I've spoken about default thinking and reflective thinking. These two thinking styles play an important role in our lives. According to the dual-processing theory,[1] the brain processes information and triggers thoughts in two specific ways:

1. Automatically (default system)
2. Reflectively (reflective system)

Both the default system and the reflective system are necessary to survive. Without the default system, our brain would be overloaded if it had to process everything it comes across consciously. Evolution has helped the brain to process information in a fast way so that we can do multiple things at the same time without consciously thinking about it. Biases, habits, stereotypes, associations, trauma responses and other automatic reactions to situations and people are centred in the default system of the brain. The reflective system, on the other hand, is the part of the brain that processes information more consciously and deliberately (which costs lots of mental energy). In our formative years, we develop the first version of our default system, which I call our *internal iOS*, version 0.6 or 0.7, which corresponds with our childhood age of 6 or 7. As we get older, our mental iOS becomes more complex but is still very much driven by its initial design. When you are 29, your internal iOS is at version 2.9. If your 2.9 version is a bit faulty, it's hard to go back to version 0.6 to change it. However, it is important to dig deep inside to see if and how previous versions are impacting version 2.9. Once the bugs have been identified, full updates, workarounds and/or patches can be made to the current programming to find ways to make version 3.0 even better. Using the reflective part of the brain, you can identify, analyse and work on those parts of the mental programming that need an upgrade. However, when the brain is stressed or scared, or we just don't have time or the energy to think things through, the reflective system runs out of energy and falls back onto the default system to dictate thoughts and behaviours again. This explains why, for many, breaking habits is so hard to do and how your brain makes you feel guilty or uncomfortable when you are attempting to change your existing programming. Just remember that feelings of discomfort during times of change are actually a sign you are doing something right (not something wrong). So, keep at it! The continuous and deliberate practising of new beliefs about yourself and others, and experimenting with new behaviours in the moment, can steadily help you upgrade your internal iOS, making new beliefs and behaviours part of your improved default response.

Red flags and green flags help you reflect

After reading this book, I am also sure that you will never look at red and green flags in the same way again. Besides their popularity in modern-day conversations and contemporary pop culture, red and green flags serve a much deeper purpose. We are quick to label someone as a red flag the moment we don't like something about them, but who says they are truly a red flag? Sometimes our interpretation of a red flag actually means we are the red flag. Red flags are also very subjective and come in different shades of red (some red flags are redder than others). In this book, I have presented a new way of looking at red and green flags. A way to also slow down thinking and become more reflective of what you are observing to improve the quality of your thinking and decision-making. RED stands for **R**eflect, **E**ngage, **D**ecide, so when you believe you have identified a red flag in someone's behaviour, take your time to investigate it. Don't run at the first sign of a red flag, as that could be a trauma response or a sign that your abilities to deal with difficult situations are declining. Red flags help us to kick in the reflective part of our brain, which can help us make better decisions in the moment. Green flags are equally reflective, as GREEN teaches us not to take positive behaviours for granted. When we see green flags, we need to make sure they are *Genuine*, and to *Respect*, *Empathize with*, *Elevate* and *Nurture* these behaviours. If we take green flags for granted, they might disappear over time. Make sure you acknowledge, praise and nurture people's green flags if you want to see them repeated and develop further. This book helps you to appreciate process over quick decision-making and helps you to strengthen your relationship intelligence.

Beige flags

Recently, the beige flag has been added to the flag collection. Beige flags are defined as behaviours that you are not sure about but catch your attention and may even annoy you at first. However, after a quick thought, you let it go because it doesn't mean anything significant to you. Think, for example, of your boyfriend calling his mum every day for a couple of minutes. It might make you think, 'Is this normal?' or 'Should it be every day?', but after some consideration you might say, 'He is a true family guy and I appreciate the connection he has with his mother', and let it go. Or when your girlfriend enjoys picking scabs from your arms or back when you are watching a movie. For some, super cute, while for others, irritating. Though you might feel irritated by it, you know it comes from a good place, so you just let it happen. Beige flags help us categorize pet peeves and minor issues into their own space for us to realize that not all annoying behaviours have to be red flags. Choosing to pick your battles and not be a Karen (I mean this for both men and women) in every situation is important to one's own resilience building and emotional regulation.

The perils of modern dating

Today's dating world seems counter-intuitive. When you give people attention, they ignore you; when you text them regularly, they lose interest; and when you tell them you like them, they ghost you. Sexual chemistry is prioritized over emotional connection, which makes dating more of a transaction, leaving many feeling lost and not knowing why anyone should date any more if not for something more serious. Modern dating has put people in limbo, which is best encapsulated by a quote on social media that says something along the lines of, 'Why do I miss my boyfriend, who is not really my boyfriend, just in my mind, but I still feel like I miss him but also so happy I don't have him'. It seems with the abundance of options we have today, we have become paralysed, wanting everything but doing nothing significant.

Technology is a major cause for these troubles in the dating world. Mobile apps have been intentionally designed to manipulate behaviour, if not only to make you more engaged or spend more money. It's clear that our devices and mobile apps are also doing something more sinister. They are making us vulnerable and dependent, affecting our abilities to think critically and making us less willing to emotionally connect and empathize with others. A machine that keeps us psychologically trapped in a mental vacuum, hooked on dopamine and scared of physical or emotional connection. Social media is not that social. It starts as a candy – being able to connect with so many people; it then turns into a vitamin – as we now use it every day, thinking it is good but not knowing how it really impacts us; and, eventually, it turns into an addictive painkiller that we consume on a daily basis to help deal with negative emotions and discomfort.

Technology usage has been linked to all kinds of relationship, physical and mental health issues. If technology design has created this mess, then technology design can also reverse it. Dating apps, messaging services and other social network platforms need to be created in a more humane way,[2] first tackling these issues we currently face and, second, finding ways to build stronger and healthier connections. It will take a company with strong morals to be able to do this, one who cares about human properties and who is not scared to push investors away if their mission is being jeopardized.

Making human relationships work in a hyper-individualized environment

We live in a world that heralds self-love and self-help, even at the expense of letting go of people who are close to us. At times, it is necessary to let go, but too much focus on self, and not establishing true connections with people in the real world (focusing primarily on social media and text-based conversations instead of face-to-face chats) are making people hyper-individualized. Focusing too much on yourself is not healthy, nor is it good for maintaining strong connections with others who are close to us. Being social and able to interact effectively with other people, be it at home, with friends or at work, requires social and interpersonal skills. Focusing too much on yourself makes you lose these skills, which motivates people to be even more by themselves. You find yourself trapped in a vicious circle, not noticing the mental and physical consequences of your choices taking place inside of you. The more alone you are and the more you depend on digital interactions for social connection, the less connected you will feel and the less capable you become to deal with difficult (interpersonal) situations.

Red, green and beige flags are your mental signposts to stop relying so much on your default system in today's digital and hyper-individualized world, especially if your fast thinking leads you astray. They are your mechanisms to help you think more critically about your interactions with other people and to become more aware of the internal triggers hampering your relationships. It is so easy to be stuck on your phone watching TikTok videos or DMing random strangers on Instagram or Facebook (instead of meeting people in person), or to block or ghost someone when something goes wrong in a friendship or relationship (instead of letting others know what annoys you to find ways to improve). It is so easy to get upset by an email a colleague sent (instead of going to that person and having a chat about the issue) or to walk away from a relationship when it feels boring (instead of trying to find out where the boredom is coming from and addressing it). All human relationships face challenges. And your ability to deal with these challenges is what makes your relationships stronger and makes you a better person. Put the phone away during social meet-ups, agree to disagree in friendships and relationships and see it as a way to better understand the differences in perspective, taking time to reflect on what triggers you and why as a way to be a better person.

What's next?

As you keep on getting better at identifying healthy and unhealthy behaviours in various domains of your life, your decision-making and interactions with others will gradually improve. You will also become more aware of your own red and green flags and find ways to work on them. This book supports you in making good, quick decisions when it is needed and, at the same time, helps those who are looking to improve their thinking and behaviour to do so through the tools and behavioural strategies provided. You now understand the importance of practise and that, without action, there is no real change. You repeat what you don't repair. So, start by preparing an action plan for yourself to help you become the best version of yourself yet. Focus on the red and green flags you see in others and you see in yourself. Here are some things you can include in your action plan:

- **Identify your red and green flags**
  - Write down five green flags and five red flags about yourself (which you knew about yourself already or have discovered after reading this book).

- Look at the green flags that you most appreciate about yourself and find ways to further nurture them. Also, look at the five red flags you don't like about yourself (or which prevent you from fostering strong relationships with others), and identify which flags you want to work at first and which could have the biggest impact on your life.
- **Identify red and green flags in others**
  - Consider which domains of your life are the most important to you right now and where you want to improve your relationships (e.g. friends, family, work, dating, relationships/marriage).
  - Then identify which red flags you see in others. Consider why they are red flags to you (e.g. general dislikes, don't align with your values) and how red (severe or unhealthy) you find the behaviours.
  - Reflect on and engage with the red flags. Are they something you want to address? If yes, how? If no, why not? What could be the consequences of staying or leaving?
- **Taking action when working on your own red and green flags**
  - Now that you have considered your personal red and green flags, decide what you want to do about it. Make an action plan on how you will address the red flags and how you will nurture the green flags.
  - Be intentional about your plan: make your personal development plan SMART and set clear deadlines for when you want to work on each thought process or behaviour. Consider how you will measure success in your personal development.

- ○ Experimentation is important when you want to try out new ways of thinking or behaving in the moment. Try slowly exposing yourself to situations that normally are nerve-wracking (e.g. social events) or be more assertive in behaviours that you normally don't engage in (e.g. speaking up). Remember, challenging the default mindset will make you feel uncomfortable. Start learning how to step out of your comfort zone.

- ○ Don't beat yourself up if you don't always follow through with what you plan. Celebrate milestones. And, if necessary, seek external support from a friend or a therapist to help you with your journey. Or listen to my podcasts and watch my videos on social media and engage with me and my online community.

- **Taking action when addressing the red and green flags of others**
  - ○ Now that you have identified which flags you want to address in others, it's time to do something about them. A first step in addressing the red and green flags in others is to write down what you will say to the other person or do about their behaviours.

  - ○ It is also important to consider how addressing the healthy or unhealthy behaviours can make you feel. You might feel uncomfortable talking about feelings, but you know how important it is to help nurture your partner's green flags. How could you address this? Or you might feel guilty to communicate your boundaries to someone, especially when you expect them to push back. How to deal with feelings of guilt or push back in the moment to have others understand your needs? Addressing the emotion while you are still in your rational state can help you be more effective in communicating your concerns to the other person when it happens.

○ Find the right moment to address the target behaviours of your friends, partner, family or colleagues. Try to meet with people face to face and not discuss the problem via text message. If you are not in the same proximity, have a video call instead. Make sure you can see each other. Be clear on what you want to see change.

○ If the behaviour is something too serious to address, then consider your alternatives. Walking away and not coming back (or ghosting or blocking someone) is an option, but only should be considered in serious situations (e.g. when further engagement with the other person is dangerous or negatively impacts your mental health). In all other situations, be courteous and explain why things are not working anymore so you can end the relationship for both of you.

Putting words into action will help you become the best version of yourself. It's all about taking control of how you think and engage with others, and how you decide to look at the world. Today's technology and lifestyles have made it easy to be more independent and to be more driven through our default settings. Let's improve the way we think and the quality of our relationships by being more reflective and by being a better person. And through our improved interactions with others, relearn what it means to be human in a digital society and hopefully make the world a better place to live in. It is only with positive intention that we can make a difference.

Additional resources

There was much more that I wanted to put in this book to help you better identify healthy and unhealthy behaviours in everyday life and build stronger relationships. On my website www.drfenwick.com I offer reader-exclusive content to supplement the book, which includes personal development and reflection tools; additional red flag, green flag exercises; video content and much much more. The reader-exclusive content will be updated regularly with new items, so make sure to check out my website.

To further supplement this book you can also enjoy my content on social media and engage with me and my audience via TikTok, Instagram, Facebook, YouTube, LinkedIn and Twitter. I post almost daily so be sure to check out my content online. Here are my social media handles:

Instagram: modern.day.psychologist
TikTok: modern.day.psychologist (or DrTikTok)
Youtube: modern.day.psychologist
Facebook: Dr. Ali Fenwick
Linkedin: Ali Fenwick, Ph.D.
Twitter: DrAFenwick

If you enjoy listening to podcasts, then be sure to listen to the official *Red Flags, Green Flags: Modern Psychology for Everyday Drama* podcast, which you can find on all major podcast platforms. Links to my podcast can be found on my website.

And if you are interested in taking your personal development to the next level (or helping your team or organization to develop), then check out my online courses, personal development sessions, and corporate training and keynote offerings on my website.

25 red and green flag questions to help you build a deeper connection and find love

When working with clients, especially couples or people who are dating, I find that helping them to discover each other's perspectives on life, values, needs, desires, fears and inner thoughts is a powerful way to build connection and to find love. It is a beautiful journey to be on when you get to know the other person better, especially from the inside out.

For people dating, the physical intimacy and compatibility might be the initial reasons for the connection they have. By having deep and structured conversations with each other (beyond simple chitchat), you can steadily find compatibility in other areas, such as in the emotional, spiritual and psychological space. Creating a more rounded and deeper connection is what will help you fall in love with each other and keep the spark alive in your bond. Or it might help you realize that the person you are with is not someone compatible in all areas of life. What to do about it? Stay and find ways to make it work, or go?

Also important is to stop trying to be someone else. The bigger the mask you put up, the more shocking it will be when people really get to know you. Don't change who you are to fit someone else's desires. Sure, you need to adjust your ways when being together, but don't exchange your authenticity for connection.

For people in a relationship, even after being years together, you will be surprised by how much you can still learn about your partner. People often leave so much untouched in relationships, especially when they get caught up in the daily hustle and bustle of life. Also, not everyone in a relationship is capable of opening up to the other person about what they truly want or what holds them back. People's needs change with time, but they don't always communicate these needs, which can lead to all kinds of problems in relationships.

That's why I have developed my 25 red and green flag questions to help you find clarity, safety and vulnerability and develop a stronger bond together worth sustaining and fighting for. The premise of these questions is based on what science shows us leads to more lasting relationships: effort, grit, vulnerability, compatibility, empathy and compassion. You don't have to engage with all the questions at the same time, rather find moments to sit together to address a couple of them at a time. Allow a conversation to develop, hear each other out (even when you don't agree with each other), dare to be vulnerable and open up to each other, have fun and laugh with each other, but also feel OK to shed a tear. True love is based on how people treat you and how they make you feel. It is also about knowing the inner workings of someone, seeing them for who they are, acknowledging and accepting them with their greatness and their flaws, and providing support where needed to help not just the other person to grow, but both of you to flourish.

1. What are your green flags and what are your red flags?
2. Which red flags terrify you the most and why?
3. Which green flags do you see in me?
4. How have your life experiences shaped your behaviours into red and green flags?

5. Do you believe you can turn red flags into green flags? If yes, which ones and how?

6. Do you think it is a red, beige or a green flag if someone calls their mum every day? Explain why.

7. Finish the sentence: 'I compare your red flags to <choose an animal or fruit>.'

8. Which red flags behaviours or fears get triggered when we are together or away from each other?

9. Which red flags are a deal-breaker in a relationship? And which would you tolerate?

10. What is the best way for me to nurture your green flags?

11. Pretend you reached the fruitful age of 99 and you looked back at the person you are today. Which personal red flags (e.g. fears, concerns, regrets) do you wish you had addressed? As the older you, what advice would you like to give to your younger self to improve how you live today?

12. Explain how your life goals can be a green flag or a red flag. Could they be both?

13. What do you consider a red flag in friendships, family and work?

14. Do you find a red flag attractive or sexy in any way?

15. When is making a joke a red flag? Give some examples and explain why.

16. Finish the sentence: 'Your beige flag is when you . . .'

17. Is crying a red flag or a green flag? When was the last time you cried?

18. Is believing in unconditional love a red flag? Explain your answer in detail.

19. Is opening up a relationship to be intimate with other people a red flag or a green flag?

20. Finish the sentence: 'Emotionally, your biggest red flag is . . .'
21. What is a relationship green flag we should strengthen to help us deal with current or future red flag situations?
22. How do you non-verbally tell me that something annoys you when you see a red flag in my behaviour?
23. Finish the sentence: 'Mentally, your strongest green flag way of thinking is . . .'
24. When is liking someone's post on social media a red flag?
25. Which green flag behaviours should we cultivate more in our relationship moving forward?

Assessing the importance of red flags and green flags in your relationship

Red and green flags can be extremely subjective. In this fun exercise, you can both indicate your top five to seven red flags and green flags in relationships. Write them down *individually* in order of importance.

Red Flags	**Green Flags**
1. _____	1. _____
2. _____	2. _____
3. _____	3. _____
4. _____	4. _____
5. _____	5. _____
6. _____	6. _____
7. _____	7. _____

Now that you have written down your top red and green flags in a relationship, I want you to assess how red or green you believe the flags are that your partner chose. You can take their flags and put a 'x', 'xx' or 'xxx' behind the flags to indicate how severe or how important those red and green flags are to you. This way, you can learn how both you and your partner align on certain ideas and values and where you differ. It's a great way to make the invisible visible; to create a better understanding of each other and find ways to work towards each other's needs in the relationship.

Notes

Red Flag 1 'Stop meddling in my life'

1 It's not only narcissistic parents who try to control or dictate their children's lives in an unhealthy way, but also parents who are overprotective or naturally anxious.

2 It could very well be that you're continuously comparing yourself to older brothers or sisters and their academic or professional success, which makes you feel inadequate and pressures you to conform to your parents' guilt-tripping.

3 Part of boundary setting is creating an agreement with your parents regarding how you will communicate with each other. For example, agree to call each other three times a week or meet for lunch once a week. You should adjust your agreement on how to connect with each other based on the context and what you feel is normal. Having an agreement in place and honouring the conditions helps to manage the anxiety parents feel when they have a hard time letting go.

4 www.hindustantimes.com/sex-and-relationships/tied-in-knots-the-problem-with-mothers-in-law-in-india/story-fzVnq9Td Bl82TnIE9Rm6HK_amp.html

Red Flag 2 'Why were you never there for me?'

1 Bugental, D. B., Blue, J., and Lewis, J. (1990). Caregiver beliefs and dysphoric affect directed to difficult children. *Developmental Psychology*, 26, 631–8.

2 Pollak, S. D., Vardi, S., Putzer Bechner, A. M., and Curtin, J.J. (2005). Physically abused children's regulation of attention in response to hostility. *Child Development*, 76, 968–77.

3 Briere, J., and Runtz, M. (1990). Differential adult symptomatology associated with three types of child abuse histories. *Child Abuse Neglect*, 14, 357–64.

4 Spinhoven, P., Elzing, B. M., Hovens, J., Roelofs, K., Zitman, F. G., Van Oppen, P., and Penninx, B. W. (2010). The specificity of childhood adversities and negative life events across the life span to anxiety and depressive disorders. *Journal of Affective Disorders*, 126(1–2), 103–12.

5 Sun, L., Canevello, A., Lewis, K. A., Li, J., and Crocker, J. (2021). Childhood emotional maltreatment and romantic relationships: The role of compassionate goals. *Frontiers in Psychology*, 12, 723126.

6 Maguire, S., Williams, B., Naughton, A., Cowley, L., Tempest, V., Mann, M. K., Teague, M., and Kemp, A. M. (2015). A systematic review of the emotional, behavioural and cognitive features exhibited by school-aged children experiencing neglect or emotional abuse. *Child: Care, Health and Development*, 41(5), 641–53.

7 Glantz, M. D., and Leshner, A. I. (2000). Drug abuse and developmental psychopathology. *Development and Psychopathology*, 12(4), 795–814.

8 Sroufe, L. A., and Rutter, M. (1984). The domain of developmental psychopathology. *Child Development*, 55(1), 17–29.

9 Maguire et al. (2015).

10 DiLillo, D., Peugh, J., Walsh, K., Panuzio, J., Trask, E., and Evans, S. (2009). Child maltreatment history among newlywed couples: A longitudinal study of marital outcomes and mediating pathways. *Journal of Consulting and Clinical Psychology*, 77, 680–92.

11 Gross, J. J. (1998). Antecedent- and response-focused emotion regulation: Divergent consequences for experience, expression, and physiology. *Journal of Personality and Social Psychology*, 74(1), 224–37.

12 www.dailymail.co.uk/tvshowbiz/article-10207219/amp/Adele-says-alcoholic-father-walking-led-hurting-partners.html

13 We have to accept the fact that we can't always change people. Not everyone wants to be changed. Even when people say they want to change, they might not. Some people just feel comfortable being stuck in familiar patterns of behaviour. Changing is fearful and might bring other issues to the surface they are not willing to engage with. It is important to meet people where they are and not compare them to the version you want them to be. Give people time to realize themselves when change is necessary.

Red Flag 3 'Middle Child Syndrome'

1 Gass, K., Jenkins, J., and Dunn, J. (2007). Are sibling relationships protective? A longitudinal study. *Journal of Child Psychology and Psychiatry, and Allied Disciplines*, 48(2), 167–75.

2 Lange, S., and Lehmkuhl, U. (2012). Kann eine Geschwisterbeziehung bei der Bewältigung kritischer Lebensereignisse protektiv wirken? [Can a sibling relationship be protective in coping with parental illness/stressful life events?]. *Praxis der Kinderpsychologie und Kinderpsychiatrie*, 61(7), 524–38.

3 Rodgers, J. L., Cleveland, H. H., Van Den Oord, E. and Rowe, D. C. (2000). Resolving the debate over birth order, family size, and intelligence. *The American Psychologist*, 55(6), 599–612.

4 Perry, J. Christopher, Bond, Michael and Roy, Carmella. (2007) Predictors of treatment duration and retention in a study of long-term dynamic psychotherapy: childhood adversity, adult personality, and diagnosis. *Journal of Psychiatric Practice*, 13(4), 221–32.

5 news.umich.edu/firstborn-asians-feel-added-pressure-with-family-responsibilities/

6 Zajonc, R. B., Markus, Gregory B., Berbaum, Michael L., Bargh, John A., and Moreland, Richard L. (1991). One justified criticism plus three flawed analyses equals two unwarranted conclusions: A reply to Retherford and Sewell. *American Sociological Review*, 56(2), 159–65.

7 Dr Murray Bowen's work shows that unique situations can change one's typical sibling position in the family dynamic (and thus the behavioural and situational impact of one's birth order).

8 It's important to keep in mind that growing up together doesn't automatically mean you and your siblings share the same experiences.

Red Flag 4 'OMG, did you hear what happened to Wendy!'

1 journals.sagepub.com/doi/abs/10.1177/1948550619837000

2 Dunbar, R. I. M., Marriott, A., and Duncan, N. D. C. (1997). Human conversational behaviour. *Human Nature*, 8, 231–46.

3 Brondino, N., Fusar-Poli, L., and Politi, P. (2017). Something to talk about: Gossip increases oxytocin levels in a near real-life situation. *Psychoneuroendocrinology*, 77, 218–24.

4 However, the balance between negative and positive gossip between the sexes seems to be fairly equal.

5 Reynolds, T., Baumeister, R. F., and Maner, J. K. (2018). Competitive reputation manipulation: Women strategically transmit

social information about romantic rivals. *Journal of Experimental Social Psychology*, 78, 195–209.

Red Flag 6 'Can you pay this time?'

1 Schino, G., and Aureli, F. (2008). Grooming reciprocation among female primates: A meta-analysis. *Biology Letters*, 4(1), 9–11.

Red Flag 7 'This company is your family'

1 Christian, Michael and Slaughter, Jerel. (2007). Work engagement: A meta-analytic review and directions for research in an emerging area. *Academy of Management Proceedings*, 2007(1), 1–6.
2 Schaufeli, W. B., and Baker, A. B. (2004). Job demands, job resources, and their relationship with burnout and engagement: A multi-sample study. *Journal of Organizational Behaviour*, 25, 293–315.
3 Kahn, W. A. (1990). Psychological conditions of personal engagement and disengagement at work. *Academy of Management Journal*, 33, 692–724.
4 Personally, I have done a lot of research in this space to find new ways to build stronger relationships at work and beyond.
5 Tajfel, H., and Turner, J. (1979). An integrative theory of intergroup conflict. In M. J. Hatch and M. Schultz (eds.), *Organizational Identity: A Reader*. Oxford University Press: New York (2004), 56–65.
6 Fenwick, A. (2018). *Creating a Committed Workforce – Using Social Exchange and Social Identity to Enhance Psychological Attachment within an Ever-Changing Workplace*. Nyenrode Business Universiteit Press: Breukelen.

7 www.mckinsey.com/capabilities/people-and-organizational-performance/our-insights/the-great-attrition-is-making-hiring-harder-are-you-searching-the-right-talent-pools

8 Deutsch, M., and Gerard, H. B. (1955). A study of normative and informational social influences upon individual judgement. *Journal of Abnormal Social Psychology*, 51(3), 629–36.

9 www.gallup.com/workplace/398306/quiet-quitting-real.aspx

10 knowledge.insead.edu/leadership-organisations/your-organisation-cult

11 Curtis, J. M., and Curtis, M. J. (1993). Factors related to susceptibility and recruitment by cults. *Psychological Reports*, 73(2), 451–60.

12 'Jonestown Audiotape Primary Project'. Alternative Considerations of Jonestown and Peoples Temple. San Diego State University. Archived from the original on 20 February 2011.

13 www.ft.com/content/656518ca-0933-11e2-a5a9-00144feabdco

14 hbr.org/2021/10/the-toxic-effects-of-branding-your-workplace-a-family

15 www.theguardian.com/business/2015/dec/10/volkswagen-emissions-scandal-systematic-failures-hans-dieter-potsch

Red Flag 8 'Can you work this Sunday?'

1 www.forbes.com/sites/sallypercy/2020/04/01/has-covid-19-caused-your-team-to-start-panic-working/#289452734884

2 youtu.be/ycoewY5uwxs?si=ROgjDtBlKWOoVG5n

3 Reflect on your personal boundaries in terms of work–life balance. Do you switch off at 5pm and go home or do you allow colleagues or your manager to call you in the evening? Under what circumstances would you allow a colleague to contact you after office hours?

Red Flag 9 'Don't complain! That's how we do things around here!'

1 Framing mental health at work as productivity- and resilience-enhancing requires dedicated approaches that focus on improving people's well-being. Transformative practices such as coaching, mindfulness, emotional regulation training and communication and conflict management skills improve how people work together and also one's quality of life. Too often companies waste money on one-off company events, offsite retreats, and inspirational speakers, who are engaging and fun but don't have a lasting impact on improving people's well-being.

Red Flag 11 'You can trust me!'

1 Office politics, workplace politics and organizational politics are used interchangeably in this chapter to refer to the same phenomenon.
2 It is interesting to note how extroverts and introverts build relationships in organizations and how their unique approach to showing up and providing value internally impacts their perceived power and abilities to influence others.
3 Expert power is particularly interesting for people who are not strong in forging strong ties in and outside of the organization, but seek a level of protection from change or political attacks. It is harder to replace someone with mission-critical knowledge or expertise.
4 sychology.org.au/news/media_releases/13september2016/brooks

www.cnbc.com/2019/04/08/the-science-behind-why-so-many-successful-millionaires-are-psychopaths-and-why-it-doesnt-have-to-be-a-bad-thing.html

www.forbes.com/sites/jackmccullough/2019/12/09/the-psychopathic-ceo/?sh=4ff78a5b791e

www.frontiersin.org/articles/10.3389/fpsyg.2021.661044/full?ref=jackclose.com

scottlilienfeld.com/wp-content/uploads/2021/01/smith 2013-1.pdf

5 Glenn, Andrea, Efferson, Leah, Iyer, Ravi, and Graham, Jesse, and (2017). Values, goals, and motivations associated with psychopathy. *Journal of Social and Clinical Psychology*, 36, 108–25.

6 Mullins-Sweatt, Stephanie, Peters, Natalie, Derefinko, Karen, Miller, Joshua, and Widiger, Thomas (2010). The search for the successful psychopath. *Journal of Research in Personality*, 44, 554–8.

7 www.cam.ac.uk/stories/cambridge-festival-spotlights/clive-boddy#:~:text=According%20to%20Corporate%20Psychopathy%20Theory,had%20in%20more%20stable%20times.

Red Flag 12 'Next time, you will achieve your targets!'

1 Ayoko, Oluremi, Callan, Victor, and Hartel, Charmine (2003). Workplace conflict, bullying, and counterproductive behaviors. *International Journal of Organizational Analysis*, 11, 283–301

www.shrm.org/resourcesandtools/hr-topics/people-managers/pages/narcissism-and-managers-.aspx

lizbethzaguirre.com/2023/04/29/how-moving-goalposts-sabotages-your-progress/

2 SMART stands for Specific Measurable Achievable Relevant and Time-bound.

Red Flag 13 'I just don't feel like dating!'

1 Apostolou, M. (2017). Why people stay single: An evolutionary perspective. *Personality and Individual Differences*, 111, 263–71

Apostolou, M., and Wang, Y. (2019). The association between mating performance, marital status, and the length of single-hood: Evidence from Greece and China. *Evolutionary Psychology*, 17(4)

www.pewresearch.org/short-reads/2022/04/06/most-americans-who-are-single-and-looking-say-dating-has-been-harder-during-the-pandemic/

2 A term that quickly became popular on TikTok referring to someone giving you an exaggerated look of disapproval.

3 One psychological reason to help explain why people like to (over)schedule their lives is that it provides a sense of control over their environment. Especially when things outside are changing so rapidly and often in an unpredictable manner, scheduling, checklists and other forms creating a structure to life provide a sense of control (especially things you have control over).

4 The usage of 'We' in an app's name isn't exclusive to Asian mobile applications. It can also reflect the collaborative nature of the service the app is trying to promote.

5 I emphasize the word 'friends' because the definition (and thus the meaning) of a friend can differ from generation to generation. In the digital age, we might consider a friend someone who is a contact we met once in the real world. It is important to be mindful of what people consider a friend to be.

6 www.euronews.com/next/2023/02/15/fewer-friends-less-time-to-hang-out-what-data-says-of-our-friendships-post-pandemic-world

7 The IKEA effect gets its name from the Swedish furniture store IKEA. The idea behind the IKEA effect is that people get immense satisfaction and pride from building stuff with their own hands. When you invest your time into things (or people), you value them more: myscp.onlinelibrary.wiley.com/doi/10.1016/j.jcps.2011.08.002.

8 www.healthline.com/health/what-is-asexual#myths

9 www.mckinsey.com/featured-insights/mckinsey-on-books/author-talks-the-worlds-longest-study-of-adult-development-finds-the-key-to-happy-living

10 Walker, Esther (21 May 2008). 'Top cat: how 'Hello Kitty' conquered the world'. *The Independent*. London.

11 A parasocial relationship is a one-sided relationship in which the person being adored is unaware of the other person's interests, feelings or existence. A parasocial relationship is often created with a celebrity or someone (famous) online and can also be with a fictional character.

12 Matanle, Peter, McCann, Leo, and Ashmore, Darren-Jon (2008). Men under pressure: Representations of the 'Salaryman' and his organization in Japanese Manga. *Organization*, 15(5), 639–64.

13 Karhulahti, V.-M., and Välisalo, T. (2021). Fictosexuality, fictoromance, and fictophilia: A qualitative study of love and desire for fictional characters. *Frontiers in Psychology*, 11, Article 575427.

14 lagente.org/narco-cultura-the-harmful-idolization-and-romanticization-of-the-mexican-drug-world/

15 According to the American Psychiatric Association (DSM-5,) fictophilia is not considered a mental health condition.

16 www.tripsavvy.com/worlds-best-restaurant-for-eating-alone-4118153

17 She based her AI lover on Eren from the Japanese anime *Attack on Titan*.

18 www.euronews.com/next/2023/06/07/love-in-the-time-of-ai-woman-claims-she-married-a-chatbot-and-is-expecting-its-baby

19 There is a study that equates prolonged loneliness to being as bad for your health as smoking 15 cigarettes a day: extension. unh.edu/blog/2022/05/prolonged-social-isolation-loneliness-are-equivalent-smoking-15-cigarettes-day#:~:text=According%20to%20the%20National%20Institute,as%20many%20as%2015%20years

Red Flag 14 'I prefer not to label it yet'

1 www.wordsense.eu/situationship/

2 In the dating app Tinder, you can swipe right to accept someone's chat request or swipe left to reject.

3 An interesting study conducted by Dr Evita March in 2018 found that there might be differences in mate selection for both men and women in booty-call relationships compared to mate selection in traditional short- or long-term relationships. Her study found that besides physical attractiveness, both men and women consider kindness as a necessity for a booty-call mate.

4 https://sfstandard.com/2023/01/21/gen-z-is-all-about-mutually-exclusive-situationships-but-are-they-really-different-from-dating/

5 Gibson, T. J. (2020). 'If You Want the Milk, Buy the Cow: A Study of Young Black Women's Experiences in Situationships', MA thesis, University of Memphis.

6 Choudhry, V., Petterson, K. O., Emmelin, M., Muchunguzi, C., and Agardh, A. (2022). 'Relationships on campus are situationships': A grounded theory study of sexual relationships at a Ugandan university. *PLoS One*, 17(7), e0271495.

7 An effective strategy to deal with letting go of abusive partners and not to relapse is to find ways to fill the void of specific routines or moments in your relationship. If you always met for dinner on Fridays, then try to plan the next couple of Fridays by creating new routines or experiences with other people.

8 Blocking in general is a very immature thing to do. However, if your mental or physical health is at stake due to abusive or manipulative behaviour, then I do recommend you terminate all contact immediately.

Red Flag 15 'Sorry I didn't text you for the past nine months. I lost my charger but now I've found it. WYD tonight?'

1 Hentai refers to a type of Japanese manga or anime containing explicit/pornographic content. The word hentai (変態性欲 in Japanese characters) is a combination of the words 'strange' and 'attitude', often used in Japan to refer to someone as a 'pervert' or someone 'doing something perverted'.

2 Schmitt, David, Shackelford, Todd, and Buss, David (2001). Are men really more 'oriented' toward short-term mating than women? A critical review of theory and research. *Psychology, Evolution & Gender*, 3, 211–39.

3 Implying that working on yourself first before deciding to date is a wiser strategy.

4 It's important to note that economic factors, global unrest and uncertainty, job prospects and changing gender norms also impact modern dating behaviour. Human behaviour and trends can never depend purely on one factor in itself.

5 You should now also understand why people run after people who disappear or don't show up consistently. They (unconsciously) apply the scarcity effect to keep you attached.

6 In social psychology other names are given to this effect, such as the *mere exposure effect* or the *familiarity principle* (see page 252).

7 A term coined by Ofer Zellermayer while writing his PhD dissertation and referring to the negative emotions experienced when having to pay for something, especially paying with physical cash.

8 People create fake personas for different reasons. People create fake personas of people they aspire to be or create an ideal version of themselves that doesn't exist in the real world. These personas are mental strategies to alleviate personal frustrations and can feel very validating.

9 A 2020 study conducted by Western Sydney University found that users of swipe-based dating apps experience more stress, anxiety and depression than those who don't: Holtzhausen, N., Fitzgerald, K., Thakur, I. et al. (2020). Swipe-based dating applications use and its association with mental health outcomes: A cross-sectional study. *BMC Psychology*, 8, Article 22.

10 www.dailymail.co.uk/tvshowbiz/article-12504877/amp/Picasso-monster-genius.html

11 Due to reduced mental resilience and less tolerance to emotional suffering.

12 When you show interest, they might walk away. And if you tell them you like them, they might lose interest. When people become hard to get, they become more interesting. The scarcity effect at its best. It's flattering when someone shows interest in you and eventually you might cave in and say yes. But playing hard to get only goes so far, and it's important to realize when someone doesn't want to be with you. Learn to stop running after people who don't want to be caught.

Red Flag 16 'I know it's only our second date, but I love you!'

1 Stranieri, G., De Stefano, L., and Greco, A. G. (2021). Pathological narcissism. *Psychiatria Danubina*, 33(suppl. 9), 35–40.

2 Freedman, G., Powell, D. N., Le, B., and Williams, K. D. (2019). Ghosting and destiny: Implicit theories of relationships predict beliefs about ghosting. *Journal of Social and Personal Relationships*, 36(3), 905–24.

3 Khattar, V., Upadhyay, S., and Navarro, R. (2023). Young adults' perception of breadcrumbing victimization in dating relationships. *Societies*, 13(2), 41.

4 Brown, R. P., Budzek, K., and Tamborski, M. (2009). On the meaning and measure of narcissism. *Personality and Social Psychology Bulletin*, 35(7), 951–64.

5 Singer, M. T., and Addis, M. E. (1992). Cults, coercion, and contumely. In A. Kales, C. M. Pierce and M. Greenblatt (eds.), *The Mosaic of Contemporary Psychiatry in Perspective*. Springer: New York, 130–42.

6 www.cps.gov.uk/cps/news/prosecutors-focus-love-bombing-and-other-manipulative-behaviours-when-charging-controlling

7 Strutzenberg, C. C., Wiersma-Mosley, J. D., Jozkowski, K. N., and Becnel, J. N. (2017). Love-bombing: A narcissistic approach to relationship formation. *Discovery: The Student Journal of Dale Bumpers College of Agricultural, Food and Life Sciences*, 18(1), 81–9.

8 Bowlby, J. (1980). *Attachment and Loss: Sadness and Depression*. Basic Books: New York.

9 Rogoza, R., Wyszyńska, P., Maćkiewicz, M., and Cieciuch, J. (2016). Differentiation of the two narcissistic faces in their relations to personality traits and basic values. *Personality and Individual Differences*, 95, 85–8.

10 Buffardi, L. E., and Campbell, W. K. (2008). Narcissism and social networking web sites. *Personality and Social Psychology Bulletin*, 34, 1303–14.

11 unfilteredd.net/how-long-does-the-love-bombing-phase-last-case-study/

12 www.psychologytoday.com/sg/basics/love-bombing

13 www.tandfonline.com/doi/abs/10.1080/03637751.2021.1985153

14 www.goldenstepsaba.com/resources/lying-statistics

15 Remember, not everyone likes the same love language. Some people might not like physical touch. Public displays of affection are not everyone's cup of tea. So, take time to explore and understand why people express their love the way they do.

16 journals.sagepub.com/doi/pdf/10.1177/0146167297234003

17 www.tandfonline.com/doi/abs/10.1080/1468199041233129 7974?journalCode=csmt20#:~:text=In%20men%2C%20 then%2C%20neuropeptide%20hormones,et%20 al.%2C%201987)

18 en.wikipedia.org/wiki/Effects_of_hormones_on_sexual_ motivation

19 www.ncbi.nlm.nih.gov/pmc/articles/PMC3633620/

20 www.womenshealthmag.com/relationships/a30224236/ casual-sex-feelings/#:~:text=%22Women%20release%20 oxytocin%2C%20a%20bonding,little%20attached%2C% 22%20she%20explains.

21 theprivatetherapyclinic.co.uk/blog/13-signs-you-are-having-sex-with-a-narcissist/

22 www.sciencedirect.com/science/article/pii/S0306453013003326

23 www.dovepress.com/sexual-dimorphism-of-oxytocin-and-vasopressin-in-social-cognition-and--peer-reviewed-fulltext-article-PRBM

24 elifesciences.org/articles/59376

25 nypost.com/2022/01/07/did-kanye-lovebomb-julia-fox-
dating-tactic-is-dangerous/amp/

Red Flag 17 'Why do I like my partners with more mileage?'

1 Believe it or not, UFOs and aliens were repeatedly in the news
in late 2022 and early 2023. Besides aliens, a potential zombie
apocalypse originating in the US or China is also keeping
many people awake at night.

2 Generation Z was born between 1997 and 2008.

3 www.themudmag.com/post/ dating-older-new-trend-for-gen-z
blog.seeking.com/2023/10/06/why-gen-z-women-prefer-
dating-older-men/
graziadaily.co.uk/relationships/dating/younger-women-
older-men/
onlinelibrary.wiley.com/doi/full/10.1002/ejsp.2854

4 Most studies investigating age differences in romantic relationships have focused on heterosexual relationships. However,
studies investigating same-sex unions are steadily increasing.

5 The average being 2.3 years in the US according to the Census
Bureau, 1.7 years in China and about 2.5 years in the UK
according to Google results.

6 The Republic of Congo being 8.6 years and Gambia 9.2 years
on average in 2017: www.un.org/esa/population/publications/
worldmarriage/worldmarriage.htm

7 www.researchgate.net/publication/31174590_Marriage_
Systems_and_Pathogen_Stress_in_Human_Societies

8 royalsocietypublishing.org/doi/10.1098/rsif.2018.0035

9 Lee, W.-S., and McKinnish, T. (2018). The marital satisfaction of
differently aged couples. *Journal of Population Economics*, 31, 337–62.

10 www.taylorfrancis.com/chapters/edit/10.4324/978020387
4370-7/may–december-paradoxes-exploration-age-gap-
relationships-western-society-western-society-justin-
lehmiller-christopher-agnew

11 www.deakin.edu.au/seed/our-impact/mind-the-gap-does-age-
difference-in-relationships-matter

12 www.psycom.net/relationships/age-difference-in-
relationships

13 www.ncbi.nlm.nih.gov/pmc/articles/PMC6785043/

14 bmcpsychiatry.biomedcentral.com/articles/10.1186/s12
888-015-0388-y

15 Lehmiller, Justin J., and Agnew, Christopher R. (2008). Commitment in age-gap heterosexual romantic relationships: A
test of evolutionary and socio-cultural predictions. *Psychology
of Women Quarterly*, 32(1), 74–82.

16 This chapter discusses age differences in dating and romantic
relationships where partners are adults and at or above the
legal age of consent.

17 Socially acceptable as well as what makes sense if you're looking for something more durable.

18 No one is quite sure where this rule of thumb comes from.

19 This rule of thumb only relates to people in their adult years
and who can consent to being with each other.

20 According to Felicia Brings and Susan Winter, authors of
Older Women, Younger Men: New Options for Love and Romance, this
is due to the emotional stability, wisdom and life experience,
clarity and new perspectives to life and boost in self-esteem
older women generally give younger men.

21 thesocietypages.org/socimages/2015/07/03/ok-cupid-data-
on-sex-desirability-and-age/

22 theblog.okcupid.com/undressed-whats-the-deal-with-
the-age-gap-in-relationships-3143a2ca5178

23 Mirandé, A. (1977). *Hombres y Machos: Masculinity and Latino Culture*. Boulder: Westview Press.
24 For more on cultural dimensions, see Geert Hofstede or Erin Meyer's work.
25 Age-hypogamy refers to woman-older relationships and age-hypergamy refers to man-older relationships.
26 This question only relates to people who are serious about dating younger and looking for someone who wants them for who they are. If you are looking for a sugar baby, then shower away.
27 Millennials are born between 1981 and 1996.
28 It still surprises me how many middle-aged men believe that they can find long-lasting love on Instagram by liking and engaging with people who are only on social media to show their bodies. I am not saying it is impossible to find a long-term partner on Instagram but thirst-trap pictures are not an entry point to commitment.

Red Flag 18 'I think I found the right person, but I don't feel anything!'

1 Koob G. F. (2015). The dark side of emotion: The addiction perspective. *European Journal of Pharmacology*, 753, 73–87.
2 Berenbaum, H., and Oltmanns, T. F. (1992). Emotional experience and expression in schizophrenia and depression. *Journal of Abnormal Psycholology*, 101, 37–44.
3 Litz, B. T., and Gray, M. J. (2002). Emotional numbing in post-traumatic stress disorder: Current and future research directions. *Austalian and New Zealand Journal of Psychiatry*, 36, 198–204.
4 Foa, E. B., and Hearst-Ikeda, D. (1996). Emotional dissociation in response to trauma: An information-processing approach. In L. K. Michelson and W. J. Ray (eds.), *Handbook of*

Dissociation: Theoretical, Empirical, and Clinical Perspectives. Springer: Boston, MA, 207–24.

5 Herpertz, S. C., Schwenger, U. B., Kunert, H. J., Lukas, G., Gretzer, U., Nutzmann, K., et al. (2000). Emotional responses in patients with borderline as compared with avoidant personality disorder. *Journal of Personality Disorders,* 14, 339–51.

6 Opbroek, A., Delgado, P. L., Laukes, C., McGahuey, C., Katsanis, J., Moreno, F. A., et al. Emotional blunting associated with SSRI-induced sexual dysfunction. Do SSRIs inhibit emotional responses? *International Journal of Neuropsychopharmacology,* 5, 147–51.

7 Sifneos, P. E. (1973). The prevalence of 'alexithymic' characteristics in psychosomatic patients. *Psychotherpy and Psychosomatics,* 22, 255–62.

8 Picardi, A., Toni, A., and Caroppo, E. (2005). Stability of alexithymia and its relationships with the 'Big Five' factors, temperament, character, and attachment style. *Psychotherpy and Psychosomatics,* 74, 371–8.

9 Hayes, R. M., and Dragiewicz, M. (2018). Unsolicited dick pics: Erotica, exhibitionism or entitlement?, *Women's Studies International Forum,* 71, 114–20.

10 www.ncbi.nlm.nih.gov/pmc/articles/PMC5321660/

11 Bressan, P. (2020). In humans, only attractive females fulfil their sexually imprinted preferences for eye colour. *Scientific Reports,* 10, Article 6004.

12 A study conducted in 1992 by Harvard researchers Ambady and Rosenthal found that students evaluate a professor in as quickly as 6 seconds, based on non-verbal cues seen on a video of an unknown professor. What was even more startling about this study is that there was hardly any difference between the evaluations of the group of students who were taught by the professor for a full term and the students who only saw the video of the

professor they had never met before. The researchers were able to ascertain that the first impression of the professor was good enough to create a favourable impression, which led to the overall evaluation of the professor: Nalini Ambady and Robert Rosenthal (1993), Half a minute: predicting teacher evaluations from thin slices of nonverbal behaviour and physical attractiveness, *Journal of Personality and Social Psychology*, 64, 431–41.

13 Zajonc, Robert B. (1968). Attitudinal effects of mere exposure. *Journal of Personality and Social Psychology*, 9(2, Pt. 2), 1–27.

14 Bornstein, Robert F., and D'Agostino, Paul R. (1994). 'The attribution and discounting of perceptual fluency: preliminary tests of a perceptual fluency/attributional model of the mere exposure effect'. *Social Cognition*, 12(2), 103–28.

15 Bartholomew, K., and Horowitz, L. M. (1991). Attachment styles among young adults: A test of a four-category model. *Journal of Personality and Social Psychology*, 61, 226–44.

16 Bereczkei, T., Gyuris, P., and Weisfeld, G. E. (2004). Sexual imprinting in human mate choice. *Proceedings of the Royal Society. Biological Sciences*, 271(1544), 1129–34.

17 Seki, M., Ihara, Y., and Aoki, K. (2012). Homogamy and imprinting-like effect on mate choice preference for body height in the current Japanese population. *Annals of Human Biology*, 39, 28–35.

18 Bressan (2020).

19 Little, A. C., Penton-Voak, I. S., Burt, D. M., and Perrett, D. I. (2003). Investigating an imprinting-like phenomenon in humans: Partners and opposite-sex parents have similar hair and eye colour. *Evolution and Human Behaviour*, 24, 43–51.

20 Rantala, M. J., Pölkki, M., and Rantala, L. M. (2010). Preference for human male body hair changes across the menstrual cycle and menopause. *Behavioural Ecology*, 21, 419–23.

21 Gyuris, P., Járai, R., and Bereczkei, T. (2010). The effect of childhood experiences on mate choice in personality traits: Homogamy and sexual imprinting. *Personality and Individual Differences*, 49, 467–472.

22 Campbell, Natalie M., (2015). Nuclear family dynamics: Predictors of childhood crushes and adult sexual orientation. *Theses, Dissertations and Capstones*, paper 944.

23 Little, A. C., & Jones, B. C. (2006). Attraction independent of detection suggests special mechanisms for symmetry preferences in human face perception. *Proceedings. Biological sciences*, 273(1605), 3093–3099.

24 www.nature.com/articles/s41598-020-62781-7

25 Orosz, G., Tóth-Király, I., Bőthe, B., et al. (2016). Too many swipes for today: The development of the Problematic Tinder Use Scale (PTUS). *Journal of Behavioural Addictions*, 5(3), 518–23.

26 www.sciencedirect.com/science/article/pii/S0736585323000138#b0175

27 Cemiloglu, Deniz, Naiseh, Mohammad, Catania, Maris, Oinas-Kukkonen, Harri, and Ali, Raian (2021). The fine line between persuasion and digital addiction.

28 Fenwick, A. (2016). Why is social media so addictive? Hult Blog. www.hult.edu/blog/why-social-media-is-addictive/

29 Studer, Joseph, Marmet, Simon, Wicki, Matthias, Khazaal, Yasser, and Gmel, Gerhard (2022). Associations between smartphone use and mental health and well-being among young Swiss men. *Journal of Psychiatric Research*, 156, 602–10.

30 To my fellow penises reading this, mobile phone over-usage has also been linked to ED problems in men.

31 Fenwick, A., and Molnar, G. (2022). The importance of humanizing AI: Using a behavioural lens to bridge the gaps between humans and machines. *Discover Artificial Intelligence*, 2, Article 14.

32 www.manasquanschools.org/cms/lib6/NJo1000635/Cen-
tricity/Domain/174/millennials_themememegeneration.pdf

33 time.com/6271915/self-love-loneliness/

34 Roberts, T. and Krueger, J. (2021), Loneliness and the emotional experience of absence. *Southern Journal of Philosophy*, 59,
185–204.

35 Eva Illouz, in her book *The End of Love*, speaks about how
modern relationships are more about the freedom to with-
draw from relationships than choosing to be in a relationship,
a concept that she connects to the economic behaviour
of disloyalty and non-commitment as a sign of self-
empowerment: Illouz, Eva (2019). *The End of Love: A
Sociology of Negative Relations*. Oxford University Press: New
York. Or, as I like to call it, toxic consumerism, pushing
people to buy products to stay focused on themselves and
seek out less connection.

36 www.newyorker.com/culture/cultural-comment/the-rise-of-
therapy-speak

37 My 15-second social media videos also contribute towards
this trend of therapy-speak, but more as clickbait to later
stimulate critical thinking and sharing of experiences in my
comment section, where people can actually learn from each
other. People's online comments help me also study contemporary (dating) behaviour.

Red Flag 19 'Stable relationships are boring!'

1 Harasymchuk, C., Cloutier, A., Peetz, J., and Lebreton, J.
(2017). Spicing up the relationship? The effects of relational
boredom on shared activities. *Journal of Social and Personal Relationships*, 34(6), 833–54.

2 Coolidge, F. L., and Anderson, L. W. (2002). Personality pro-files of women in multiple abusive relationships. *Journal of Family Violence*, 17, 117–31.

3 Coolidge and Anderson (2002).

4 If you want to address the inner chaos and the behaviours you once believed to be normal, it is good to work on a plan to desensitize yourself and (re)learn effective communication strategies (e.g. tonality, handling disagreements, word choice) to deal with conflict and build a healthy relationship.

5 I know that sounds wishy-washy and no one wants to experience utter boredom in their relationship, but it's absolutely fine, and even beneficial at times.

6 Mann, Sandi and Cadman, Rebekah (2014). Does being bored make us more creative?, *Creativity Research Journal*, 26, 165–73.

7 www.psychologytoday.com/us/blog/surprise/202205/the-power-surprise

8 Psychologist Dr Michael Rousell explains in his book *The Power of Surprise* that surprises not only help to improve the memory of specific events but can even change people's hard-held beliefs.

Red Flag 20 'You're out of my league!'

1 www.researchgate.net/publication/298066956_SelfEsteem_and_the_Quality_of_Romantic_Relationships

2 It can be very tiring to deal with negative self-talk and insecurities on a daily basis. It's important to gradually reorient oneself towards a more balanced mindset and to find ways to positively reframe experiences. Anxiety can happen to both partners at different times of their lives, so it can be useful if

both partners work together towards improving the way they think and communicate.

3 Shaver, P. R., Schachner, D. A., and Mikulincer, M. (2005). Attachment style, excessive reassurance seeking, relationship processes, and depression. *Personality and Social Psychology Bulletin*, 31, 343–59.

4 www.healthline.com/health/healthy-sex/average-number-of-sexual-partners

5 www.ncbi.nlm.nih.gov/pmc/articles/PMC3752789/

6 www.sciencedirect.com/science/article/abs/pii/S007961231730016X

7 link.springer.com/referenceworkentry/10.1007/978-94-007-0753-5_2624 academic.oup.com/her/article/19/4/357/560320

Red Flag 21 'Let's open things up!'

1 According to a study in the *Journal of Sex & Marital Therapy*, close to one in five Americans have been in an open relationship at least once in their life. There are few alternative studies to draw on in the UK, but with the broadening understanding of what it means to be in a CNM or non-exclusive relationship, my bet is that this number could be even higher.

2 pubmed.ncbi.nlm.nih.gov/34100145/

3 www.usnews.com/news/health-news/articles/2022-12-19/people-in-open-relationships-face-stigma-research-shows

4 www.elle.com.au/celebrity/celebrities-open-relationships-20980

Red Flag 22 'Why can't you realize it's your fault!'

1 languages.oup.com/word-of-the-year/2018-shortlist/
2 Stark, Cynthia A. (2019). Gaslighting, misogyny, and psychological oppression. *The Monist*, 102(2), 221–35.
3 www.medicalnewstoday.com/articles/long-term-effects-of-gaslighting#what-to-do
4 psychcentral.com/health/effects-of-emotional-abuse#short-and-long-term-effects-in-adults
5 Stern, R. (2018). *The Gaslight Effect*. Harmony Books: New York.
6 When pushing back, it is important to be firm and use a controlled voice in communicating your demands, even when a partner yells at you or threatens you. Avoid being pulled into screaming and using bad language when pushing back.
7 www.forbes.com/sites/chasewithorn/2022/02/09/tinder-swindler-simon-leviev-claimed-to-be-the-son-of-a-diamond-billionaire-meet-the-very-real-and-very-rich-lev-leviev/#:~:text=Leviev%20also%20owns%20a%20gold,a%20deputy%20mayor%20in%20St.

Red Flag 23 'I never meant to hurt you!'

1 Definition of infidelity according to Webster's Dictionary.
2 A fantasy-rich form of cheating – like porn – but with a cyber-physical component to it. The first component of the word 'Sci' has a similar pronunciation as cy-ber and the second component of the word 'fi' has a similar pronunciation as phy-sical. Sci-fi cheating is different from digital cheating because in digital cheating the digital realm serves as a medium to facilitate

emotional/physical cheating between two or more humans, whereas with Sci-fi cheating someone chooses to get off on a virtual program and/or robot instead of their human partner. The virtual aspect triggers the fantasy, while the machine engages with the human if both are used at the same time. Still find it hard to fathom? Just imagine having sex with C-3PO from *Star Wars* while R2-D2 is showing you a get-your-freak-on projection.

3 www.sciencedirect.com/science/article/pii/S0747563218
303625

4 www.tandfonline.com/doi/abs/10.1080/00224499.2022.
2104194

5 www.psychologytoday.com/au/blog/drawing-the-curtains-back/202205/infidelity-revenge

6 eprints.whiterose.ac.uk/93281/12/IPV_systematics_review_Pakistan.pdf

7 A 2021 study in the *Journal of Sex Research* provided evidence that online and offline infidelity can be predicted (using AI) by looking at interpersonal factors, such as relationship satisfaction, love, desire and length of the relationship.

8 When Will and Jada Pinkett Smith sat at the *Red Table* to talk about their marriage, Jada used the word 'entanglement' as a euphemism to refer to her romantic relationship with rapper August Alsina (which the rapper said started prior to an unofficial break-up between Will and Jada). Jada tells Will during the interview that she went with August because 'I just wanted to feel good': https://www.youtube.com/watch?v=mjL5wrGhqoU

9 Studies are inconclusive about the exact percentage of how many men cheat. This depends on various factors such as country of investigation and what counts as cheating.

10 ifstudies.org/blog/who-cheats-more-the-demographics-of-cheating-in-america

11 Most common forms of physical cheating are one-night stands and short-term flings. More serious forms of physical cheating are long-term sexual relationships and extramarital affairs.

12 academic.oup.com/edited-volume/44606/chapter-abstract/378217290?redirectedFrom=fulltext

13 link.springer.com/article/10.1007/s10508-014-0409-9

14 worldpopulationreview.com/country-rankings/infidelity-rates-by-country

15 It should be noted that in some countries adultery is punishable by law. In no way does this book promote breaking local laws.

16 people.com/movies/ben-affleck-denies-affair-with-nanny-christine-ouzounian-she-says-it-was-love/

Red Flag 24 'When the situationship ghosted me, but at least I got over my damn ex'

1 I would say less than three months, but research says around six weeks after the previous relationship terminated: see Cassie E. Shimek and Richard S. Bello, 'Distress due to relational termination and attachment to an ex-partner: The role of rebound relationships'. Paper presented at the 83rd Annual Meeting of Southern States Communication Association, Louisville, KY, 10–14 April 2013.

2 Brumbaugh, C. C., and Fraley, R. C. (2015). Too fast, too soon? An empirical investigation into rebound relationships. *Journal of Social and Personal Relationships*, 32, 99–118.

3 Choo, Patricia, Levine, Timothy, and Hatfield, Elaine (1996). Gender, love schemas, and reactions to romantic break-ups. *Journal of Social Behaviour and Personality*, 11, 143–60.

4 Spielmann, S. S., MacDonald, G., and Wilson, A. E. (2009). On the rebound: Focusing on someone new helps anxiously attached individuals let go of ex-partners. *Personality and Social Psychology Bulletin*, 35, 1382–94.

5 Brumbaugh, C. C., and Fraley, R. C. (2007). Transference of attachment patterns: How important relationships influence feelings toward novel people. *Personal Relationships*, 14, 369–86.

6 Brain scans of people who had recently got out of a relationship show pain centres in the brain light up, reflecting pain sensations related to intense emotional experiences due to a break-up.

7 Lewandowski, G. W., Aron, A., Bassis, S., and Kunak, J. (2006). Losing a self-expanding relationship: Implications for the self-concept. *Personal Relationships*, 13, 317–31.

8 Fenwick, A. (2018). *Creating a Committed Workforce – Using Social Exchange and Social Identity to Enhance Psychological Attachment within an Ever-Changing Workplace.* Nyenrode Press.

9 When the routine, rituals and the common people suddenly disappear, it can make you feel very empty. It's like a geographical memory of people and places, and the emotions attached to them, which get lost when you break up.

10 Anxious attachment styles reflect people who have a negative view of self and who are always on the lookout for potential relationship threats due to the fear of losing a partner or being alone.

11 Cope, M. A., and Mattingly, B. A. (2021). Putting me back together by getting back together: Post-dissolution self-concept confusion predicts rekindling desire among anxiously attached individuals. *Journal of Social and Personal Relationships*, 38(1), 384–92.

12 Field, T. (2011). Romantic breakups, heartbreak and bereavement. *Psychology*, 2, 382–7.

13 Brumbaugh, C. C., and Fraley, R. C. (2007). Transference of attachment patterns: How important relationships influence feelings toward novel people. *Personal Relationships*, 14, 369–86.

14 Wang, H., and Amato, P. R. (2000). Predictors of divorce adjustment: Stressors, resources, and definitions. *Journal of Marriage and the Family*, 62, 655–68.

15 Rusbult, C. E., Martz, J. M., and Agnew, C. R. (1998). The investment model scale: Measuring commitment level, satisfaction level, quality of alternatives, and investment size. *Personal Relationships*, 5, 357–91.

16 Wolfinger, N. H. (2007). Does the rebound effect exist? Time to remarriage and subsequent union stability. *Journal of Divorce & Remarriage*, 46(3–4), 9–20.

Concluding thoughts

1 en.wikipedia.org/wiki/Dual_process_theory

2 Fenwick, A., and Molnar, G. (2022). The importance of humanizing AI: using a behavioral lens to bridge the gaps between humans and machines. *Discover Artificial Intelligence*, 2(1), 14.

Acknowledgements

There are various people I would like to acknowledge who have supported me throughout the book-writing process. Writing a book is never a solo effort. I first want to thank the amazing team at Michael Joseph Penguin Random House, who believed in my abilities and supported me throughout the entire process. From editing and legal to marketing and translation rights, thank you so much everyone! I am sure this won't be the last book we produce together! Special thanks to Karolina and Paula for your continuous and invaluable feedback and support from start to finish. Also, a special thank you to Ella and Hattie, who made marketing this book such a fun process! And a big thank you as well to my proofreaders Isabel, Kay, and Emma for the peer review and invaluable feedback which helped dot the I's and cross the T's.

I am also very grateful for the countless conversations I have had with my friends over the years about human behaviour and modern-day relationships. Even though science and professional practice is your go-to place to validate insights, having novel ideas validated by friends is the sanity check you need sometimes. I would like to thank Ajami, Andre, Andreja, Angela, Bruno, Burcu, Jetinder, Jose, Konstantina, Konstantinos, Massimiliano, Patsy, Smith Ma, Radjesh, and Violet for the many inspiring and challenging convos!

I also want to thank the many executive students I have engaged with while writing this book, or who inspired parts of my social media journey. To remain an expert in human behaviour, you can never stop learning. Even when you teach you learn things you never realized before. A special shout-out goes to my student in Dubai Tatyana, who gave me some valuable creator tips when making my first TikToks. Another shout-out goes to Warwick for our funny discussions about red flags in dating (especially when it comes to dating in Dubai). I also remember dearly my conversations with Taj and Aline about drama at work. And my discussions about family, dating and relationships with my teaching assistant Chayanka. As for my peers, I am grateful for my conversations about red and green flags with Viktoria, Karl, Gabor, and Nick.

This book would not have been possible without the ongoing support from my social media followers. Not only the encouragement you have given me to write this book but also your continuous support and engagement on all of my platforms (and not to mention the 1000s of online and off-line conversations we have had the past two and half years about modern relationships, family, friendships, childhood trauma, and the impact of technology on our mental well-being). Your personal stories have shed so much light on what is happening to people all over the world and help to aid understanding of the causes of modern-day behavioural phenomena.

About the author

Dr Ali Fenwick is an expert in human behaviour and technology. He has studied the mind and human behaviour for over twenty years, both academically and professionally. Dr Fenwick is a professor of Organization Behaviour and Innovation at a top FT-ranked business school where for the past 10 years he has been teaching executives across the globe how to apply psychology at work, in society, and in their personal lives to achieve more happiness and success. In his capacity as professor, he also conducts scientific research and supervises doctoral candidates in the fields of organizational psychology, people development, and artificial intelligence.

Dr Fenwick is the founder and CEO of LEAD TCM&L™ – *The Center for Applied Behavioral Science & Technology*, which in 2013 was one of the first advisory and people development agencies specialized in the field of applied psychology and technology. Through his centre, Dr Fenwick has advised both the private and public sector on how to apply behavioural science within business and society to achieve positive and sustainable outcomes. In 2024, the centre was renamed to the *Dr Fenwick Lab for Human Behavior & Technology*, focusing on conducting psychological and behavioural research and providing training, workshops, assessments, keynotes, advisory, and other resources with the aim to strengthen human relationships, enhance well-being and performance, and ensure technology is used in a responsible and ethical manner.

Known online as the modern-day psychologist, Dr

Fenwick has also amassed millions of followers on social media through his engaging content, which communicates human behaviour and psychology to a global audience in a creative and unique way. Through a combination of science, eight words of wisdom, modern-day perspective, humour, music, technology, and creative design, he is able to explain complex topics in an accessible way which has resulted in mass behavioural change and mindset improvement amongst many of his followers. Dr Fenwick's purpose is to make the world a better place. He believes that the study and application of psychology is more than just the 'disease model' or fixing 'symptoms'. Mental health and human relationships should be considered from a more holistic perspective, where learning how to strengthen the mind, improve behaviour and become a better person is the focus of sustained mental and physical well-being. Dr Fenwick and his team aim to find novel ways to achieve these goals through the use of technology (including social media) in today's digital world.